THE FARMERS' GAME

THE FARMERS' GAME

Baseball in Rural America

DAVID VAUGHT

The Johns Hopkins University Press
Baltimore

Printed in the United States of America on acid-free paper
2 4 6 8 9 7 5 3 1

The Johns Hopkins University Press
2715 North Charles Street
Baltimore, Maryland 21218-4363
www.press.jhu.edu

Library of Congress Cataloging-in-Publication Data

Vaught, David, 1958–
The farmers' game : baseball in rural America / David Vaught.
p. cm.
Includes bibliographical references and index.
ISBN 978-1-4214-0755-5 (hdbk. : alk. paper)—ISBN 978-1-4214-0833-0 (electronic)—ISBN 1-4214-0755-8 (hdbk. : alk. paper)—ISBN 1-4214-0833-3 (electronic)
1. Baseball—United States—History. 2. Baseball—United States—Social aspects. 3. Country life—United States—History. 4. Farm life—United States—History. 5. United States—Rural conditions. I. Title.
GV863.A1V38 2013
796.357–dc23 2012017647

A catalog record for this book is available from the British Library.

Special discounts are available for bulk purchases of this book. For more information, please contact Special Sales at 410-516-6936 or specialsales@press.jhu.edu.

The Johns Hopkins University Press uses environmentally friendly book materials, including recycled text paper that is composed of at least 30 percent post-consumer waste, whenever possible.

For R. J. Q. Adams

CONTENTS

ACKNOWLEDGMENTS

With great pleasure, I express my gratitude to the following individuals and institutions:

My thanks begin with those who made the research possible. I extend my deepest appreciation to the staffs of the A. Bartlett Giamatti Research Center, National Baseball Hall of Fame and Museum, Cooperstown; Division of Rare Manuscript Collections, Carl A. Kroch Library, Cornell University; Dixon (California) Public Library; Fayette Heritage Museum and Archives, La Grange, Texas; Briscoe Center for American History, University of Texas at Austin; Institute of Texan Cultures, University of Texas at San Antonio; Roy R. Estle Memorial Library, Dallas Center, Iowa; State Historical Society of Iowa Library and Archives, Des Moines and Iowa City branches; Dallas County Archives, Adel, Iowa; Bob Feller Museum, Van Meter, Iowa; Van Meter Public Library; Minnesota Historical Society, St. Paul; North Carolina Collection, Wilson Library, University of North Carolina at Chapel Hill; North Carolina Collection, Joyner Library, East Carolina University, Greenville; Francis Manning Room, Martin Community College Library, Williamston, North Carolina; Martin Memorial Library, Williamston.

Special thanks go to Wayne Wright, New York State Historical Association, Cooperstown; Joe Amato, Jan Louwagie, and C. J. Molitor, Southwest Minnesota Regional Research Center, Southwest Minnesota State University; and Elinor Mazé, Baylor University Institute for Oral History. At Texas A&M University, generous and greatly appreciated financial support from the Melbern G. Glasscock Professorship in Undergraduate Teaching Excellence, Program to Enhance Scholarly and Creative Activities, and Department of History paid for much of my travel and research expenses.

Many others graciously offered assistance as well. Tom Heitz shared his knowledge of Cooperstown history and gave me an insider's tour of the village. Joanne Doherty of the Burton (Texas) Cotton Gin Museum answered many of my questions on local history or found someone else in town who could. Barbara Judkins, from the Farmers Branch Mustangs, introduced me to vintage base ball in central Texas. Several generous colleagues read portions of the manuscript and offered criticism, support, and valuable insights: Dale Baum, Joe Bax, Walter Buenger, Doug Helms, Doug Hurt, Walter Kamphoefner, Brian Linn, Bill Page, Don Pisani, Adam Seipp, Leslie Seipp, Rebecca Sharpless, Ethel Vaught, and Melissa Walker. Harold Livesay shared my enthusiasm for baseball history, read chapter drafts and the entire manuscript with a keen editorial eye, and helped me sharpen my arguments. And many thanks, as always, go to Robert J. Brugger at the Johns Hopkins University Press. He remains the consummate editor.

Like many academics before me who dared to combine their passion for history with their passion for baseball, I am deeply indebted to Jules Tygiel, whose death a few years ago took from the historical profession one of its ablest practitioners. Unlike many others, I remain inspired not just by his pioneering books and articles on Jackie Robinson, race, and baseball history but by his teaching and mentoring as well. While an undergraduate at San Francisco State University in the mid 1980s, I benefited enormously from several of his stimulating and rigorous classes in American history and from his advice, insight, and encouragement in long conversations in his office. I still think of him not as a baseball historian but as my history professor. Jules was a true scholar—wise, generous, and kind. He is missed very much.

While conducting research for this book, I published three articles as a means to introduce key themes and work on specific problems. An earlier version of chapter 6 was published as "From Tobacco Patch to Pitcher's Mound: Gaylord Perry, the Spitter, and Farm Life in Eastern North Carolina," *Journal of Southern History* 77 (Nov. 2011): 865–894, and I thank the editors for permission to include this material. I also wish to thank the Agricultural History Society for granting permission to use material that appeared previously in my article "Abner Doubleday, Marc Bloch, and the Cultural Significance of Baseball in Rural America," *Agricultural History* 85 (Winter 2011): 1–20. I am grateful to the History Department at the University of Texas at Arlington for permission to publish a revised version of my essay "'Our Players are Mostly Farmers': Baseball in Rural California, 1850–1890," in *Baseball in America and America in Baseball* (Walter Prescott Webb Memorial Lecture Series no. 38), ed. Donald G. Kyle and Robert B. Fairbanks (College Station: Texas A&M University Press, 2008), 8–31.

My family continues to sustain me through good times and bad. "What's new and exciting in the world of history?" my wife, Ethel, asks me most every day at dinnertime. Sometimes she gets more than she bargained for, but she continues to ask anyway. Diana, my daughter, pretends to listen (sometimes), even while deeply engrossed in Harry Potter. I would not have it any other way. They give my life perspective and joy, as does my mother, Marilyn, who I am delighted to report has become a baseball fan of late, much to my utter astonishment.

Over the years at Texas A&M, I have been very fortunate to have made good friends with so many colleagues in the History Department. I would like to pay tribute to one in particular. Quince Adams does not like baseball and prefers British to American history. But he is a dear friend, a distinguished scholar and teacher, and a mentor beyond compare. I am a better person, colleague, and historian for having known him all these years. I dedicate this book to him.

THE Farmers' Game

Abner Doubleday and Baseball's Idol of Origins

Abner Doubleday led an eventful life and achieved considerable fame as a career officer in the United States Army and Union general in the American Civil War. Following in the footsteps of his grandfather, who fought in the American Revolutionary War, and his father, a veteran of the War of 1812, he entered West Point in 1838 and graduated four years later, twenty-fourth in a class of fifty-six cadets. Doubleday fought in the Mexican-American War from 1846 to 1848, took part in campaigns against the Seminoles in Florida from 1856 to 1858, and was promoted to captain for his efforts. As the Civil War approached, Doubleday found himself second in command of the garrison at Fort Sumter, South Carolina, where in response to the Confederate attack on April 12, 1861, he ordered the first Union cannon fire of the great conflict. He then distinguished himself on a succession of battlefields, including Bull Run, Antietam (where he was wounded), and Fredericksburg. In perhaps his finest hour, Doubleday, by then a major general, played a pivotal role in the early fighting at Gettysburg, taking command of the entire battlefield when General John F. Reynolds fell to Confederate fire. Some military analysts after the war accused him of indecision as a commander (unfairly, many historians now insist), but Doubleday nonetheless enjoyed an admirable postbellum career, serving mostly in San Francisco and Texas, until his retirement in 1873. Thousands saw him lie in state in New York City after his death in 1893, and a seven-foot obelisk monument still marks his grave at Arlington National Cemetery.[1]

But Doubleday's major claim to fame—though he never actually claimed it himself—rests not with his military service but with his association with baseball.

It began, innocently enough, with a long-running, spirited debate on the origins of the game between two pioneers of professional baseball—Albert Spalding, a former star pitcher and the leading sporting goods entrepreneur and sports publisher in America, and Henry Chadwick, a popular and highly respected British-born baseball writer. Since the late 1880s, in the most widely read sports publications of the day, including *Spalding's Official Base Ball Guide*, Chadwick had maintained that baseball evolved from the English stick and ball games that he had played as a child, most notably rounders, whereas Spalding insisted that the game was entirely an American product. The debate became more heated as the stakes rose after the turn of the twentieth century. With big league professional baseball not yet a big-time commercial success, and at a time of rampant nationalist fervor and anti-British chauvinism, Spalding realized that a purely American origin and a heroic American inventor could work wonders to promote both the game and his business interests. With considerable fanfare he convened, in 1905, a "special commission," chaired by former National League president Abraham G. Mills and including two senators and several prominent businessmen, "to settle the matter definitely and . . . for all time."[2]

With little pretense of objectivity, the commission began its work. Its secretary, James E. Sullivan of New York, president of the Amateur Athletic Union, placed ads in newspapers and sporting publications around the country inviting "old-timers of the game" to send him "any proof, data, or information" that they might have on the origins of baseball. For two years, Sullivan collected and filed the responses—several dozen in all—most of which credited the famous Knickerbocker Base Ball Club of New York City for inventing the game in the mid 1840s. That, however, was the extent of the commission's research. The five members other than Mills and Sullivan appeared to have done nothing at all except lend their names to stationery letterhead. Its rather dubious methods notwithstanding, the commission submitted its final report to the public in March 1908. Based solely on the reply of one individual, an elderly Denver resident named Abner Graves, and a follow-up exchange with Spalding, the commission concluded that none other than Abner Doubleday invented baseball while playing with his schoolmates in a cow pasture in the village of Cooperstown, New York, in the summer of 1839.[3]

And so the legend began. Few figures have ascended into American folklore so effortlessly as Abner Doubleday. Fewer still have generated a substantial body of literature so unwittingly as Albert Spalding. Far from "settling the matter definitely and for all time," the Mills Commission (as it came to be known) revitalized the debate, so much so that baseball historians to this day have remained fixated on pinpointing the game's true origins. This century-long crusade has left the game with an identity crisis. According to the Doubleday story, baseball was born in the country. According to most of the game's historians, baseball has long been a city game. Every year, 350,000 suburbanites (knowingly or not) pay homage to Doubleday by visiting the mecca of the sport, the National Baseball Hall of Fame and Museum in Cooperstown—a two-hour drive from the nearest city of Albany and four hours from New York City. Every year, scores of new books and articles continue to treat baseball as the quintessential urban game. Portrayed as rural in myth and pastoral in mystique, urban in fact and cosmopolitan in character, baseball also has a mistaken identity. How has this curious alignment come about over the years? Does baseball have a rural history—apart from the creation myth of Cooperstown—worthy of study and significant in its own right? This introductory essay addresses the first question with the assistance of a famous French historian. This book answers the second with a resounding *yes*.

Spalding himself might have preferred New York City or, perhaps, his native Chicago to the isolated hamlet of Cooperstown, an urban setting being better for business. All things considered, however, he was delighted with the Doubleday-Cooperstown story. "It certainly appeals to an American's pride to have had the great national game of Base Ball created and named by a Major General in the United States Army," he wrote. To his credit, Mills tried to find, as he put it, "a connecting link between Doubleday at Cooperstown and the beginning of the game in New York." It had come to his attention that one of the Knickerbocker players, whom Mills knew only as "Mr. Wadsworth," had lived at one time in or near Cooperstown. Could he have learned Doubleday's "plan for the game" there, brought it with him to Manhattan, and then taught it to his teammates? An "exhaustive examination of the records" found, however, that Mr. Wadsworth did not actually join the Knickerbockers until 1852, well after "the game was a fixture" in New York City. The Doubleday story would have to stand on its own.[4]

Not that Mills and Spalding were particularly worried. They teased readers with speculations about the mysterious Mr. Wadsworth at the end of the commission's report, only to learn the actual details of his whereabouts three months after its release to the public.[5] By then, the accolades had already begun to pour in. Echoing newspapers around the country, the *New York Evening Post* denounced Chadwick's "unpatriotic theory" and hailed the commission's report as a decision that settled "once and for all" the great question of baseball's origin. "Cooperstown is the birthplace of baseball," declared the village's *Freeman's Journal* with pride and joy, quoting the final report and the *New York World*'s equally jubilant response at some length.[6] Spalding himself praised and publicized the commission's findings in his book *America's National Game*, published in 1911, as did writers, popular and scholarly alike, for years thereafter. Indeed, the potent combination of nationalism, patriotic emotion, and bucolic imagery in the Cooperstown story captured the imagination of the American public, who welcomed Abner Doubleday as the nation's newest hero. Wrote Cooperstown historian Ralph Birdsall in 1917, "It is pleasant to fancy young Doubleday standing there, surrounded by an eager crowd of boys, amid the golden sunlight and greenery of long ago, as he traces on the earth with a stick his famous diamond, and from these shades goes forth with his companions to begin the national game of America." Even Columbia University professor John Allen Krout, in a monograph on the history of sport published by Yale University Press twelve years later, swallowed the commission's verdict uncritically.[7]

In the minds of most observers, nothing remained to debate. Baseball had acquired an official beginning, a distinctly rural American origin, and a romantic pastoral appeal. Over the decades, such sentiments were reinforced by the celebration of the game's "centennial" in 1939 in Cooperstown at the grand opening of the Hall of Fame (where for years a portrait of Maj. Gen. Abner Doubleday hung prominently over a large brick fireplace on the first floor); by children's schoolbooks and, through the early 1980s, college history textbooks; by more than a few Gary Cooper and Kevin Costner movies; and by the words of seemingly every baseball broadcaster on every Opening Day, depicting, in nostalgic bliss, the green grass, blue sky, fresh air, and carefree atmosphere of the ballpark. Even the prestigious *Time* magazine got into the act when, in 1938, it trumpeted, "The world will probably little note nor long remember what he did at Gettysburg, but it can never forget what he did . . . in that sleepy little New York village 99 years ago." In its haste to wax poetic, *Time* seemed oblivious to the irony that Spalding's obsession with baseball's American origins had, over time, all but obliterated Doubleday's true military legacy.[8]

The commission had its critics, however. In May 1909, just one year after the commission released its report, Will Irwin, a muckraking journalist best known for his investigative reporting of the San Francisco earthquake for the *New York Sun*, wrote a series of detailed, well-researched articles on baseball history for *Collier's* magazine. In an aside, he questioned the commission's findings, insisting that baseball predated Doubleday, predated rounders, and originated in, of all places, England. Later that same year, veteran baseball writer William Rankin, who earlier had sided with Spalding over Chadwick in the debate over the game's origins, called the commission's report "the latest of all the fakes," claiming that a mere check of War Department records in Washington, DC, put Doubleday at West Point, not Cooperstown, in 1839. Both Irwin and Rankin argued that if anyone deserved credit for "inventing" the game, it was Knickerbocker pioneer Alexander J. Cartwright, whose set of twenty new and modern rules, written down and published in 1845, constituted "the Magna Charta of baseball."[9]

Few seemed to heed these early criticisms, however. Three full decades passed before the commission's report met another challenge—this one considerably more substantial. In two articles appearing in the late 1930s and a book published in 1947, Robert W. Henderson, chief curator of the main reading room at the New York Public Library, dismantled the Doubleday-Cooperstown story, showing its protagonists no mercy.[10] The commission arrived at its decision, Henderson emphasized, on the basis of "one solitary document without any supporting evidence of any kind." The so-called invention it described "germinated in the senile brain of the ancient Abner Graves," a seventy-one-year-old man "groping dimly into his youthful experiences" to narrate specific events of long ago—sixty-six years ago, in fact. Henderson corroborated the earlier assertion that Cadet Doubleday could not have been in Cooperstown in 1839 and added that the future major general was at least fifteen years older than Graves and his other "playmates." Mills and Doubleday, Henderson also discovered, had known each other for thirty years, but somehow the latter's association with baseball had never come up in conversation. In all of Doubleday's extensive writings, including sixty-seven diaries and a two-volume memoir, he never once mentioned the fast-growing sport of baseball, let alone that he had invented it. The closest Doubleday had come to the subject, Henderson maintained, was in a letter recalling his youth. "In my outdoor sports," he wrote, "I was addicted to topographical work, and even as a boy amused myself by making maps of the country." And several of the new rules of the game attributed to Doubleday in the commission's report, Henderson pointed out, did not appear in Graves's letter and thus existed only "in the fertile imagination of Spalding."[11]

What left Henderson most "amazed and incredulous," however, was that Spalding and Mills had "utterly disregarded" several references in a few of the letters sent to Sullivan to various forms of baseball *prior* to 1839. Henderson took this as a personal challenge. He then wrote *Ball, Bat, and Bishop*, not to create controversy but to showcase his own, impressive research. For thirty years, Henderson had immersed himself in the New York Public Library's rich and extensive collections of books, documents, and old periodicals to develop his own theory of the origins of baseball—indeed, of all modern "hit-the-ball games." Baseball, polo, tennis, golf, cricket, and even billiards, Henderson postulated, all derived from ancient religious rites and evolved through the centuries. By 1700, one such derivative became known by a variety of names, including "base ball," and developed most fully in France, England, and eventually the United States. Henderson discovered clear descriptions of baseball's most distinguishable feature, the diamond-shaped infield, in the illustrations and written rules found in *A Little Pretty Pocket-Book* (1744), *Les jeux des jeunes garçons* (1810), *The Boy's Own Book* (1829), and *The Boy's Book of Sports* (1838). And in the writings and reminiscences of such luminaries as Jane Austen, Daniel Webster, William Latham, Thurlow Weed, and Oliver Wendell Holmes, Henderson found still more evidence of baseball's early popularity.[12]

Ball, Bat, and Bishop did not circulate widely when it was first published in 1947, and thus, despite its many insights, it made little impact on the public's widespread belief in the Doubleday story. For a new generation of baseball researchers coming of age in the 1950s and 1960s, however, Henderson's book marked a crossing of the Rubicon. No historian worth his or her salt could take the Doubleday tale seriously any longer, and most took their own swings at Spalding, Mills, and Graves by adding a few corroborative details to Henderson's critique. Graves's credibility as a witness, most notably, took an even bigger hit when it emerged that in 1924, at the age of ninety, he was convicted of murdering his wife and committed to a state asylum for the criminally insane. He died two years later, with a legacy among baseball historians as "a ne'er-do-well who liked seeing his name in the paper."[13]

Dumping Doubleday raised new questions, namely, "If not Doubleday, who, and if not Cooperstown, where?" For years, the focus returned to Knickerbocker Alexander Cartwright, the Johnny Appleseed of baseball, as Harold Peterson labeled him in a 1969 *Sports Illustrated* article and subsequent book. Henderson himself, though reluctant to name "a patron saint of baseball," selected Cartwright for the honor of "contributing most to the origin of organized baseball as it is known in America today."[14] And indeed, a standard narrative of the development of modern baseball soon emerged that owed its beginnings to Henderson's devotion to research and emphasis on New York City as "the birthplace of organized baseball." It linked the "New York game," played by Cartwright's rules, to intercity competition among clubs across the nation in the 1850s and '60s, to the advent in 1868 of the Cincinnati Red Stockings (said to be the first openly professional team to sign players to contracts at a negotiated salary for the season), to the launching of the National League in 1876, to the emergence of a robust sports journalism in American cities, to the full evolution of baseball as a spectator sport, to the labor-management "wars" of the 1880s and 1890s, and so on into the twentieth century. With Doubleday and Cooperstown out of the picture, the central theme of nineteenth-century baseball history became the commercialization and professionalization of the game in an emerging urban, industrial America.[15]

All along, however, researchers never stopped searching for the roots of the game, and by the turn of the twenty-first century, staking a claim to baseball's origins had become a virtual cottage industry. More attention went to other members of the Knickerbockers—Doc Adams, Duncan Curry, and William Wheaton—all of whom had as much, or perhaps more, to do with drawing up the famous set of twenty rules than did Cartwright himself.[16] But the larger emphasis has focused on making "finds" in obscure sources that document baseball and "baseball-type" games before 1845. We have come to know, for example, that New York ball clubs in the 1820s, '30s, and '40s—Gotham, Washington, Eagle, Magnolia, and Olympic—actually preceded the more famous Knickerbockers;[17] that nine ballplayers from Hamden, New York, just fifty miles south of Cooperstown in Delaware County, published a notice on the front page of the *Delhi Gazette* on July 13, 1825, challenging "an equal number of residents of any town . . . to play the game of bass-ball for the sum of one dollar each per game";[18] that the town council of Pittsfield, Massachusetts, passed an ordinance in 1791 banning baseball within eighty yards of the town meeting house; and that Revolutionary War soldiers and, before them, English colonists played ball.[19] "Baseball," moreover, was the name of a game played in England still earlier in the eighteenth century, even before rounders existed, and the name of a game played in Germany as early as 1796. Just how far back baseball's history extends then depends on how much one wants to stretch its definition. Various bat and ball games were played in France in the thirteenth and fourteenth centuries, in England following the Norman invasion of 1066, in Central America by Mayan tribes in the 900s A.D., and in ancient Egypt as far back as 1500 B.C., as depicted on wall inscriptions in tombs excavated by archeologists. One leading baseball historian has gone so far as to say, with tongue in cheek, that it all began "the moment the first cave kid hit a stone with his club."[20] These and many more such "finds" appear in a seemingly endless list on Web sites, blogs, and published chronologies.[21]

In their search for baseball's roots, these empirically minded enthusiasts, through extensive research and striking discoveries, have proven that America's pastime was neither born in America—let alone Cooperstown—nor a product of nineteenth-century rural life. Still, the fascination with identifying the oldest or earliest example of bat and ball games has obscured as much as it has revealed about the broader cultural significance of baseball. The Doubleday myth, it turns out, has created a trap of a kind that often ensnares historians. As temporalists by nature, historians gravitate to the subject of beginnings and sometimes get stuck in what the great French historian and Annales school founder Marc Bloch famously called the "idol of origins," which is to say, the tendency to so fixate on the origins of a process or phenomenon that the process or phenomenon itself gets lost in the shuffle.[22]

Baseball's idol of origins has often stifled alternatives to the standard narrative of the rise of the commercial, professional urban game—though not without occasional objections. "Much of what passes for baseball history concerns only major league baseball," wrote one historian in a landmark essay in 1994, "and is presented without qualification as though 'baseball' and 'major league' were synonymous." Even those scholars who have studied the game's history prior to the advent of the Cincinnati Red Stockings have treated its coming of age as but a prelude to the professional game. Such an approach has obscured the fact that as both a spectator and participant sport, baseball in America has always been primarily nonprofessional. For every Alexander Courtwright, Harry Wright, Albert Spalding, Cap Anson, and John Montgomery Ward who played organized baseball of some kind, many thousands of amateur and casual players felt just as passionate about their teams and the game itself. A whole occluded world of baseball exists outside the professional game and, as a result, the relationship between baseball and American culture remains partially eclipsed.[23]

The debunking of the Doubleday myth and the focus on baseball history as an urban game played by professionals has rendered the world of rural baseball—the game played by farmers and residents of small towns—most obscure and most elusive of all. While the standard narrative often acknowledges that an earlier version of baseball (most often called townball) migrated from farm to city around the turn of the nineteenth century, it all but abandons the rural game thereafter.[24] Here, the idol of origins strikes again. In their zeal to debunk the myth of baseball's rural origins in upstate New York and to expose the propagandists who have long sought to give the sport a pastoral image, historians of the game have virtually neglected the enduring phenomenon of rural baseball. While the game as we now know it did develop most fully in New York City in the 1840s and 50s, the corollary, indeed the axiom, that baseball "was a city game for city men" ever since bears empirical scrutiny no better than the Doubleday myth itself.[25] From the very beginning, whenever that was, rural people embraced the game as passionately as city people—though not always for the same reasons.[26]

What does a rural perspective actually add to the game's history—if anything—a skeptical reader might ask? Even the casual observer, after all, already recognizes baseball's intrinsically pastoral qualities. Who could argue with former baseball commissioner and Yale University president A. Bartlett Giamatti, who waxed poetically, "The game begins in the spring, when everything else begins again, and it blossoms in the summer . . . and then as soon as the chill rains come, it stops and leaves you in the fall alone." Who could quarrel with renowned broadcaster Jon Miller, a self-proclaimed "baseball purist," who declared, "So now it's springtime, and baseball draws us back. Baseball is good company. It's everyday. It's dependable. Baseball is like the friend you have for life. Baseball is a vacation from the real world, whenever you want it." Who could find fault with Roger Angell's delight in the "country sweetness" of baseball, Bruce Canton's opinion that baseball's very popularity stems from its agrarian mystique, or Thomas Boswell's insistence that time itself "begins on opening day," when "the pastoral pleasures of baseball" capture our attention? Such expressions invoke to one's heart's content rural *imagery* and rural *nostalgia* but pay little if any heed to rural *culture*. However alluring, these abstractions tell us nothing about how farmers and small-town residents in different regions and different time periods saw their world and experienced day-to-day life, let alone the impact of baseball on their lives. Why has rural baseball remained largely in the hands of romanticists? Why have baseball historians—scholarly and popular alike—bought the assumption that farmers and baseball do not belong on the same field, let alone in the same culture?[27]

Part of the problem may lie in the nature of culture itself. Few concepts are used by historians with more abandon—some might say reckless abandon—than *culture* (*crisis*, *transformation*, and *revolution* also come to mind). Culture has a plethora of meanings and applications—rural culture, urban culture, American culture, agriculture, wheat culture, cotton culture, tobacco culture, folk culture, Czech culture, German culture, southern culture, popular culture, just to cite a few used in this book alone. By any definition, moreover, the historical process of reconstructing culture from its various elements, expressions, and features functions inexactly and indirectly. We know it when we see it, historians tend to believe. But there are also times when we see it but do not know it. Indeed, the fact that historians of the game have not recognized the cultural significance of baseball in rural America—despite the abundance of evidence before them—indicates how embedded the game has become in both the past and the present. Culture can often be opaque, invisible to its natives—so taken for granted that it seems unworthy of comment.

The present study relies on no single interpretive or cutting-edge theory of culture. It does, however, share the tried and true assumptions of anthropologist Clifford Geertz and others that popular patterns of play both influence and reflect social and cultural behavior. Consider the photograph on page 56—cotton farmers playing ball in a pasture in south-central Texas in the early twentieth century. The scene is analogous to the famous Balinese cockfights analyzed by Geertz in the early 1970s. Geertz viewed these contests not as simple pastimes but as expressions deeply symbolic of the way the Balinese perceived social reality. By practicing "thick description"—examining in as much detail as possible these sorts of guiding symbols—the careful observer interprets not just the activity at hand but also the totality of the culture itself. Just as the cockfight opens up hidden dimensions to Balinese culture, so too does baseball offer an opportunity to improve our understanding of American rural culture. The game's intricate set of rules and rituals, competitive drama, and widespread and long-lasting popularity among farm people strongly suggest a cultural meaning far more profound than heretofore acknowledged.[28]

This is not to say that baseball at any point in time was exclusively rural or that connections between baseball and rural culture were necessarily causal. Baseball has mesmerized city people for over a century and a half and has appealed over the years to many different groups, Americans and non-Americans alike. But the game has long had a special resonance with rural people. That cultural dynamic constitutes the central theme of this book and promises to broaden and enrich the standard narrative of the game's history. A full-scale, systematic revision falls beyond the scope of this project, however. My goal is exploratory and suggestive rather than definitive or comprehensive. A fresh understanding of baseball in rural America can emerge through a series of intensive case studies—core samples or postholes, one might say—of specific themes, regional characteristics, people, and events.

What follows, then, are six essays (and an epilogue) conceived along these lines, organized as chapters, and presented chronologically—from the early nineteenth century through the present. Each stands alone as a separate inquiry into a particular time and place. Each follows an analytical strategy that historian Jules Tygiel called "taking one's eye *off* the ball"—meaning, paying as much, if not more, attention to the broad and wide-ranging historical context of the game as to the game on the field itself.[29] Each essay also adheres to a time-honored approach shared by two generations of social and cultural historians—inform attentive readers about the particular while encouraging them to reflect upon the general. In each of the settings examined, the rise of baseball—an important story in its own right—also speaks to the places, the people, and the times in a part of rural America. Together, the essays reveal that baseball has reflected broad changes in agrarian society and maintained a prominent place in American rural culture. The game has had the capacity to generate change as well. It has both exposed and mitigated class relationships, ethnic rivalries, economic tensions, and rural/urban conflicts.

We would do well, in short, to adhere to the words of historian Jacques Barzun, which ring just as true today as when he first penned them in 1954. Historian after historian has quoted the first half of his pronouncement: "Whoever wants to know the heart and mind of America had better learn baseball." Few, however, have added the rest: "and do it by watching first some high school and small town teams."[30] Barzun sensed that the essence of the game—its widespread popularity and cultural meaning—has always been fundamentally local. Rural baseball, therefore, needs to be understood in its rural context, not as a by-product of the developing urban-professional game. Baseball may have been, and may still be, a source of rural nostalgia for city people. For country people, it served as the sport of choice, a powerful cultural agent, and, in the end, the true legacy of Abner Doubleday.

What better way to begin than by focusing directly on the game in—yes—Cooperstown during the formative years of the American republic in the first half of the nineteenth century. With farmers, craftsmen, a dwindling genteel class, and the landscape itself in constant flux and rapid transformation—and both the Market Revolution and Second Great Awakening in full swing—ball-playing in Cooperstown had great symbolic importance to the region's social and cultural relations. The essay sheds new light on the Doubleday family in Cooperstown and, along the way, makes a "find" or two of its own.

CHAPTER ONE

Playing Ball in Cooperstown in the Formative Years of the American Republic

Seth Doubleday led a full life by any measure. Born August 16, 1761, in Lebanon, Connecticut, he was the thirteenth of twenty-five children sired by his father, Elisha (who married three times), seventeen of whom survived into adulthood. His great-grandfather (also named Elisha) had migrated to Massachusetts from Yorkshire in 1676, making Seth a fourth-generation Yankee. Along with six of his brothers, Seth enlisted in the continental army during the Revolutionary War. In his three-year term of service, he participated in the battles of Trenton, Princeton, Brandywine, Germantown, and Monmouth and wintered with Gen. George Washington's army at Morristown and Valley Forge. Upon his return to Lebanon, Seth learned the weaver's trade as an apprentice. He married Barthena Clark in 1783, but he remained restless. Like many of his generation, he was determined to set the course of his own life. His desire to own a substantial freehold farm drove him from Connecticut, where poverty, population growth, and land depletion prevailed. The promise of cheap, fertile land and generous credit lured him to the densely forested, hilly region around Otsego Lake, between the Mohawk and Susquehanna Rivers in central New York.

In 1793, he purchased sixty acres from Otsego's leading land speculator, William Cooper. In the small farming community of Pierstown on the west shore of the lake, Doubleday built a log house and began the arduous task of clearing the land and preparing it for crops and livestock. He and Barthena had eight children, four of whom eventually moved to the larger village of Cooperstown four miles to the south. For forty years until his death in 1836, Seth devoted his energies to converting his tract of forest land into a profitable farm.[1]

Neither his military service nor his farming expertise most impressed his grandson, Rufus O. Doubleday, and other Pierstown teens in the 1820s and 30s. "No one," reminisced one of them years later, "was more highly esteemed and held a warmer place in the hearts of his neighbors and acquaintances" than "Uncle Seth." He delighted in hosting Fourth of July gatherings, military parades, and election day parties (he was a staunch Democratic-Republican). The Doubleday homestead always welcomed siblings, grandchildren, cousins, and more distant relatives from New York and New England. One older brother, Abner, arrived with his wife and four children from Connecticut in the late 1790s and purchased a plot of land in Pierstown a few years later. Uncle Seth loved to tell old war stories, discuss theology with his neighbors, and organize various sporting activities, including wrestling (he claimed that his fellow soldiers had wrestled to keep warm at Valley Forge), shooting matches, foot races, horseshoe pitching, rail splitting, and fishing and hunting contests. Even after his advancing age limited his participation, Uncle Seth remained the center of attention. He especially liked, as one neighbor remembered, to "keep the tally . . . when the young people were playing ball." Since ball (or townball) games went on until one side achieved a requisite number of "rounds" or "tallies" (usually 100), players chose only respected, fair-minded persons to serve as tallymen (or scorekeepers). Thus, Uncle Seth, the extended Doubleday family, and his Pierstown neighbors regularly played ball on the farm long before his great-nephew (brother Abner's grandson) supposedly invented the game.[2]

But the historical significance of Uncle Seth the tallyman runs much deeper than just another documented "baseball-type" game before 1839, even one played by the Doubleday family near Cooperstown. Rufus knew that "the experience of my grandfather was similar to that of the other settlers." Thousands of Yankees from crowded New England flocked into upstate New York between 1780 and 1820, a period of explosive demographic growth, territorial expansion, and environmental change. Like Seth, these new settlers occupied, cleared, and farmed the land and, in the process, transformed (or "improved") 63 percent of the old growth forest in Otsego Township into grain fields and cow pastures. Seth's experience differed in one important aspect, however: he stayed put while his neighbors behaved not as a rooted population of farmers but one in constant flux. Many of his brothers, for example, pulled up stakes and relocated several times over the course of their lives. All Otsego residents, farmers and townspeople alike, experienced the great economic and social trends of the early American republic and Jacksonian era: the transportation and market revolutions, immigration, religious upheavals, community building, and the rise of a new middle class. Ball-playing provided them with more than just a leisurely activity to cope with the pressures of the times. It became deeply ingrained in the region's rural life and a cultural symbol of the unprecedented and accelerating changes that characterized America's frontier margins.[3]

Seth Doubleday's relative stability in Pierstown reflected not only his own hard work and persistence but also his favored status as an early arrival to the area. The American Revolution had severely disordered colonial society and property, which allowed savvy speculators such as William Cooper opportunities to accumulate profits and authority in the new republic. When he saw an opening in 1786, Cooper put together a complex financial deal to purchase 40,000 acres in the Otsego country from its elite proprietors, who were anxious to sell because of unclear titles. Unlike the great landed barons of eastern New York of the seventeenth and eighteenth centuries, Cooper wholeheartedly opposed the old leasehold system, which he felt suppressed initiative. Cooper knew that for him to succeed—to meet his own pressing debts and generate profits from his purchase—his buyers needed to succeed. Thus motivated, he shrewdly pursued an aggressive, fourfold strategy to attract industrious, enterprising (if cash-poor) settlers: he sold freehold title at modest prices; he sold on comparatively long credit (ten years as opposed to the customary three or five); he sold "the best lots to the first comers" at the standard price; and he maintained a strong presence in Otsego as a reassuring, resident landlord. As a "first comer," Doubleday snatched up one of the prime (relatively flat) lots near the lake, seeking to cultivate a marketable surplus as well as family subsistence from the land. Doubleday received his deed by signing a mortgage with no down payment, and his subsequent efforts to clear and farm the land promised to enhance the value of Cooper's unsold lands and overall investment.[4]

When choosing his tract, Doubleday, like other new settlers to the area, judged the economic potential of the land by paying close attention first and foremost to the trees. Trees, he knew, represented commodities in lumber, firewood, syrup, and especially potash. Even more importantly, he judged the fertility of the soil just as previous Doubledays had done in Connecticut—by the presence or absence of native vegetation, timber in particular. Wherever forests of tall, thick deciduous hardwoods predominated, good soil surely lay beneath. Upon removing the trees, Doubleday anticipated using a small portion of the cleared land for pasture and vegetable gardens, but most of it would go to wheat, the crop that Yankees identified with economic growth. Wheat, they knew, flourished on the rich soils of the frontier. It required little cash and only a limited amount of unskilled labor. A first crop often returned a sizeable profit. Moreover, since American and European diets centered on bread, wheat invariably brought the best market prices of any grain. Wheat was also nonperishable and transportable at minimal cost to distant markets in oceangoing ships. When bad harvests and devastating warfare disrupted the European supply in the 1780s and '90s, a vigorous trans-Atlantic trade developed, enhancing prices and profits for American farmers and merchants. The hard part for Otsego settlers was getting the crop to Albany, the linchpin of the wheat trade in upstate New York at the junction of the Hudson and Mohawk Rivers, a hundred miles to the east over roads so bad that farmers actually preferred to make the five-day round-trip in the winter on heavy horse-drawn sleighs carrying twenty to twenty-five bushels at a time. "It was a curious sight," one settler recalled, "to observe the immense number of sleighs, on approaching the city; a string a mile long was no uncommon occurrence in those days."[5]

As long as settlers like Doubleday could exploit the export market for wheat, both Cooperstown and Cooper stood to benefit. As the emerging service center for the surrounding agricultural community, Cooperstown attracted increasing numbers of craftsmen, merchants, and professionals by the close of the eighteenth century. Blacksmiths, carpenters, coopers, cobblers, cabinetmakers, millwrights, printers, and other artisans offered skills and resources that quickly became indispensable to farmers. Storekeepers provided a variety of items including dry goods, groceries, soap, shoes, crockery, coffee, tea, liquor, and hardware. Lawyers, physicians, clergymen, and schoolteachers soon became prominent citizens in the community as well. This second wave of settlers freed farmers from the weary demands of self-sufficiency, which in turn gave them more time to improve their farms and increase production. More time also opened for leisure, enjoyed at taverns, churches, or, as Seth Doubleday came to favor, wrestling rings and ball grounds. The commercial growth of Cooperstown and the surrounding countryside's emergence from frontier conditions did wonders for Cooper as well by facilitating land payments from the older settlers, inflating the land prices he could charge newer settlers, and creating a local market to supply Otsego County's surging population (1,721 in 1790; 21,251 in 1800; 38,425 in 1810).[6]

While the local economy flourished, deep-seated social tensions—characteristic of Cooperstown in particular and America in general—simmered just beneath the surface. Citizens of the new republic, while subscribing to democratic values and practices, nonetheless remained bound by hierarchical conceptions of social worth from their colonial past. This dichotomy resulted in the persistence of both a genteel class (the "better sort"), whose members believed that only their benevolent power could impose order on the fragile new nation and protect citizens from danger, and the lower and middling classes (the "common sort"), increasingly determined to reject elite concepts of society and take control of their own lives. At issue lay the establishment of a new basis for authority on the foundations of an act—the American Revolution—that had repudiated an earlier authority. This great paradox prevailed on the frontier every bit as much as in established eastern cities as Americans having won home rule grappled with the question of who would rule at home.[7]

In Cooperstown, prosperity appeared for a time to mitigate the tension between gentility and commonality. Cooper maintained settlers' loyalty by tolerating irregular payments on their loans, occasionally forgiving a portion of a mortgage, assisting poor or struggling farmers, and subsidizing community services, such as the local general store, the Episcopalian church, and a new, improved road to Albany. In return, settlers deferred to Cooper and accepted his patriarchal rule by publicly affirming their loyalty and affection and, in most instances, voting as directed. Even when settlers failed to fulfill their purchase contracts but wanted to retain their farms, Cooper often gave them the option to remain as tenants, paying annual rent in cash or in produce. Cooper believed he personified this mutually beneficial coexistence, having risen from humble origins to riches, influence, and authority. All Otsego residents—indeed, Americans in general—celebrated the opportunity, equality, and mobility that Cooper's life seemed to represent.[8]

This fragile equilibrium depended on a stable wheat trade, but a disruption came in December 1807, when President Thomas Jefferson declared an embargo on commerce with the British empire. While some Otsego farmers managed to smuggle their produce northward across the St. Lawrence River to a thriving black market in Canada, the virtual closing of the Albany port left most settlers without a means to sell their high-value crop. Even after the embargo was lifted two years later, the war of 1812-1815 and subsequent economic downturn that culminated in the Panic of 1819 made for stubbornly hard times for most of the decade. No crop at all in 1816, "the year without a summer" as it became known for its late snows (well into June) and early frosts, did not help either. The Otsego country had grown rapidly in both population and prosperity largely because of the European demand for wheat, but when the bottom fell out of the international market, Otsego lost its reputation as a promising frontier county. The dominoes fell quickly. Without a market, the settlers had no cash to make payments on their mortgages, and without payments from the settlers, Cooper and his heirs (he died in 1809) could not repay his speculating partners and other creditors. Cooper now personified not the rise but the decline of "his" town. With his fortunes hinging on the prospects of the thousands of farmers who had settled his Otsego lands over twenty years, Cooper's estate collapsed into financial ruin during the prolonged economic hardships of the 1810s, the troubles now exacerbated by his heirs' mismanagement and his own overspeculation. As for the settlers themselves, more of them rented than owned their lands by the end of the decade, and more migrated out of the county to the west than moved into it from the east. That Seth Doubleday stayed put suggests he probably had already paid off his mortgage on his prime plot of land, but if so, he was one of the privileged few. Indeed, contrary to Cooper's initial hopes and aspirations, Otsego's rising proportion of tenant farmers and high degree of transiency left it much like the older counties of eastern New York.[9]

Nor did the cordial (but tenuous) social relations in Otsego survive the demise of the wheat trade. In Cooperstown in particular, economic growth through the end of the first decade of the nineteenth century created an exclusive, ever-widening social circle of genteel families—not only the Coopers, but also the Phinneys, Averells, Pomeroys, Metcalfs, and Campbells, to name just a few. They transformed the village from a crude collection of log cabins and stump-filled pastures to a cosmopolitan community featuring two dressmakers, a bookstore, three newspapers, two fine hotels, two schools, two churches, a young men's debating club, a Young Ladies Benevolent Society, at least a dozen elegant mansions, and a new brick courthouse built in 1807 at a cost of $7,000. In terms of fashions, mores, and manners, Cooperstown's better sort imitated their counterparts in New York City, Boston, or Philadelphia and flattered themselves as their equals. The leading families, however, increasingly complained in the 1810s that the common sort in and around Cooperstown no longer provided the proper deference to which they had become accustomed. Anecdotal evidence of popular discontent—difficulties finding dutiful and modest servants, increased petty vandalism, trespassing on their estates, vulgar language, disrespectful behavior—filled their conversations and the columns in the local newspapers. With rumors abounding of rowdy bands of arsonists conspiring to burn down the village, the thought of the wood buildings that lined the streets fed the gentility's anxiety. Hard evidence, however, suggests that farmers and townspeople, with wheat prices plummeting, worried more about their own lives than the aristocratic pretensions of the village's gentlemen and ladies.[10]

Cooperstown's gentility did more than fret about the decay of deference that, in their minds, had brought the village to the brink of social anarchy. To calm their anxieties and regain their mastery over the village and its hinterland, they set out to impose their will on their common neighbors. If the unwritten social contract that had worked so well in the 1790s and 1800s no longer seemed adequate, then they would, in essence, write a new one, one clause at a time, and create institutions to enforce it. They began in June 1812 by pushing a bill through the state legislature incorporating the village of Cooperstown. The act established a new village government, consisting of an annually elected board of five trustees assisted by one clerk-treasurer. Isaac Cooper, William's son, emerged as the board's president and presided over the trustees through 1818. His brother-in-law, George Pomeroy, served as clerk-treasurer from 1812 to 1819. Other board members over the course of the decade included Robert Campbell (the Cooper family's lawyer), Isaac's brother Samuel, John Russell, Elijah Metcalf, Peter Goodsell, James Averell Jr., Cyrus Clark, Henry Phinney, and John Prentiss—all of them prominent lawyers and/or businessmen and leading members of Cooperstown's high society.[11]

Taken together, the ordinances passed by the Cooperstown Board of Trustees the first few years read like a practical guide for restoring order and decorum in the village. They began on November 23, 1812, with "A Law Relative to the Streets," which fined anyone caught cluttering the village's new plank sidewalks with wood, timber, wagons, carts, sleighs, wheelbarrows, or other "obstructions" the considerable sum of twenty-five cents. The trustees also ordered villagers, under threat of the same fine, to keep their geese, swine, and cows fenced in their own yards and pastures. Poorer townspeople and nearby farmers had loosed their animals to forage the village streets for grass and rubbish, creating a spectacle that their more prosperous neighbors found displeasing to the eye, ear, and nose. Such negligence also forced them to build fences around their own gardens to keep out the roaming livestock. To the dismay of the trustees and their backers, the law met considerable resistance and proved ineffective. The following year, and for several years thereafter, they reissued the street ordinance, virtually word for word, doubled the fines for each infraction, and added new rules and regulations. In the fall of 1813, for example, the board declared that it would seize and put up for sale "the swine with which the streets are infested" and impose an enormous fine of ten dollars on anyone attempting to rescue an impounded pig, a not uncommon practice, apparently. When the common sort continued to ignore "the several ordinances heretofore passed, relating to swine running at large in the streets of the village of Cooperstown," the trustees repealed them in June 1816 in favor of a new, more simplified and straightforward law mandating fines of $2.50 "for each and every swine so found running at large." The board also banned horse racing in the streets and, to guard against their worst fear, required the owner of every dwelling, house, office, shop, or store to keep at hand at least one leather fire bucket under the penalty of one dollar "for neglect or refusal to do so."[12]

The leading villagers crusaded for greater order through private institutions as well, most notably the Otsego County Bible Society and the Otsego County Agricultural Society. Once again, the village trustees, all of them Episcopalians or Presbyterians, played leading roles in organizing the ecumenical association in 1813, with Cooper's sons emerging as the most generous donors. Dedicated to purchasing bibles and Christian testaments for free distribution to the poor, the bible society reinforced the gentility's efforts to reform the appearance, morality, and discipline of the common people. The very act of offering systematic charity revitalized the hierarchical notion among the better sort that they could not only earn popular gratitude but also rescue society from "innumerable vices and disorders" with daily readings of the bible. In a similar manner, members of the agricultural society, founded in 1817, cared more about promoting their vision of social harmony than advancing new farming techniques and approaches. Very few, in fact, even were farmers. The society set out, for example, to replace crude log cabins and their vulgar inhabitants with "comfortable and elegant habitations and a happy community," but again they met resistance from the common folk. Before the year's end, one prominent member conceded that Otsego farmers suspected "that all societies of this kind are bodies not organized for their good, but for the express purpose of debasing and oppressing them." James Cooper, along with the rest of the society's founders, might have done well to take heed of his father's insight from the previous decade that common farmers knew "their interests better than strangers can instruct them."[13]

In all likelihood, Seth Doubleday neither joined nor paid much interest to these two voluntary associations, nor did the various village ordinances cause him, as a nonresident of Cooperstown, much concern. One, however, surely caught his eye. On June 6, 1816, the board of trustees posted two new ordinances in the *Otsego Herald*—the revised swine act and, right below that, an anti-ball measure: "Be it ordained, that no person shall play at Ball in Second or West street, in this village, under a penalty of one dollar, for each and every offence."[14] The irony of banning public ball-playing in the place known for the birth of baseball has not escaped scholars, but few (if any) have placed the ordinance in its immediate or long-term historical context.[15] Isaac Cooper and his fellow trustees found townball on the streets of the village just as distasteful, immoral, and threatening as foraging swine, Sabbath breakers, excessive profanity, and vandalism. While they had no control over it in the countryside—on Doubleday's farm, for example—they made getting rid of the game a top priority in their crusade to take back their village. Why, the question remains, did ball-playing strike such a sensitive nerve? In part, simply because playing ball caused a ruckus, and the genteel found just about any ruckus inherently offensive. The fact that the popular (or notorious, depending on one's perspective) Red Lion tavern stood at the particular intersection mentioned in the ordinance (know by the locals as "The Four Corners" in the center of town) no doubt did not sit well with the better sort either. The more commotion they could remove from the streets, they wholeheartedly believed, the greater their perfection of self-control.[16]

But what really got under the village leaders' skin was that the game so enthused the common sort. Townball little resembled the ordered, rational game that we recognize today as baseball. In most versions, the infield was square, with no foul lines or fixed positions in the field. Eight to fifteen persons—and sometimes as many as fifty—played on a side. The "feeder," the least important player, had only to toss the ball to the "striker," who could actually demand just where he wanted the ball and could wait as long as he wanted until he got his pitch. He could hit the ball in any direction, including directly behind him. A single out retired the side, and a runner was out if the ball was caught either on the fly or on one bounce, or if he was "soaked" or "plunked," which is to say hit with a thrown ball when running the bases. A fixed number of runs, usually 100, won the game, and the rules varied from region to region, even from town to town. A game required only the rudest preparation—driving sticks into the ground as "goals" or bases at approximate distances—and minimal equipment, such as a wagon tongue for a bat and a stuffed leather ball made by a local shoemaker.

The game's simplicity, informality, and spontaneity made for great popularity and wide participation. Children, young adults, and middle-aged men all played together at the same time, thus making townball overwhelmingly *democratic*—the very essence of commonality and the everlasting dread of gentility. As such, it symbolized the mounting social tension in Cooperstown and its hinterland.[17]

While common farmers were skeptical of, if not hostile to, the gentlemen of the Otsego County Agricultural Society for telling them how to farm, they might have done well to listen when the society warned that the time had come to retool the local economy. Though they faced seemingly insurmountable odds for success with prices in free fall for over a decade, farmers hesitated to give up on wheat, even with the additional devastation wrought by the Panic of 1819. Wheat, after all, had built a way of life for them not just in Otsego County during the past twenty years but, in many cases, dating back several generations to their roots in New England. Moreover, news of the construction of the Erie Canal through the

Mohawk Valley, just thirty miles to the north, revitalized their spirits with the promise of a resurgent wheat trade. When the canal opened in 1825, wheat was indeed one of the principal commodities it carried east, but not wheat from Otsego County and other geographically isolated regions of central New York. A community already under stress, torn by social, cultural, and economic crosscurrents, now faced an even darker future. For families like the Doubledays, playing ball became their passion in this period of adjustment and disillusion.[18]

The notion of the Erie Canal as savior had legitimacy. In the second quarter of the nineteenth century, everything in the northern United States seemed to be expanding, from transportation networks to markets to people's horizon of experience—with the Erie Canal as one of the key catalysts of this "great transformation." Changing patterns of world trade set in motion by the end of the Napoleonic wars in 1815 prompted American merchant capitalists to redirect their focus from Europe toward the American continent itself. They began investing in the construction of roads, canals, bridges and, later, steamboats and railroads to link the urban markets of the Northeast to growing regions of the West and thus open the way for internal commerce to flourish. Built between 1817 and 1825, the Erie Canal stretched 364 miles from Buffalo to Albany, connecting, by extension, the Great Lakes and Ohio Valley to the Hudson River, New York City, and the trans-Atlantic world. This engineering marvel reduced the cost of shipping a ton of goods from Buffalo to Albany from about a hundred dollars to just ten, and the transit time dropped from twenty days to eight. The Erie Canal also offered the cheapest and fastest way to send goods from Philadelphia to Tennessee. In its first full year of operation, the canal generated three-quarters of a million dollars in profits. The flood of farm products from America's interior soon made New York City the most important commercial center in the nation. It was hard to say who was more ecstatic, Western farmers or Eastern businessmen.[19]

Everyone looked like a winner—but not, as it turned out, Otsego farmers. Before the decade of the 1820s ended, they realized, much to their dismay, that they simply could not compete with farmers who had access to low-priced Western lands subject to little or no taxation, as well as proximity to the canal itself. With transportation cheap and the cost of cultivating wheat on the vast, untouched, flat, and fertile lands of the Ohio and Michigan territories low, the more inland soil broken by the plow, the more acute the crisis became for the suddenly old sequestered communities of central New York. In 1835, more than 86,000 barrels of flour and 95,000 bushels of wheat moved eastward from Buffalo to the Hudson River; five years later those quantities had expanded to an astounding 633,000 barrels of flour and 881,000 bushels of wheat. Local efforts in the early

1830s to construct an artificial watercourse from Otsego Lake to tap the Erie Canal in the Mohawk Valley found few investors and never got off the ground. This turn of events demoralized Otsego farmers and drove them, grudgingly, to consider their genteel antagonists' earlier suggestion that they abandon wheat and try something else. In the 1830s, they began to turn primarily to dairying and wool growing, both of which proved moderately profitable, though as soon as Western farmers entered the sheep market a decade later, local agriculturalists again found the competition too keen. By the mid 1840s, hops became a major crop—until new hop-raising districts in the Far West in the 1880s doomed that strategy as well. Grain growing, what little remained, went toward the production of whiskey and flour, and virtually all farm produce in Otsego County sold to local and state markets.[20]

Local merchants, manufacturers, and craftsmen also found themselves at a crossroads. While Otsego County had never numbered among the more heavily industrialized sections of the state, its decline in this sector from 1830 to 1850—particularly the reduction in sawmills, gristmills, and tanneries—sharply contrasted with the explosive economic growth in canal towns such as Rochester and Utica (the latter just forty miles away). By the 1850s, the main products manufactured in Otsego County—rope, hoes, rakes, silverware, paper, medicines, glue, matches, barrels, ladders, bricks, and gloves—mostly sold no farther away than Otsego and its adjacent counties.[21] While the organization of work in Rochester and other thriving canal towns changed dramatically in the 1830s and '40s—moving from the artisan system to one based more heavily on wage labor—shoemakers, coopers, cabinetmakers, and other craftsmen in Cooperstown continued, well into the second half of the nineteenth century, to run their shops with journeymen and apprentices and board them in their homes. In the 1850s, a cash economy still had not replaced a complex barter-exchange system.[22] Carrying on traditional work relations did not bring stability, however. While the population of Otsego Township changed little between 1820 and 1860 (about 1,300), the community continued to experience heavy in- and out-migration. Throughout this period, one-ninth of Otsego's population transferred out and an equivalent number transferred in during an average year. The same enterprising spirit that had carried settlers into the region before the opening of the Erie Canal drove many of their descendants to Ohio and Michigan, including Demas Abner Doubleday, Seth's nephew, who moved his family from Otsego to Kalamazoo in 1837.[23]

A major exception to Cooperstown's stunted economic growth was the printing establishment founded by Elihu Phinney in the 1790s and carried on by his two sons, Henry and Elihu Jr., through the first half of the nineteenth century.

Originally founded to publish the *Otsego Herald*, Cooperstown's first newspaper, the Phinney firm greatly expanded under the two sons' leadership to include book publishing and selling. In the process, they became famous in upstate New York for their original methods of conducting business. In the 1810s, they began constructing "locomotive bookstores"—large wagons with movable tops for easy access and shelves stocked with hundreds of volumes. Traveling agents drove them to villages throughout much of central New York, where books were scarcely attainable otherwise. The Erie Canal actually opened up more fields of enterprise for the Phinneys. They turned ordinary canal boats into "floating bookstores," serving towns from Buffalo to Albany. Unlike most other freight, books, light in weight and high in value, could bear the cost of transportation. By 1838, the Phinney's stereotype foundry in Cooperstown had five presses and employed forty people. Each year they printed approximately 200,000 almanacs, 8,000 bibles, and 60,000 other volumes, mostly children's schoolbooks. In 1850, with their business worth an estimated $100,000, they, too, found it expedient to move the publishing department of their firm to Buffalo, from where they could better access the entire Great Lakes region, leaving behind only a bookstore in Cooperstown.[24]

While the Erie Canal passed farmers and townspeople in Otsego County, they did benefit from the expansion of political democracy that moved steadily across the nation between 1800 and 1830—and straight through New York in 1821. That year, the state revised its constitution, instituting universal white male suffrage (with minimal restrictions). The effects of the electoral reform were far-reaching and swiftly felt. As political parties sought votes from a much broader electorate, the tone of politics became more open and competitive, swayed by the interests and values of ordinary people. In Cooperstown, over the course of several years, the rich and well-born lost their political authority to the self-taught village lawyer, small merchant, newspaper editor, respectable farmer, and well-established craftsman. Seth Doubleday Jr., son of the pioneer farmer and owner of a prosperous grocery store on the Four Corners, epitomized this new class of leaders who took responsibility for ordering public life. Known for his generosity of credit, firm grasp of community affairs, and "plain-speaking," Seth was elected to several offices: to the Cooperstown Board of Trustees in 1830, as first officer of the newly organized Universalist church in 1831, as librarian of the local branch of the Franklin Society Library for much of the 1830s, to the local arrangements committee that welcomed President Martin Van Buren to Cooperstown in 1839, as trustee of the Otsego Academy in 1840, and as village supervisor in 1847—the sorts of positions that the Coopers and other genteel families had held earlier in the century. Many of Seth's brothers and cousins—William, Rufus, Lewis, Lester, and Elisha among them—also played prominent roles in the public life of the village and county.[25]

This sort of activist energy had powerful religious underpinnings. Starting at the turn of the nineteenth century and accelerating through the 1830s, a wave of evangelical fervor swept through upstate New York. While Otsego County lay just east of the famous "burned-over district," many of the region's leading itinerant preachers—Charles Finney, Charles Giles, Thomas Nash, Billy Hibbard—frequently worked the "Otsego circuit" between Rochester and Cooperstown. Giles found one Cooperstown resident's conversion account so moving that he often highlighted it in his sermons: "While at the quarterly meeting on the Sabbath, I was awakened, and saw myself as a great sinner. I came home with a burden of misery resting on my mind, which was discovered by a young lady in the family, who inquired to know the cause of my sadness. I told her my feelings, and that I desired to be saved from my sins: the young lady advised me to read prayers; but I told her that I chose to pray out of my heart. So I went on sorrowing, praying, and seeking the Lord, till, on a certain day, as I was bowed before the throne of mercy, praying, *righteousness struck me*; my burden rolled off, and I was happy: all my sins were forgotten." The account dramatized a fundamental difference between what contemporary evangelical leaders termed the Second Great Awakening and its original or first incarnation led by George Whitefield and Jonathan Edwards the previous century. While both awakenings stressed the sinful nature of humans, nineteenth-century ministers rejected the belief that salvation lay in God's hands alone and insisted that humans had the capacity, and indeed the duty, to repent their sins and embrace moral agency. What counted was not people's belief in formal church doctrines but their will to seek redemption. Salvation took more than reading scripture or attending revivals; it required action.[26]

With this great sense of participation and responsibility, Methodists, Baptists, Presbyterians, and a new sect of Universalists established churches in Cooperstown in the 1830s. While Universalists, Seth Doubleday included, criticized what they regarded as the excessive drama of revivalism, they too repudiated the Calvinist doctrine of predestination and emphasized that exercise of free will could lead to a Christian conversion. More representative of the time and place was the First Baptist Church of Cooperstown, founded in 1834 by eight crusading charter members. Baptists' evangelical fervor fostered lay preaching, emotional worship, and communal singing, all of which created an egalitarian religious culture. No bishops or governing bodies stood above the religious congregation, and most church decisions rested with church members. These democratic features, along with the efforts of dedicated local missionaries such as Henry Smith, Moses Lippitt, and Lewis Raymond; a spectacular site for baptisms at the source of the Susquehanna River on Otsego Lake; and friendly competition with the Methodists, Presbyterians, and Universalists generated constant revival and remarkable growth, especially given the transient nature of the local population. Between 1834 and 1840, the First Baptist Church of Cooperstown annually baptized one person for every four already in the church, and expanded, over the same period, to more than 200 members, a rate of growth similar to the other evangelical churches in the village. In contrast, the Episcopalian church declined in relative membership. Its leaders and members seemed content to maintain the existing congregation and grow slowly through natural increase.[27]

Tellingly, most converts to the new Protestant churches came from Doubleday's "new middle class." The rise of an evangelical conception of social order affected not only their religious lives but also their politics, their social outlook, and even their sporting diversions. The new evangelicalism created a new kind of Christian citizen, driven by enterprise, self-importance, and a spirit of independence and repelled by eighteenth-century notions of hierarchy and authority.[28]

This did not mean that the genteel simply gave up without a struggle—quite the contrary. Leading the way for the Cooperstown's well-to-do was none other than William Cooper's youngest son, James Fenimore Cooper, the single most influential American writer of the early nineteenth century, best known for his famous series of Leatherstocking Tales: *The Pioneers* (1823), *The Last of the Mohicans* (1826), *The Prairie* (1827), *The Pathfinder* (1840), and *The Deerslayer* (1841). A major theme running through these and many of his other thirty-two novels was the "great moral descent" of America's social order in its postrevolutionary decades. To dramatize this theme, Cooper set four of his novels in Cooperstown ("Templeton") and the surrounding forests and countryside, with characters based on village residents, including his father ("Judge Marmaduke"). Beguiled by his vivid and realistic depictions of village life and the Otsego landscape, contemporary critics often referred to his novels as history rather than fiction. In truth, Cooper wrote a wishful history at best. In *The Pioneers*, his first major novel, he sought to quiet his own fears, and those of other elite Americans, that the ever-widening social divide between gentility and commonality would eventually destroy the republic. By novel's end, Templeton's better sort emerges triumphant to exercise a unified authority over an increasingly deferential and harmonious community. Meanwhile, in Cooper's real life, his father's estate crumbled into ruins and resistance to gentility waxed rapidly. To remind Cooper of that reality, an arsonist torched his mansion on the west shore of Otsego Lake on July 23, 1823, prompting the novelist to flee to New York City and, later, Europe, alienated from his native village and yearning for the company of well-mannered, like-minded aristocrats.[29]

Cooper returned to America in 1833, rich, famous, and hoping to find the Cooperstown of his youth. Much had changed over the years but not, in his mind, for the better. He took up residence at Otsego Hall, the former home of his father and of his youth. The five-acre estate, situated squarely in the center of the village between Second and Third streets on a two-block lot, created a conspicuous open space on the town grid that prevented Fair Street from continuing straight through from one side to the other. On the death of William Cooper's widow in 1818, Otsego Hall was closed and sold, as none of the heirs could afford to maintain it. During the fifteen years that elapsed before Cooper bought it back in 1833, "the noblest mansion west of Albany" fell into considerable disrepair—the roof rotted, the interior neglected, and the grounds overgrown. An attempt to set it on fire in 1823 had failed. At enormous cost, Cooper remodeled the building into a lordly manor (after a palace he admired in La Grange, France), with Gothic architecture, ornate furniture, an extensive art collection that included an original Rembrandt, and a marble bust of himself made in Paris by David d'Angers, a famous French sculptor. Cooper also intended to build a high stone wall all around the grounds with a castellated gatehouse at the Second Street entrance to keep out intruders and riffraff, but because of the cost he had to settle for a two-foot stone wall in front and a wooden fence around the rest. Village residents, much to his chagrin, had fallen into the habit of taking a short cut across the grounds and around the house from one side of Fair Street to the other. The villagers could easily have chosen an alternate route without much trouble or additional time. Their trespassing protested what they regarded as Cooper's arrogance—not only for his pretentious mansion in the middle of town but also, as one observer put it, for his "fastidiously undemocratic" tastes and mannerisms. He had, for example, a tendency to lecture the neighbors on their manners upon meeting them on the street. In turn, Cooper, utterly unconscious of any arrogance in his behavior, found the townspeople rude and ungrateful.[30]

Another dispute led Cooper to similar conclusions about the locals and, in addition, to a long series of libel suits. At issue was Three Mile Point (originally known as Myrtle Grove) on the west side of Otsego Lake, a small wooded area with a sandy beach and sweeping vistas, owned by the descendants of William

Cooper and, for years, a family recreation spot that had produced many fond memories. "I have myself seen children of my family sporting in the shades of Myrtle Grove, as I saw their parents sporting as children, before them," wrote James Fenimore Cooper. But when he returned from Europe in 1833, he found that the villagers had turned the point into a public picnic ground and had chopped down a couple of trees (which he termed "extensive vandalism"). Furious once again, he posted a warning in the *Freeman's Journal*, promising to have all trespassers arrested and prosecuted. An equally furious group of villagers resolved, in print, to resist the "arrogant pretensions of James Fenimore Cooper," claim title to the point for themselves, and, for good measure, remove all Cooper's novels from the local library. Cooper quashed this plan by producing a copy of his father's will. But when the village's other newspaper, the *Otsego Republican*, denounced Cooper with a series of unflattering characterizations, the novelist became the lawyer, suing the paper (and eventually two others as well) for libel, arguing his own case in court. Though he eventually won his verdicts from reluctant juries, he became profoundly disillusioned with his neighbors and they with him. When deemed an un-American aristocrat on one occasion, Cooper retorted, "In this part of the world, it is thought aristocratic not to frequent taverns, and lounge at corners, squirting tobacco juice."[31]

Cooper had more in store. In 1838, he openly satirized Cooperstown (and, by extension, Jacksonian America) in *Home as Found*—a work of fiction in which much of the plot and content, as in *The Pioneers*, mirrored events in the novelist's life. *Home as Found*, in fact, continued the storyline of *The Pioneers*, though with a significantly revised central theme and an altogether different tone. Edward Effingham (Cooper's alter ego) and his family, descendants of the pioneer frontiersman who founded Templeton, return to their native village after several years abroad in Europe. In contrast to the optimistic conclusion reached in *The Pioneers*, Cooper depicts Templeton not as a mature harmonious village of modest and deferential commoners but as a sink of vulgarity, hypocrisy, and demagoguery—as illustrated most prominently by dramatizations of the Otsego Hall ("the Wigwam") and Three-mile Point ("Fishing Point") controversies. The generation who succeeded the pioneers, Cooper now maintained, had lost the character and values of their fathers and grandfathers and lacked any appreciation for the price of liberty or any sense of how free men should conduct their lives. Midway through the novel, the narrator expresses hope that Templeton, as it grew in population and complexity, could eventually evolve to a third stage of development where "men and things come within the control of more general and regular laws" and society in general assumes the proper "division into castes that are more or less rigidly maintained." That wishful scenario manifested in neither fiction nor fact, however. By novel's end, the Effinghams withdraw into the private sanctity of their estate, as did Cooper himself in the last years of his life.[32]

In a revealing passage, dripping with sarcasm, "a game of ball" becomes a vehicle for Cooper to pontificate on the decline of order and decorum in Templeton. Aristabulus Bragg, the village lawyer and a local "booster," tries his best to negotiate a settlement of the ensuing controversy.

> As they came in front of the hall windows, a party of apprentice-boys were seen coolly making their arrangements to amuse themselves with a game of ball, on the front lawn directly in front of the house.
>
> "Surely, Mr. Bragg," said the owner of the [house], . . . "you do not countenance this liberty?"
>
> "Liberty, sir! I am an advocate for liberty wherever I can find it. Do you refer to the young men on the lawn, Mr. Effingham?"
>
> "Certainly to them, sir; and permit me to say, I think they might have chose a more suitable spot for their sports. They are mistaking liberties for liberty, I fear."
>
> "Why, sir, I believe they have always played ball in that precise locality."
>
> "Always! I can assure you this is a great mistake. What private family, placed as we are in the centre of a village, would allow of an invasion of its privacy in this rude manner? . . . I beg, Mr. Bragg, that you will at once desire these young men to pursue their sports somewhere else."
>
> Aristabulus received this commission with a very ill grace; for, while his native sagacity told him that Mr. Effingham was right, he too well knew the loose habits that had rapidly been increasing in the country during the last ten years, not to foresee that the order would do violence to all the apprentices' preconceived notions of their immunities. . . . In passing the ball-players, he called out in a wheedling tone to their ringleader, a notorious street brawler.
>
> "A fine time for sport, Dickey; don't you think there would be more room in the broad street than on this crowded lawn, where you lose your ball so often in the shrubbery?"
>
> "This place will do in a pinch," bawled Dickey, "though it might be better. If it weren't for that plagued house, we couldn't ask for a better ball-ground."
>
> . . .
>
> "Well, Dickey, there is no accounting for tastes; but, in my opinion, the street would be a much better place to play ball in than this lawn. . . . There are so many fences hereabouts. . . . It's true the village trustees say there shall be no

ball-playing in the street, but I conclude you don't much mind what they think or threaten."

"Let them sue me for that, if they like," bawled a particularly amiable blackguard, called Peter, who struck his ball as he spoke, quite into the principal street of the village. "Who's a trustee, that he should tell gentlemen where they are to play ball!" . . .

The bait took; for what apprentice, American apprentice in particular, can resist an opportunity of showing how much he considers himself superior to the law? Then it had never struck any of the party before, that is was vulgar and aristocratic to pursue the sport among roses, and one or two of them actually complained that they had pricked their fingers in searching for the ball.

"I know Mr. Effingham will be very sorry to have you go," continued Aristabulus, following up his advantage, "but gentlemen cannot always forego their pleasures for other folks."

"Who's Mr. Effingham, I would like to know?" cried Joe Wart. "If he wants people to play ball on his premises, let him cut down his roses." . . .

The lawn was now evacuated en masse.[33]

The scene had a clear purpose. Cooper did not have to explain the significance of townball to his readers. Villagers may not have "always" played ball on the grounds of Otsego Hall, the streets of Cooperstown, or Seth Doubleday's farm, but they had clearly played the game for years. Cooper took for granted not only his readers' familiarity with the game but also their understanding of its cultural meaning. He no more sought to ban ball-playing than to recover the small piece of property from trespassing picnickers or shut down a shortcut through his yard. The principle alone mattered, and for Cooper that meant the preservation of the natural social order. The villagers, on the other hand, greatly resented Cooper's sarcasm and condescension. To them, the ball-playing men do not mistake liberties for liberty; Effingham mistakes liberty for gentility. The key character, in the end, is Bragg, who finds himself caught in the middle of the confrontation. Effingham relies on him not only to communicate with Dickey, Peter, and Joe Wart but also, in the long run, to convince them that only genteel guidance can lead Templeton to the all-important third stage of the settlement's maturity. Bragg agrees, but then Bragg will agree with just about any principle that offers him an advantage.[34]

Ironically, shortly after Cooper's death in 1852, men of lawyer Bragg's new class exploited the novelist's literary success by turning Cooperstown into a profitable summer resort. In the second half of the nineteenth century and into the twentieth, tourists flocked to Otsego Lake and its surrounding hills and forests to see for themselves all the exotic places made famous in *The Pioneers* and *The Deerslayer*—Mohican Canyon, Leatherstocking Falls, Council Rock, Mount Vision, Natty Bumppo's Cave, Chingachgook's Grave, and the Echo of Glimmerglass, to name just a few. In town, signs inscribed with similar names lured visitors into taverns, inns, restaurants, parks, churches, and cemeteries. Cooperstown had finally found its niche, as a dignitary speaking at the village's centennial celebration in 1907 well understood. "Had our village become a canal feeder," he asked the crowd, "could author have immortalized or poet glorified the 'Glimmerglass'?" References to *Home as Found*, which proved too close to home, were nowhere found, however. It remains one of Cooper's most obscure works.[35]

Just a few months after Cooperstown's centennial celebration, the Mills Commission, based on Abner Graves's two letters to Albert Spalding, announced their conclusion that Abner Doubleday invented baseball in Cooperstown in 1839, just one year after Cooper had published *Home as Found*. Graves was mistaken about the identity of the "inventor"—that much is sure. The significance of Graves's letters and the entire Doubleday "myth," for that matter, has really nothing to do with the origins of baseball. Finding the game's originator is a futile search, for all the energy that has been devoted to it. As one historian observed, "To ascertain who invented baseball would be equivalent to trying to locate the discoverer of fire."[36] The significance of Graves's letters lies in the fact that baseball—an earlier version of it, anyway—had already become rooted in the region's rural life by the time Abner Doubleday supposedly invented it, and this embeddedness is a cultural phenomenon that has in large part escaped the attention of baseball historians and rural historians alike.

Given the history of playing ball in Cooperstown on the streets, on the grounds of Otsego Hall, and on Seth Doubleday's farm, might there be some element of truth to Graves's reminiscences? Did Uncle Seth's great-nephew Abner really not "know a baseball from a kumquat," as so many Doubleday myth busters have quipped? Have we misjudged both Graves and Doubleday over the years? Though neither right nor consistent in his recollection of *all* the details, Graves was, after all, a seventy-one-year-old man trying to summon from memory events and individuals from his early childhood. He responded, typing his first letter on April 3, 1905, just two days after Spalding's request for "proof, data, or information" on the origins of baseball appeared in the newspaper. It seems highly unlikely that he meant to mislead anyone and eminently possible that he had actually played ball in Cooperstown, perhaps even with Abner Doubleday. Indeed, leaving aside the "inventor" claims (Graves himself never actually stated that he had witnessed the "invention"), Graves's reminiscences as a whole, rather remarkably, ring true—from the names of his playmates, to where they actually played, to many of the details of Doubleday's involvement.[37]

Graves made a point to mention, by name, eight of the "boys" with whom he had played ball in Cooperstown, and not one was a figment of his imagination. They ranged in age from five to twenty-one and spanned the social spectrum of the village. Elihu Phinney III, seventeen years old at the time, was the son of the most prominent businessman in town, publisher and bookseller Elihu Phinney Jr. Both father and son were known to be frequent guests of James Fenimore Cooper and his son Paul at Otsego Hall (though no Coopers made Graves's list).[38] John Starkweather, eleven, was the eldest son of George A. Starkweather, a village lawyer and booster whose career bore a strong resemblance to that of Aristabulus Bragg. John went on to become a general in the Union Army during the Civil War.[39] John Doubleday, Abner's cousin, was the nine-year-old son of Seth Jr., whose grocery store (and its location at the Four Corners) Graves accurately identified.[40] Nels Brewer, also nine, was the son of wagonmaker John Brewer, whose shop was a few doors down Second Street from Seth Doubleday's store.[41] At age five, Tom Bingham was the youngest of the group; his father was a shoemaker and a village trustee in 1846.[42] Cousins Abner and John Graves, aged six and fourteen, respectively, were grandchildren of tailor Calvin Graves and great-grandchildren of pioneer Abner Graves, who came to Otsego Township from New Hampshire in 1794.[43] Joseph Chafee's father, Samuel, was a laborer who resided in Otsego County no more than a few years.[44] The boys' wide range of ages and social backgrounds should come as no surprise. Such inclusiveness had long been a characteristic of townball, whether on Uncle Seth's farm or the streets of Cooperstown. While Graves acknowledged Doubleday's new game of "base ball," with far fewer players (eleven instead of twenty to fifty) and specifically assigned positions, as "an improvement," he remembered that at the time, "we smaller boys didn't like it because it shut us out from playing, while Town Ball let in everyone who could run and catch flies, or try to catch them."[45]

Just where the boys played has never been questioned all these years, but it probably should have all along. Graves mentioned several locations in town, including the Otsego Academy campus, but he emphasized "the 'Phinney farm' on the west shore of Otsego lake" as the boys' "favorite place" to play. It has always been assumed that Graves meant Phinney's lot, an irregularly shaped open field bounded by Main, Chestnut, Susquehanna, and Elm Streets, two blocks *south* of Otsego Lake in the center of the village. After all, the Cooperstown Chamber of Commerce, in 1917, had chosen to build Doubleday Field, which it dubbed "the birthplace of baseball," on this site. But Phinney's lot and Phinney's farm were not one and the same. Phinney's farm lay two miles from town up the west side of the lake at Brookwood Point (Graves initially wrote "half a mile" but later, and more accurately, stated "a mile or two"), about halfway to Uncle Seth's farm in Pierstown. Graves and his friends knew that playing ball in the village could mean trouble, making it well-worth the short walk out of town for a ball grounds where they had plenty of space to play without fear of repercussion.[46]

As for Abner Doubleday, one particular aspect of the standard myth-busting argument cries out for myth-busting itself. Doubleday, at West Point all year long in 1839, could not have been in Cooperstown. True. But the Mills Commission, not Graves, selected that particular year (for reasons never made clear). Graves dated his reminiscences to "the spring prior, or following the 'Log Cabin & Hard Cider' campaign of General Harrison for President," which he acknowledged could have meant either 1839, 1840, or 1841. In fact, the campaign took place in the summer and fall of 1840. And sure enough, a simple check of West Point's personnel records reveals the existence of "Order No. 30," signed by Major R. Delafield on June 18, 1840, granting Cadet Doubleday "a leave of absence until the 28th of August, next."[47]

Once Order No. 30 comes into play, other indications of Doubleday's whereabouts and doings that summer begin to fall into place as well. Abner's father, Ulysses Freeman Doubleday (son of Abner and grandson of Elisha) was baptized November 3, 1802, at the Presbyterian Church in Cooperstown and apprenticed to a village printer in 1809 before serving for several months against the British in the War of 1812. He eventually settled in Ballston Spa, New York (where Abner was born in 1819) and later moved to a farm in Scipio, about 100 miles west of Cooperstown. While several claims, none of them documented, maintain that Ulysses sent Abner to Cooperstown to live with his uncle and attend Otsego Academy, no hard evidence exists that he ever resided in Cooperstown for any extended period of time. But the Doubledays were a large, very close family, and Abner in particular was known to visit relatives whenever the opportunity presented itself, in Cooperstown and elsewhere across the state. On his leave from West Point, he almost assuredly traveled to Scipio to see his father and very likely could have stopped along the way in Cooperstown, where he still had many cousins.[48] Too old? Doubleday, twenty-one at the time and a take-charge type, as later demonstrated at Fort Sumter and Gettysburg, certainly might have been the older one organizing the others, just as Graves described it. His later correspondence and memoirs? Yes, no mention of baseball appears, but Doubleday also barely alludes to his experiences at West Point and all but passes over his boyhood. His writings concern the military, nothing more, nothing less. Might Graves have confused Abner the future general with Abner Demas Doubleday his cousin, as recently suggested? Perhaps, though Graves specifically remembered a sixteen- or seventeen-year-old Doubleday, and Abner Demas was only eleven at the time.[49]

Thus, it does seem entirely within the realm of possibility that at some point in his travels, Abner Doubleday acquired knowledge of a new variety of ball called "base ball" and shared it with his mates—with a young, impressionable Abner Graves perceiving, mistakenly but understandably, that the older boy he so admired had actually invented the new game.

Abner Graves and Rufus Doubleday were not the only ones to reminiscence about playing ball in Cooperstown. On August 11, 1877, thirty-two villagers gathered on the west grounds of the Cooper House Hotel to play townball, "the old-fashioned game of our boyhood." The game had "feeders" and "strikers," runners getting "plugged" on the base paths, no foul lines, no balls or strikes, and a "soft" ball made by a shoemaker in town especially for the occasion. Though none of the players were direct descendants of Graves, Doubleday, or any of their playmates from 1840, they were all of roughly the same age—now in their late thirties, forties, or early fifties. They came from all walks of middle-class life—"doctors, lawyers, editors, bankers, merchants, mechanics, office-holders, and others," the *Freeman's Journal* reported. "Others" included three farmers, four store clerks, two bartenders, and a bank teller. Fully half belonged to one of Cooperstown's five fire companies, which regularly sponsored dances, carnivals, parades, fireworks displays, and baseball games to raise funds and promote an esprit de corps among the ranks. Everyone took the game seriously. They chose Otsego County judges Hezekiah Sturges and Samuel Edict to captain the "Reds" and the "Blues," respectively, and upon the captains fell the responsibility of "choosing sides." Sixty-seven-year-old Luther Burditt, a second-generation Otsego County lawyer, was entrusted with keeping the tally. A "lively" time was had by all, including the "large number of people" who came out to watch the festivities. When the game ended, the Reds gave the victorious Blues three cheers and asked for a rematch the following week.[50]

Baseball (the game as we know it) had long since replaced townball with a more ordered, rational approach. But on this day, players, fans, and readers of the extensive coverage in the two local newspapers recalled how much the "old-fashioned game"—its spontaneity, simplicity, and egalitarian nature—had meant to them and to their parents' generation during the formative years of Otsego County and, more generally, the America republic. Cooperstown's true baseball heritage lies in this cultural memory, not with the "invention" of the game.

CHAPTER TWO

Baseball and the Transformation of Rural California

On a hot Sunday evening in June 1887, the Davisville Oletas and the Dixon Etnas played the fifth of fourteen ballgames between the two rivals that summer. Several hundred fans crowded around the diamond at "the Y," a triangle-shaped grounds bounded by the three railroad lines that converged at the Davisville depot. Sitting on grocery boxes, empty kegs, rocks, and small benches under the broiling sun, the spectators—"highly desirous of witnessing the contest," as the local scribe put it—waited anxiously for the first pitch. The game did not meet their expectations, however. "The local nine played listlessly" and lost by a score of 18 to 7. The Etnas took home the hundred dollar purse, and the betting in the stands amounted to hundreds more. Fortunately for the "disappointed" Oletas fans, another game was already scheduled for the following Sunday at Driving Park in Dixon, where their team would have a chance to "redeem themselves." Sure enough, the Oletas returned the favor, beating the Etnas on their diamond and sending the Dixon fans home equally disheartened. By season's end, the two teams had split their summer series evenly, with fans from both towns "mourning the defeats" and cherishing the victories.[1]

Baseball (an earlier version of it), introduced to rural California during the gold rush, gradually gained a stronger foothold over the next two decades, and then caught fire in the 1880s, when farmers and townspeople began spending lots of time watching, playing, and reading about it in the local newspaper. By 1885, according to the same reporter, they had become "devoted to the game"—so much so that on the rare occasions when a Sunday evening in the summer went by without "their accustomed amusement," life became "unbearably dull" for players and fans alike. The scheduled games, well-established venues, large crowds, newspaper coverage, fierce rivalries, high-stakes gambling, and close bonds between teams and residents all reveal that baseball—largely regarded by historians as an urban phenomenon—had by the late nineteenth century become deeply rooted in the region's rural culture. One farmer went so far as to say that attending church on Sunday—or, more specifically, "seeking the salvation of our immortal souls"—had become "a matter of secondary importance."[2]

The farmers' devotion to the game in the 1880s raises interconnected questions, the answers to which root in California's post–gold rush history. First, just how "rural" (and in what sense) was baseball in towns such as Dixon and Davisville? Did the farmers themselves play it? Second, rural California underwent a series of dramatic transitions—economic, generational, and environmental—during the second half of the nineteenth century. How did these transformations affect patterns of recreation—horse racing, gambling, and baseball, in particular—in communities such as Davisville and Dixon? Third, why did baseball itself become so popular in rural California at precisely this time? What about the 1880s—socially, culturally, economically—compelled rural residents to embrace the game so wholeheartedly?

By focusing on one region, two towns, and a relatively small number of players and fans, this chapter offers a starting point for answering such questions. On a broad level, we know much about agriculture and rural life during this period and a great deal about baseball's development from a primitive game into a profession and "the national pastime." For at least three decades, in fact, practitioners of both the new rural history and the new sport history have emphasized culture and society. But the two subfields have rarely intersected. At the grassroots level, consequently, we know little about baseball in late-nineteenth-century rural California. Players and fans in Davisville and Dixon perceived the game from a local, not a national, perspective and, indeed, as a local, not a national, pastime.[3] The rivalry needs understanding that way—in its rural context, not as a by-product of the developing urban, professional game. "Our players are mostly farmers," wrote the Davisville correspondent, words that should be taken seriously. The history of the game in the region, he knew, intertwined with the history of the region itself.[4]

Were the players, in fact, mostly farmers? The limited literature available suggests otherwise. Even the few scholars who have promised to emphasize "barn raisin' games" and "down home" baseball in the late nineteenth century rarely focus on farmers themselves. Recent studies have found that the Miamisburg Actives in western Ohio, the Kalamazoo Champion Base Ball Club in western Michigan, and other such "village" teams consisted primarily of local townspeople—clerks, merchants, artisans, bankers, and lawyers—not farmers from the surrounding countryside.[5] Like those towns, Davisville and Dixon owed their existence to the railroad, in this case the Southern Pacific Railroad. Both sat on the last leg of the first transcontinental line, with Davisville the first depot out of Sacramento, fifteen miles to the west, and Dixon the next stop, another nine miles down the tracks. Both towns had small but fairly stable populations of about 500, with more than enough workers and young professionals to fill two teams. Yet the Davisville correspondent got it right. Of sixty-nine players identified in box scores and feature stories between 1878 and 1895, census records and biographical sources in fact identify forty-four of them (68 percent) as farmers.[6]

Not that there was much reason to doubt the word of the Davisville correspondent, a longtime resident named Elijah W. Brown, one of the most trusted and in-the-know members of the community. After migrating to the region from Missouri in 1855 via the Isthmus of Panama, Brown had tried his hand at a little bit of everything. He ran a cattle and grain ranch on Putah Creek with his half-brother, Gabriel, for a few years; worked as a bookkeeper for local wheat merchant William Dresbach; owned and operated his own hardware store in Davisville after the town was established in 1868; speculated in town lots from time to time; and organized the Sinclair Windmill Company, which helped promote a local irrigation movement in the 1880s. For most of that decade, he also wrote a weekly "Davisville Doings" column, under the byline J. O. N., for the *Dixon Tribune* (and later for the *Yolo County Democrat*). Brown left no subject of local interest untouched, from county politics (he was an avid Democrat) to crop conditions, community gossip, and baseball. No one knew the history of the region, its farmers, the two towns, their residents, the game, and its players better—or expounded upon such matters more—than he did.[7]

That history began in the wake of the gold rush. Rural communities in northern California proliferated in the 1850s—not in the standard American fashion of settlers moving westward along a broad front, cultivating the land homestead by homestead, but communities nonetheless. Putah Creek, named for the river that ran west to east out of the coast mountains across the lower Sacramento Valley, typified such communities. The majority of the 900 transplanted Midwesterners who settled it over the course of the decade came not to farm but to seek riches in gold. Those unfortunate to arrive after 1851, however, found surface deposits already depleted by the 100,000 forty-niners who had gotten there ahead of them.

Many of them, too ashamed to return home, turned to agriculture and rural life with the same intensity of expectation that brought them to California in the first place. Dread of admitting failure a second time infused them with a furious drive to succeed.[8]

Farming along Putah Creek, though often extraordinarily productive, proved immensely challenging. Using all the latest technology, including McCormick reapers and treadmill threshers, farmers cultivated the region's virgin soils to produce bumper harvests of sixty to eighty bushels of wheat per acre—four to five times the average "back home"—most of which helped feed the escalating populations of San Francisco and Sacramento. "The lands of Putah," proclaimed one wide-eyed newspaper reporter in the fall of 1852, revealed "the magnificent results of agriculture under the bold and energetic patronage of its farmers." Yet not one of these farmers made a profit in the 1850s. High production costs at the beginning of the decade and falling prices at the end, the result of the boom and bust of the gold rush, gave farmers little chance. Greed and arrogance did not help either. Had they paid even the slightest heed to the human and natural history of the region—in particular how Indians and Mexicans before them had coped with periodic floods and droughts—they might have limited their mistakes and excesses. The sheer power of seduction, the abundance of natural advantages, amazing new technology, gigantic yields, and instant fame, all on the heels of the disillusionment of the gold rush, wooed these farmers to pursue market opportunities aggressively despite odds stacked against them.[9] Their eagerness to keep pumping money into their farms even overpowered the unresolved question of title to the land itself. Three Mexican land grants engulfed the region, which meant that farmers, under the provisions of the Treaty of Guadalupe Hidalgo and the California Land Act of 1851, had to defend their property rights before federal authorities. Until the mass of litigation was resolved—a process that took almost two decades with one of the grants—no one truly owned the land.[10]

In their haste to succeed in California, farmers committed themselves not only to material pursuits but to community life as well. Neither the legal chaos caused by the land grants nor the seductions of farming in the Sacramento Valley nor the unfulfilled dreams of the gold rush dampened the community sentiments the migrants brought with them from the Midwest. In just a few years, residents shared a specific sense of place ("Putah Creek," as they called it), similar patterns of everyday life, common obligations, and public rituals and institutions that pulled men, and eventually women, together as a social unit. They gave names to bends in the creek, crossings, roads, bridges, and other elements of the landscape.

They gathered to celebrate holidays, weddings, births, and other community activities; formed strong religious ties; and felt obligated by tradition and necessity to participate in all facets of township and county government.[11]

Putah Creek farmers also shared a favorite pastime: horse racing. Those with southern roots imported trotters and built racetracks. Virtually everyone cheered their favorite horses and reveled in the attention that winners, particularly at the state fair in Sacramento, gave their community. Rattler, the most celebrated trotting stallion from Putah Creek, won more races, took more premiums, and earned more in stud fees than any horse in northern California in the late 1850s and early 1860s. When Rattler died in 1863, the *Sacramento Daily Union* ran his obituary as its feature news story, lamenting, "The death of this fine animal will be regretted by turf men throughout the state"—especially settlers along Putah Creek. The tradition of fine horsemanship, originally imported by the gentry in colonial Virginia before spreading northward and across class boundaries by the early nineteenth century, took root in Putah Creek and throughout the Sacramento Valley almost immediately and lasted well into the twentieth century. Indeed, horse racing symbolized how quickly rural life in California matured in the decade after the gold rush.[12]

Baseball, though not nearly as popular as horse racing, also made its way to the Sacramento Valley in the 1850s. Legend has it that none other than Alexander Cartwright, whose reputation for "inventing" the game is second only to Abner Doubleday's, brought baseball with him from New York City by literally carrying a bat, ball, and a copy of the rules of his beloved Knickerbocker Base Ball Club overland to the gold country of California. While most serious accounts acknowledge that such a feat cannot be attributed to Cartwright alone, if at all, most do agree that early Californians did in fact play the game that the "father of modern baseball" (as Cartwright's Hall of Fame plaque in Cooperstown reads) helped create in 1845. The twenty rules that the Knickerbockers codified (or at least popularized) that year included the diamond-shaped infield, the inclusion of foul lines, and the insistence that players on the field had to throw to a base to get a runner out rather than hit ("soak" or "plunk") him with the ball. Though less well known (and far less documented), rural Californians took up the sport in the 1850s just as eagerly as urban Californians. Farmers and farmhands, wearing no uniforms but overalls and black shirts, played informal games on Putah Creek farms between peak periods of the production cycle as early as 1857—"baseball in the olden time," as Brown remembered it. Three years later, at the state fair, Putah Creek residents numbered among the 2,000 spectators who watched teams from San Francisco, Sacramento, and Stockton play a one-day tournament with the "state title," a silver bat, and $350 in prize money on the line. Baseball, it seemed, had arrived in the Golden State.[13]

While baseball continued to thrive in San Francisco and other Bay Area cities early in the next decade, the game's popularity noticeably declined in the state's rural regions, as farmers along Putah Creek and throughout much of northern California grappled with two of the worst natural disasters in the state's history.[14] In the winter of 1861-62, a flood of almost biblical proportions hit the Sacramento Valley when a series of warm, tropical rains melted several feet of snow in the Sierra Nevada. Rampaging rivers poured out of their channels, filling much of the valley like a bathtub and spreading devastation for weeks on end, drowning cattle by the tens of thousands, burying the cities of Sacramento and Marysville deep in mud, destroying farms and ranches, and sweeping hundreds of people to their deaths. With most of the land along Putah Creek completely underwater, "nothing indicate[s] the locality of the ranches but a windmill," observed one stunned resident. The "flood of the century" immediately preceded another mammoth ecological disaster: the most severe and prolonged drought ever to hit the state. For close to three years, from the fall of 1862 to the winter of 1864-65, the rains failed. Hundreds of thousands of cattle perished, and crop loss in the Sacramento Valley was so severe that Californians had to import wheat from Chile to make their bread. The back-to-back disasters postponed the state fair for three years, and baseball fields and horse-racing tracks lay largely vacant throughout the region while farmers struggled mightily to recover.[15]

Those farmers who persisted through the end of the decade—about 35 percent in Putah Creek—reaped rewards for their perseverance. With much of the confusion over land titles finally resolved, and with the return of a more stable weather pattern, farmers resumed wheat cultivation with a vengeance. By coincidence—the type that seems to pervade American agricultural history—California produced three straight bumper crops after the drought broke in 1865, at the same time that Great Britain and other European nations suffered dangerously deficient harvests. Enterprising grain merchants in San Francisco and Liverpool, including the legendary Isaac Friedlander, exploited the opportunity to the fullest, as did farmers in Putah Creek. Production skyrocketed between 1866 and 1869, with almost three-fourths of their crop exported to the United Kingdom. Farm incomes more than tripled, and land values doubled. Thus began what historian Rodman Paul called "one of the most extraordinary of all agrarian episodes"—California's bonanza wheat era. This dramatic turn of events from devastation to profitability confirmed all the more the prevailing belief among these farmers that demand would inevitably outpace production. Developments over the next three decades eventually exposed that notion as folly, but for the time being, farmers had finally struck gold.[16]

The prosperity of the wheat boom helped revive horse racing but not baseball, at least not to the same degree. In the late 1860s and early 1870s, the sport of kings, in fact, became something of an obsession in the Sacramento Valley, with racetracks built on the outskirts of seemingly every town. Several Putah Creek farmers began training their own trotters and pacers and raced them at venues up and down the valley. Baseball remained dormant in rural areas for several years, though teams in Sacramento, Stockton, and Marysville resumed play in 1867 on a limited schedule. Horse racing, with its traditional, age-old appeal, and by far still the most popular spectator sport among rural residents in the Sacramento Valley, weathered the turbulent 1860s much better than did baseball.[17]

In late September 1869, baseball received an unexpected boost from a distant source. Just four months after the golden spike driven at Promontory, Utah, marked the completion of the first transcontinental railroad line, the Cincinnati Red Stockings barnstormed their way through California. If not the nation's first all-professional team, the Red Stockings were certainly the highest paid, the best promoted, and the most successful. The team payroll was $9,400, with four of the ten players making well over $1,000 a year. Their long road trip that season, through the East and Midwest, as well as California, covered more than 12,000 miles and entertained more than 200,000 fans. On the tour, they would win eighty-one straight games easily, disposing of one opponent after another. En route to the West Coast, the Red Stockings, in characteristic fashion, trounced two teams in St. Louis by a combined score of 101 to 18. In late September and early October, three San Francisco clubs and another from Sacramento fared little better in six games, losing 35 to 4, 58 to 4, 66 to 4, 54 to 5, 76 to 5, and 46 to 14 to the visitors.[18]

While the thrashing may have broken the spirit of the losing California teams, the Red Stockings' brief tour ignited locals' passion for the game beyond anyone's expectations. Newspapers, often on the front page, covered seemingly every movement of the players on and off the field, including gala banquets held in their honor in both cities' finest restaurants. Fans (more than 2,000 for at least three of the games) marveled at the Cincinnati nine's superior skills of pitching, fielding, batting, and running; gaped at their impressive physiques and dapper uniforms (white flannel shirts, Knickerbocker trousers, and spiked oxford shoes complemented the knee-length stockings); and crowded the Sacramento railroad depot to bid the team farewell on October 8. And in smaller towns on the Southern Pacific line, including Dixon and Davisville, rural onlookers gathered in droves to catch a glimpse of "the gallant men in stockings red" as their train passed. Indeed, with their flair for promotion and playing prowess, the Red Stockings whetted northern Californians' appetite for baseball, including thousands who never actually saw them play.[19]

Baseball's surge in popularity proved more lasting in urban areas. In San Francisco, Oakland, Sacramento, Stockton, and Marysville, heated rivalries in the early 1870s sparked "match play" tournaments and, by the end of the decade, the state's first two professional associations of baseball teams: the Pacific League and the California League (both of them forerunners of the famed Pacific Coast League). The players were well paid, and the teams drew large and enthusiastic crowds at their expansive new ballparks. When the Red Stockings returned to San Francisco in 1879 on another grand exhibition tour, they found the competition much tougher and the fans equally excited but not nearly as awestruck.[20] In Davisville and Dixon, however, no one rushed to the depot this time to welcome the Red Stockings back. Baseball continued to be played in the area during the 1870s at picnics and other informal gatherings but with little of the fanfare, much less the professionalism, exhibited in urban areas. Sporadic efforts to form teams in nearby Silveyville and Woodland went for naught, and there seemed no enthusiasm for organized play in either Davisville or Dixon. Farmers in the region continued to be consumed by wheat and horse racing. Local newspapers indicate that they read, in considerable detail every week, of developments in the world grain market and of trotting races at the neighborhood track, but the box scores and feature stories that now filled the pages of Sacramento and San Francisco papers seemed of little interest. As late as 1879, as Brown later admitted, farmers in the area "knew little more of the game" than they had when it first came west more than two decades earlier.[21]

The game had changed considerably over that time. In addition to the standardization of the diamond, the establishment of foul lines, the first grand tour by a professional team, and the organization of ball clubs in cities across the country, the essential elements of the modern game—the rules, the fundamentals of each position, the rudimentary equipment, and even the language—gradually evolved after much experimentation. Each side now consisted of nine players; three offensive failures ("outs") compelled a team to relinquish its offensive opportunity to its opponent; each team had nine such scoring opportunities ("innings"); fielders could no longer register "outs" by catching batted balls on the first bounce; hitters lost the privilege of waiting for just the pitch they wanted and instead had to confront a well-defined "strike zone"; four pitches delivered outside that zone constituted a free pass ("walk") to first base; and in the 1880s, overhand pitching (along with the dreaded curveball) gradually replaced underhand, and the modern pitching distance of sixty feet six inches became standard. Players specialized at one or two positions, with the understanding that the best all-round athletes played pitcher or shortstop, the fastest the outfield, and the "pluckiest" the infield. Catchers donned wire masks ("muzzles" or "birdcages"), fielders put on gloves, and teams everywhere adopted uniforms like the Red Stockings had. "Long ball," "hit and run," "bunt," "change of pace," "tag up," "battery," "home plate," and other expressions populated the lexicon of players, fans, and newspapermen. Indeed, by the late 1870s, shrewd publishers of the great metropolitan dailies well understood the abilities of baseball writers to sell newspapers.[22]

Although today's fan could recognize the game of baseball in the late 1870s, most contemporary rural residents did not. Farmers in Davisville and Dixon, if they played the game at all, had not yet adopted many of the basic conventions of the urban game. Recollections of men who played in such remote areas invariably mention the lack of fielding equipment. Catchers especially, but infielders and outfielders as well, suffered "swelled hands, torn nails, and crooked joints" from playing barehanded. Local conditions often dictated the number of players and the layout of the field, outfielders were known as "pasturemen," and teams played in the clothes on their backs, not in uniforms. With the newer rules and state-of-the-art equipment, city teams generally played relatively low-scoring games of two hours or so in length, but a typical rural game might come to an end only with the onset of darkness. "Two square yards of blackboard were needed to record those scores of 80 to 90," Brown recalled.[23]

While farmers continued through the 1870s to play "baseball in the olden time," big changes in their lives, the magnitude of which they had only begun to realize, lay ahead in the next great agrarian episode in California, the transition from wheat to specialty crops. Wheat growing itself posed few, if any, problems. Five times between 1872 and 1884 no state grew more wheat than California, which earned the Golden State a new reputation as "the granary of the world." Farmers, however, continued to ignore the harsh realities of supply and demand—not only the simple economics of overproduction but also the fact that farmers elsewhere in the United States and thousands of miles away in Europe, Asia, South America, and Australia could beat them at their own game, many using techniques and machines (the combined harvester, in particular) imported from California. As prices fell precipitously year after year, farmers along Putah Creek and elsewhere began to ask the question none of them wanted to hear: "Does it pay to raise wheat, our bread and butter for so long?"[24]

Their answer, moreover, split along generational lines. "Old-timers" argued, as early as 1880, that the market had bottomed out and that wheat would surely "reign king in our district" again. Their sons, however, found the question more complicated. They feared that the bottom had in fact dropped out of the market. Wheat's decline, moreover, came just as they emerged from their fathers' shadows, determined, as one put it, to look forward with "fresh energy and clear vision." For years, their fathers had tended small orchards and vineyards to supplement their grain incomes. The new generation did not abandon wheat in the 1880s but turned increasingly to fruits and nuts both as cash crops and to cultivate their own identities. To an even greater degree than their fathers, they spent their lives struggling to resolve the great paradox of agriculture in the modern economic world: farmers' very identity—their inner drive to produce, produce, produce—invariably gluts the market, brings low prices, and spreads misery and frustration.[25]

However, the transition from wheat to fruit eventually took place. As late as 1889, California remained the nation's second-leading wheat-producing state, with almost three million acres harvested and exports totaling 840,000 tons. By 1909, however, wheat acreage fell to less than 400,000 acres, with the state becoming a net importer. Over the same period, California emerged as one of the world's principal producers of deciduous and citrus fruits, grapes, vegetables, and nuts. Though no one could have known what lay ahead back in the late 1870s, farmers and their sons had embarked on the early stages of "one of the most rapid and complete transformations ever witnessed in American agricultural history," as one scholar has described it. In fact, the shift from wheat to specialty crops in Davisville and Dixon, as elsewhere in the state's rural regions, proved slow, uneven, contingent, and fraught with anxiety and conflict from the very beginning. Sons inherited their fathers' dreams of striking it rich in California and pursued them with equal, perhaps even greater, passion. With boldness, hard work, and a little luck (not necessarily in that order), they still believed that they could succeed materially and, just as importantly, bring stability and prosperity to their community. They did indeed transform agriculture along Putah Creek, but they also maintained strong cultural ties to the gold rush generation—more so than they cared to admit.[26]

In this context, baseball's popularity rose to unprecedented heights. Farmers' newfound passion for the game coincided with a period of far-reaching economic, social, and generational change in rural California. Indeed, had Brown said, "Our players are mostly farmers' *sons*," he would have spoken even more accurately. Of the forty-four farmers who played baseball for the Davisville Oletas and the Dixon Etnas in the 1880s, at least thirty-six were sons of gold rush generation settlers. These young men aged nineteen to twenty-eight, identified by Brown and confirmed by census records, in many cases became key players in the transition from wheat to almonds, the main specialty crop of the region. When, for example, the fifteen charter members of the Davisville Almond Growers' Association met in 1897 to form California's first nut cooperative, eleven of them were sons of pioneer wheat farmers from the 1850s and 1860s, and eight of the eleven had played several seasons for either the Oletas or the Etnas in the 1880s.[27]

Searching for distraction from their arduous daily routines and the uncertainties of the times, these young men found baseball the perfect antidote. They might have pursued horse racing, as their fathers had before them, but even those who raced horses found playing and watching baseball more satisfying. The two sports had much in common. Indeed, the racetrack helped develop rural people's fascination with swift motion and sudden action, which the ball field, located in the middle of the track in Dixon, cultivated to the utmost. But baseball's new rules, which local teams began adopting early in the decade, imposed a much more precise, detailed order on its participants than did horse racing. On defense, players trotted out together to the same positions every inning and tried their best to hone their specific, individual skills for the good of the team; on offense, they tried to hit the ball within the foul lines and away from the fielders, to run the bases without being tagged out, and to parlay their individual efforts into runs, the game's most meaningful measure of achievement. They performed all these actions automatically, without pause for concern, because the game itself dictated it. For young men mystified by the operations of the grain market and wary of what the future held but who, like their fathers, could not admit failure or even the possibility of failure, baseball offered excitement, respite, stability, diversion, mutuality, and gratification—all in powerful, albeit short-term, doses.[28]

Other, less tangible, factors may also have contributed to the "epidemic of baseball," to use Brown's apt description, that hit Davisville and Dixon in the 1880s. Some fathers did not want their sons playing the game, especially when games interrupted work on the farm. Brown reported one instance during the wheat harvest of 1885 when an enraged father, shotgun in hand, stormed the Davisville diamond in the fourth inning and marched his son from his outfield position back to the farm—an action that no doubt reinforced the association between baseball and rebellion in the young man's mind. Members of the Oletas and Etnas also, on occasion, spoke of the game's "manly" qualities—its ag-

Baseball game at Dixon's Driving Park, ca. 1890.
Dixon Public Library Historical Collection, Dixon, California.

gressive, competitive aspects—as did so many young Americans, both rural and urban, of this generation. And baseball may even have helped tame two interrelated ethnocultural conflicts in the two towns. Since the early 1870s, a disgruntled minority, led by leaders of the Davisville Presbyterian Church, had decried the region's lack of respect for the Sabbath and temperance. Baseball games on Sundays served only to fuel the fire, at first, but gradually, even the most militant reformers accepted and even welcomed the idea. "Some of the more thoughtful among the temperance advocates," explained Brown, "prefer to have the crowds at the ballgame rather than the alehouse." Indeed, by the end of the 1880s, the saloon-keepers were the ones grumbling over the game's popularity.[29]

The epidemic of baseball spread across racial lines as well. Two of the most valuable players on the Dixon Etnas in the mid 1880s, brothers José and Isidro Peña, had roots in the area that extended deeper than any of their teammates. Their grandfather, Juan Felipe Peña, migrated to California in 1841 and two years later became co-owner of Rancho Los Putos, one of the three Mexican land grants in the area. Although the U.S. Supreme Court confirmed Rancho Los Putos in 1857, the grantees remained mired in legal turmoil with squatters, speculators, and lawyers. By the early 1860s, only a small portion of the 44,000-acre grant remained in the Peña family. The overwhelmingly Anglo community of Dixon treated José and Isidro as social outcasts as they grew up—until both brothers demonstrated that they could hit. The "Peña boys," as Brown called them, became fixtures in the Etnas' lineup, José at second base and Isidro in centerfield, and led the team to numerous victories. Though Isidro died in a farm accident in 1894, José took advantage of his prowess on the ball field and growing acceptance off the field to become a successful cattleman. Descendants of the Peña family still reside in the area today—not entirely because of baseball, of course, but the game did help them carve out their place in the community. Even baseball, however, could not penetrate the rigid racial barriers between white farmers and Asian immigrants, who increasingly dominated the agricultural work force in the region. In the twentieth century, however, even Chinese and Japanese residents in northern California formed their own teams and become equally devoted to the game, albeit on segregated diamonds.[30]

Widespread gambling, perhaps the most febrile symptom of the baseball epidemic, permeated the life of these two rural towns and long predated baseball. Farmers, by the very nature of their enterprise, were gamblers, "staking their all upon the season," according to Brown. Most Putah Creek farmers had come to the Golden State on a gamble in the first place. Every year, they rolled the dice on the weather, the yield of their crop, and on just when to sell their crop to get the optimum price. They also bet on billiards, poker, dice games, pitching horseshoes, pigeon shooting, the number of raw eggs one could swallow at a sitting, the outcome of elections, whether or not someone would survive an illness—on just about anything. And, of course, gambling sustained horse racing. So enamored was one Davisville farmer with gambling that in 1884, he borrowed $100 to make a bet and then refused to pay it back when his horse lost the race. When his lender took him to court, the bettor insisted that anyone with any sense of honor would have given him another chance to pick a winner, and a jury of his peers agreed with him.[31]

Gambling deepened almost everyone's fascination with baseball. Paradoxically, the game provided not only an antidote to the uncertainties of modern life but also an opportunity to bet on the uncertainties of modern life. The new rules gave people their money's worth in more ways than one. The more ordered, rational version of the game allowed for more precise, sustained play and thus greatly facilitated betting. Bettors could now wager not only on a game's final score but also on whether the next batter would get a hit, the next pitch would be a strike, or the next fly ball would be caught (prompting bettors, on at least one occasion, to fire off their guns to disconcert the fielder and make him muff the ball). The players themselves were not averse to playing games for substantial, winner-take-all purses; paying "revolvers" or "ringers" from nearby teams of Vacaville and Winters to "beef up" their lineups for especially important games; or even taking bribes to throw games, a practice commonly called "hippodroming." Gambling, for all intents and purposes, played as much a part of baseball as hitting, pitching, and running, and it spread its own "epidemic" contagion along Putah Creek.[32]

The plain measure of success in baseball, as much as any one factor, attracted farmers to the game. Baseball tantalized them with the illusion that they could master reality—that they could reverse their fortunes—by simply courting Lady Luck or, when teams tried to fix games, by manipulating her. They found something inherently liberating about this notion. Win or lose, each game (and the games within the game) produced a clearly defined outcome, in sharp contrast to the difference between success and failure on their farms year after year. For players and fans alike, baseball and gambling at the Y in Davisville or at Driving Park in Dixon had a cultural meaning beyond the chance to make money. It allowed them to entertain the same impulse that had failed them during the gold rush, the gamble of the century. That impulse, along with the tradition of baseball games on Sunday evenings, persisted well into the twentieth century in Davisville and Dixon. Even as teams changed their names, adopted uniforms, and played in more organized leagues, and even as "our National game of ball," as Brown put it, became more firmly entrenched, farmers continued to experience the game first and foremost as a local and rural pastime.[33]

Farmers along Putah Creek responded culturally to the myriad problems that accompanied the transformation of rural California—not just economically or politically. When they played baseball or rooted for their favorite team, they displayed some of the central elements of rural culture in California: competitiveness, materialism, and individualism, as well as hard work, cooperation, and mutuality. Baseball offered not only an outlet for the tensions of rural life but also a means of translating a core set of values, which they inherited from their fathers, into action. Each game staged a great social drama, full of excitement, suspense, and opportunity but void of paradox. Players and spectators could express themselves freely—and take risks, even poorly calculated ones—with little regard to long-term consequences. Their very identity—their inner drive to produce, produce, produce—found expression and gratification on the ball field rather than the misery and frustration they so often experienced in their wheat fields or at the grain market. There was nothing mysterious about the game. Baseball came along at the right time in the right place to satisfy farmers' insatiable appetite for achievement in a world of change and chance. It became their sport of choice in this time of transformation.

CHAPTER THREE

Multicultural Ball in the Heyday of Texas Cotton Agriculture

Texas Czechs gathered by the hundreds in Fayetteville on Sunday, July 2, 1911, for the fifteenth anniversary of the founding of Slavanská Podporující Jednota Statu Texas (SPJST), the state's preeminent Slavonic benevolent association. The venue was most appropriate. Fayetteville, long known as the "cradle of Czech settlement in Texas," was predominantly "Bohemians and Moravians" in population (as designated by the census) and the home of the first lodge of the SPJST. Orators from as far away as Temple and Houston spoke at length (in Czech) on the virtues of fraternalism; plenty of plump spiced pork sausage and home-brewed beer kept the festivities lively; and attendees polkaed to the music of the famed Baca Family Brass and String Band well into the night. The SPJST lodge celebration showcased the endurance of an array of ethnically distinctive traits and thus seemed to confirm a Czech American historian's assessment that the culture of Fayetteville, after two generations of emigration, still resembled that of a Moravian village.[1]

One event—"the key feature of the afternoon's program," according to a local correspondent's account—seemed out of place, however. "A double header of baseball was pulled off at the park between Fayetteville and Round Top." Led by pitchers Denis Kurtz and Ed Tydlacka, the all-Czech locals beat the all-German visitors 3 to 1 in the first game and played them to a 6-to-6 tie in the second. Round Top pitchers Fritz Etzel and Arthur Sachs praised the victors but vowed to beat them on their home grounds the following Sunday, when "our whole town will be out to see the game." Remarkably, residents of two of the oldest settlements in the state (both predated the Texas Revolution), steeped in their respective folk cultures and insulated from their Anglo neighbors, crossed ethnic boundaries to play baseball, a game as American as apple pie, or so it seemed. Since the early years of the twentieth century, Fayetteville and Round Top regularly played other predominantly German or Czech community teams from Fayette, Washington, Lee, Robertson, and Austin Counties, including La Grange, Ledbetter, Carmine, Burton, Brenham, New Ulm, Greenvine, Ellinger, Giddings, Somerville, Snook, Bellville, Dime Box, and Schulenburg. And in less organized settings, baseball had penetrated many of these otherwise closed ethnic communities since at least the early 1880s.[2]

This "baseball craze," as the *La Grange Journal* called it in 1909, was all the more remarkable given that the vast majority of players and fans were small-scale cotton farmers (tending plots of 100 acres or so). In the northern states, agriculture had modernized by the 1910s—that is, in science, technology, economic organization, and cultural values, farming in the 1910s had more in common with farming today than with that of the 1880s. And baseball represented one of the more visible forms of modernity. But for the German, Czech, Anglo, and African American farm families in south-central Texas, new and old ways coexisted. On the one hand, "the heyday of Texas cotton agriculture" meant that livelihoods depended on an unpredictable world market. On the other hand, this region still functioned as a quasi-subsistence economy, where hogs and free-range turkeys roamed and where industrial noise was so rare that the thunderous roar of the cotton gin woke up the entire town when it started up early in the morning. The peculiar needs of cotton dictated the way these farmers ordered their lives, and the peculiar needs of baseball reinforced the core values of the cotton culture that cut across racial and ethnic lines.[3] Even on the flat prairies of south-central Texas, however, baseball was not played on a level playing field. While the various ethnic groups were of one mind about cotton and one mind about baseball, neither baseball nor cotton fully overcame the deep-seated cultural divisions that had engulfed them over the years. African Americans in particular found themselves shut out from interracial competition. In that regard, the game's redemptive powers, though widespread among whites, proved limited indeed.

How did baseball come to Texas? For years, the answer given to that question began with none other than Abner Doubleday. In his postbellum military career, Doubleday served two stints in Texas—in 1867 as sub-assistant commissioner of the Freedmen's Bureau for Galveston County and from 1871 to 1873 commanding the all-black Twenty-Fourth U.S. Infantry regiment in west Texas. Periodic newspaper stories have maintained (though with considerably less fanfare than Abner

Graves's remarks have generated) that Doubleday, seeking healthy recreation for his soldiers, organized the first game of baseball in the Lone Star State in Galveston on February 22, 1867, in celebration of George Washington's birthday. Though not a snippet of hard evidence substantiates these stories, baseball clubs did in fact begin to organize in Galveston about this time. Texans returning from the war or occupying Union troops might well have brought the game with them to the busy seaport. The ease with which baseball migrated offered a clear sign of its vitality. Thousands of soldiers of both armies encountered the game for the first time, took to its excitement, introduced it to their home communities, and in the process greatly enhanced the game's popularity. Since most German and Czech immigrants caught their first glimpse of Texas in Galveston, they might well have caught their first glimpse of baseball there as well.[4]

How, then, did baseball make its way to Fayette, Washington, and neighboring counties? The answer to that question involves still more speculation. Possibly, as settlers moved inland, the game slowly spread from Galveston and other urban centers to rural areas. One contemporary newspaper, for example, claimed that the first baseball game played in Fayette County took place on March 23, 1877, in Schulenburg, a railroad town founded just four years earlier. The Schulenburgers lost to the Columbus Coloradoes, 33 to 20. Both teams seemed to imitate city players, particularly in how they dressed, with the Coloradoes wearing "everyday trousers, undershirt, pants tucked into red and white 'barber pole' stockings, fancy belts on which they hooked suspenders" and the Schulenburgers "everyday dress, caps and belts, and one or two [with] white stockings into which they stuffed their pants." Though Schulenburg bore the name of the German immigrant who donated the land for the Galveston, Harrisburg and San Antonio Railway to build through the site, and observers had already dubbed the town "Little Germany," Anglo Americans still made up nearly 50 percent of its 730 residents. And of the original nine Schulenburgers only one, second baseman Joseph Wessendorf, was of German heritage. Anglo Americans, this would seem to suggest, brought the game with them to south-central Texas and, slowly but surely, taught it to German immigrants.[5]

The game in Schulenburg that day took place in the midst of a gradual but dramatic population shift in Fayette County and south-central Texas more broadly. Anglo-Americans from Stephen F. Austin's original colony in the 1820s had settled the region, a generation before the first German communities organized. Farmers from provinces in northern Germany, weary of famines, conscriptions, wars, and expensive land, began settling the area in the 1840s through the process of chain migration—trans-Atlantic networks that virtually transplanted rural communities, if not entire villages, to Texas. With the assistance of family and friends already in Texas, German farmers moved into this fertile region of rolling hills, live oak groves, forests of cedar and post oak, and open prairies. They purchased land settled earlier by Americans, while the Anglos moved on—a trend greatly accelerated by the Civil War with its devastating impact on the region's plantation economy. In 1850, 75 percent of Fayette County's white population was Anglo and 19 percent German, all recent immigrants. By 1900, those figures had almost reversed. As early as 1887, Anglos (5,212 of them) stood in fourth place among the county's population groups, behind Germans (13,901), African Americans (8,298), and Czechs (6,084). Largely because of the German influence, Fayette County had been one of the few in Texas to vote against secession. That influence continued to grow until, at some point in the 1880s, it was no longer clear just which group had assimilated the other.[6]

From an economic standpoint, German immigrant farmers adopted many of the identifying traits of Anglo Americans, who themselves migrated to Texas from the Upper South and Gulf South in roughly equal numbers. Almost immediately upon arrival, German settlers embraced cotton as their cash crop. Cotton well suited south-central Texas, not only the fertile bottom lands of the Brazos and Colorado Rivers but also the rich prairie lands of the region. Its 250-day growing season allowed ample time for it to mature, a particularly attractive feature to new, inexperienced cotton farmers. German immigrants had no qualms about raising cotton in competition with slaveowners (very few had slaves of their own), and after the Civil War, when competition with the large planters ceased, they turned heart and soul to cotton, producing it in prodigious amounts but on small farms rather than plantations. Germans also imitated certain southern yeoman methods for raising hay, hogs, kitchen gardens, poultry, draft animals, and cattle. Perhaps most striking was their immediate embrace of corn, the staff of life in the South (as both a forage and subsistence crop) but virtually absent in nineteenth-century Germany. Often to the astonishment of friends and relatives back home, German immigrants adopted cornbread as the mainstay of their diet from the very first. They did, however, continue to grow white potatoes, turnips, cabbage, and other crops not found in an Anglo garden, and the type of sausage they made remained distinctively German well into the twentieth century. Overall, German immigrants became so adept at farming in Texas that they eventually beat their native Southern counterparts at their own game.[7]

From a cultural standpoint, however, Texas Germans fiercely resisted assimilation. They stood out among all ethnic groups in the region for their passion for preserving their ancestral language, which they felt not only tied them together but bound them to their past as well. While generally having good control of English for use in the marketplace, Germans spoke German in their schools, churches, homes, agricultural societies, and festivals through the nineteenth century and well into the twentieth. In areas such as La Bahia Prairie, a vast expanse of rich cotton land straddling eastern Fayette and western Washington Counties, bounded by the towns of Round Top, Winedale, Carmine, and Burton, Germans dominated the population to such an extent that Anglo children felt obligated to learn German in school, rather than vice versa. Germans also employed their language as a source of entertainment through word games, riddles, proverbs, and characteristic wit. In addition, much of the culture they brought with them from Germany they faithfully reproduced in rural Texas. Art, newspapers, literature and literary societies, theater, music and music societies, casino clubs, and athletic associations all served to preserve the folk wisdom of the past and refresh the Germans' sense of cultural identity. And of course, wine and beer flowed freely. Germans knew how to amuse themselves, even (or especially) on the Sabbath, so much so that contemporaries often maintained that they taught their American Baptist and Methodist neighbors, who often took even their pleasure seriously, how to relax after toil.[8]

Texas Germans might very well have taught Texas Anglos the pleasures of baseball as well. Beginning in the early 1880s, as their population continued to increase in numbers both absolute and relative to other ethnic groups, Germans in south-central Texas began a love affair with baseball. Children, boys and girls alike, played baseball in school and after church in much the same manner as they played kick the can, marbles, mumblety-peg, tag, and jacks—as a matter of course, as though German youth had been hitting, pitching, catching, and running the bases on prairie dirt diamonds for generations. Boys and girls played ball with the support of their mothers and grandmothers, the principle caretakers of children under the age of twelve or so, and perhaps even under their elders' instruction. As children moved into their teen years and took on more gender-specific roles, however, the game became an all-male activity. When teams of young men coming of age played one another, the competition could turn especially fierce.[9] For many, that spirit of competition carried over into adulthood, though still on an informal basis prior to the turn of the century. With no uniforms, mitts, or umpires, and using homemade bats, balls, and bases, participants often brought their cotton hoes to the game literally to chop out a field in someone's pasture. The games themselves were equally primitive. Outfielders (as many as five or six) positioned themselves just beyond the scruffy infield; pitchers stood fifty or so feet from home plate and flung the beat-up ball side-armed or underhand; catchers stood several feet behind the batter, hoping to corral the ball on one hop; and batters tried merely to slap the ball through the infield and race toward first base in one motion. "We didn't need no umpires," asserted one farmer from La Bahia Prairie with pride. "We had good teams," added another. "Baseball was very big around here."[10]

Such enthusiasm gradually led to more organized play. "Match games" between teams from neighboring communities had their origins in the German penchant for coming together in clubs (or *Vereine*) for social activity. In Brenham, the county seat of Washington County, a Germania Verein organized in 1870 and, among its many functions, put on a major Volksfest every May to celebrate the coming of spring. Upwards of 2,000 revelers "came in from all directions" to enjoy feasts, singing, and dancing. In 1881, Volksfest became Maifest, which became even more popular but incurred great expenses, draining profits from previous years. Looking for ways to raise funds, the Maifest Association organized a baseball match in 1884 between the Saxons of Brenham and the Cochattes of Bellville and charged a small public admission. The match proved such "a grand success" that baseball became a fixture of the Brenham Maifest at Firemen's Park for decades to come.[11] Similar sequences of events took place at Round Top and La Grange in the 1880s and 1890s. Gradually, baseball became part of other festivals and holidays, including the Fourth of July, which Germans celebrated with considerably more exuberance than their teetotaling Anglo-American neighbors. In 1902, the Round Top Schuetzen Verein put on a "glorious fourth . . . that attendees would remember for many years to come," with a parade featuring the local baseball club on horseback, formal readings of the Declaration of Independence (one in German and one in English), music, food, prizes, rifle competitions, and the game itself between the Round Top Baseball Club and the Carmine Stars. The two-day event's lone disappointment was that the Verein ordered only twenty kegs of beer, "which proved insufficient."[12]

The Fourth of July coincided with another cause for celebration: a lull in the cotton-production cycle that southerners (including Germans and Czechs eventually) traditionally called "laid-by time" (or "laying-by time"). Cultivation practices—land preparation, sowing, cultivating, weeding, and harvesting—changed little over a century and a half across the South. In the late winter, farmers broke the land, made rows, and planted seeds. When the cotton began to sprout in early to mid April, workers (entire families in most cases) with razor-sharp hoes began passing through the fields, thinning out excess plants and keeping the fields clean

A game of baseball at a farming community in Fayette County, ca. 1900.
Fayette Heritage Museum and Archives, La Grange, Texas.

of weeds—a process known as "chopping," in the parlance of southern agriculture. Plowing then alternated with chopping until the plants had grown tall enough and spread wide enough to "shed out" the weeds and, in essence, prevent any further trips up the rows. At that point, usually late June or early July, farmers "laid the crop by," meaning they ended their field work and began a period of about two months waiting for the bolls on the stems to fill out and burst open into white puffs. That moment then signaled the start of the relentless period of picking the cotton and hauling it to the community gin, which, as additional bolls continued to burst through the fall months, could last into December. Laid-by time did not mean idle time, as farm families turned to such tasks as haymaking, wood-chopping, plow-sharpening, fence-repairing, food preservation, beekeeping, and winemaking. But the late-summer break in the cotton cycle did give them time for various recreations—fishing, squirreling, rabbit hunting, visiting families of nearby communities, and, increasingly, baseball.[13]

Around the turn of the century, the match games that brought so much excitement to players and fans alike at Maifest and German Fourth of July celebrations became regular features of laid-by time. With virtually every crossroads community in south-central Texas organizing a team each summer, including eight or nine on La Bahia Prairie alone, there was no shortage of competition. Homemade uniforms with the team's name or town emblazoned across players' chests,

The La Grange Boll Weevils, ca. 1910.
Fayette Heritage Museum and Archives, La Grange, Texas.

an umpire or two, and real bats, balls, and gloves became commonplace, paid for by players' own contributions and teams charging admission to the games though organized leagues with prearranged schedules, standings, pennant races, and championship games had not emerged just yet. Cotton dictated the parameters of each season. Shortly after chopping ended, team leaders began scheduling games for Sunday (and sometimes Saturday) afternoons on a week-to-week basis, often announcing them in the local newspaper. In years when the crop looked promising, teams and groups of devoted fans might travel via railroad or horse and buggy to seven or eight different towns as far away as thirty miles—Burton to La Grange, for example. But if facing a bad crop or low prices, Burton might instead play only its nearest rival, Carmine, just seven miles down to road, over and over again. The players themselves, the names of the teams, and the location of the community diamond often changed from year to year.

Three constants persisted, however. First, the games ended when laid-by time ended. In 1908, for example, the La Grange Boll Weevils, en route to play a doubleheader with the Round Top Scrubs, were called back to their farms by an unexpectedly early August harvest. Second, women, though no longer participants on the field, played significant roles as spectators, organizers of road trips, food providers, and uniform sewers. Third, the best pickers often made the best players. Picking cotton and playing ball required fine hand-eye coordination, ingenuity, and persistence. Texas Germans excelled at both.[14]

So too did Texas Czechs, in their own distinctive manner. Each ethnicity has wanted to claim that it had a more intimate attachment to the land than any other and that it went to greater lengths to preserve its cultural heritage. By most accounts and measures, Czechs really did seem even more zealous than Germans in trying to maintain their ethnic identity. Three to four generations of Czech parents in Texas reminded their children of this fact with the common expression, "*My jsme Češi; oni jsou Američané*!" (We're Czechs; they're Americans!). With tremendous pride, they created a powerful sense of otherness, not only from their Anglo neighbors but also from German and African Texans. Czechs by their own preference isolated themselves from the larger society, structuring their communities and their lives according to their own ways. Yet, as with the Germans, baseball permeated Czech culture. By the early twentieth century, the game became every bit as Czech Texan as polka dances, SPJST lodges, and *kolác* pastries.[15]

In many respects, Czech settlement in Texas mirrored that of German immigrants. Czechs also made their way to Texas through chain migration. Scholars claim to have identified the very first link in the chain, Rev. Josef Arnošt Bergmann, the "father" of Czech immigration to Texas. Shortly after arriving at the Austin County settlement of Cat Spring in 1850, Bergmann began writing letters to friends and family in Europe about the wonderful opportunities in "this wildly beautiful region with many trees," thereby stimulating the first wave of Bohemian and Moravian immigration. Czechs came to Texas pulled by good, relatively inexpensive farmland and pushed by generations of bitter experience in political turmoil, wars, and conquering invaders. By nature clannish in their social relations, they created cultural islands out of many of their settlements in Texas. Like Germans, Czechs suffered persecution during the Civil War for their half-hearted support of the Southern cause but benefited thereafter when the giant plantations were divided up and sold cheaply to newly arriving settlers. Czechs also felt duty bound to maintain their national identity by preserving their language. They placed great value on religion, education, and fraternalism. And they loved well-seasoned food and good beer every bit as much as Germans did.[16]

Important differences existed as well, however. Germans began immigrating to Texas about twenty years before the first groups of Czechs and, over the course of the nineteenth century, came in significantly larger numbers. On the eve of the Civil War, 20,000 German-born persons resided in Texas compared to just 700 Czechs. While a crescendo of new immigration began for both ethnic groups after the war, by 1900 Texas was home to 160,000 first- and second-generation Germans and 9,200 Czechs. Even in Fayette County, where the greatest number of Czechs came to settle, Germans outnumbered them by more than two to one.[17] Though their relative levels of poverty resist precise measurement, immigration scholars generally describe Germans as "poor but not destitute" and Czechs as virtually penniless upon arrival, often deeply in debt to family or friends for paying their passage. Nor did Czechs feel much of a political or cultural affinity with Germans. In fact, the great majority of Czech-speaking immigrants from Bohemia and Moravia did not consider themselves German at all. They regarded German nationalism and even the German language as symbols of oppression, the hostility stemming from their political, religious, and economic persecution during the period of Habsburg Absolutism. Nonetheless, because Germans constituted the largest European minority in Texas, Czechs tended to settle in areas that already had a significant German population. Czechs and Germans, both Protestant and Catholic, commonly coexisted in many communities, particularly in Fayette, Austin, and Washington Counties. Nevertheless, Czechs generally formed their own ethnic enclaves within those communities, as in La Grange, for example. Eventually, as immigration continued to increase, Czechs formed settlements of their own, including twenty-two in Fayette County alone by the turn of the century.[18]

This pattern of settlement worked not only to keep Czechs isolated from their German and Anglo neighbors but also to create a tightly knit social structure centered around family, community, and their attitude toward the land. For the typical Czech farm family, success meant owning land, which for centuries under the Habsburg empire had remained agonizingly out of reach for most peasants. Czech immigrants transplanted this burning desire for land to Texas and then transmitted it to the younger generations. Purchasing land presented no easy task, given Czech immigrants' deprived backgrounds. Most began as tenants, renting land not from Anglos or Germans but from their own relatives already in Texas. Communities such as Fayetteville, Snook, Praha, Dubina, Hostyn, and Ammannsville, as a consequence became networks of extended families, nearly all of whom placed great value on hard work, manual labor, and cooperative effort. Even after families could buy their own farms (which in the Snook area took eleven years, on average), they remained poor, frugal, and dependant on one another. To cope with such limited resources, they established cooperative stores and cotton gins that extended much-needed credit to poor farmers, beef clubs designed to provide families with a weekly supply of fresh meat during the spring and summer, reading clubs that accumulated small libraries of hard-to-find

Czech literature, community newspapers, schools, churches, and fraternal societies (such as the SPJST) that paid benefits to farm families in case of sickness or death. So many organizations sprang up in these communities that another common expression about Texas Czechs emerged by the end of the century—"Where there are two of them, there are three clubs"—which Anglos took as a joke but Czechs took very seriously. Founded by Czechs and for Czechs, these organizations served the needs of the community, preserved the integrity of their culture, and maintained the social distance from other ethnic groups that Texas Czechs so valued.[19]

Central to the overall ethic of Texas Czech rural life was the concept of *hospodářství*, which in English translates loosely to "husbandry." The term suggests a series of interrelated attitudes and practices including intensive farming, the utmost use of resources, conservation, careful attention to detail, and an overall conservative view of the world that defined standards for behavior both on the farm and in the community. In the fields, hospodářství meant not just cultivating healthy cotton plants but also planting meticulously neat and evenly spaced rows, chopping weeds methodically (if not compulsively), preventing farm buildings or fences from deteriorating, and taking proper care of one's livestock. Czechs typically went over their cotton rows an average of twenty-one times each crop year—half again as many as other ethnic groups—plowing seven times, chopping five times, and picking four times, including a final scraping to wipe the fields clean. If a stranger went by on the road at any time of the year, so it was said, he would know the field belonged to Czechs.

Hospodářství also placed a strong emphasis on cooperation. Czech farmers had a deep-seated tradition in assisting one another in their field work and pooling their resources. Neighbors routinely swapped farm equipment and, when one fell sick or disabled, worked the afflicted's fields or harvested their crops at no cost. In Snook, a Ladies' Aid Missionary Society associated with the local Brethren church helped coordinate these substitute work crews and, in the process, turned an otherwise dire situation into a social event. The society even had its own cotton crop, harvested by volunteers from land donated by a local farmer, and used the proceeds to fund church projects. Ingenuity, mutuality, and pride in the execution of day-to-day duties—passed down from generations of farming small plots of poor soil in Bohemia and Moravia—went a long way toward explaining how Czechs farmers survived and, in many cases, thrived in south-central Texas.[20]

Because Texas Czechs "ate, drank, and slept farming," as one put it, they seemed to have little time or inclination for leisure. Social life, as defined by hospodářství, revolved around family, community, and tradition, with barn raisings, beef club days, hog killings, trips to the local cooperative gin at harvest time, picnics, weddings, and church bazaars occasionally bringing the scattered settlers together. Their main form of entertainment consisted simply of talking as a family in the evenings after the long days in the fields. A letter from relatives in Europe would make an especially lively topic of conversation and often circulated among families in the community for months. Music had long enlivened the social life of Czech settlements on both sides of the Atlantic, and in Texas, towns organized community orchestras to play traditional polka and waltz music at celebratory events. For adult males, meetings at fraternal lodges became important places to relax, drink beer, and share local gossip, perhaps over a hand of *taroky*, a Slovenian card game that Czech immigrants brought with them to Texas. More organized recreational activities for adults or children, however, were few and far between.[21]

Except, that is, for baseball—as revealed with special clarity, by the experiences of the Skrabanek family of Snook early in the twentieth century. No one took hospodářství more seriously than John Skrabanek. His idea of entertainment was to repair a farm implement in the evening. Farming dominated his very existence; his fields were immaculate. A highly respected community leader, he held offices in the SPJST, beef club, cemetery association, school board, and the Snook Brethren Church. But even with all those demands on his time, he almost never missed a meal at home. If he returned late, his family waited for him, no one daring to complain about hunger or ask for a presupper snack. Yet, this family and community patriarch—duty-minded, frugal, and fiercely proud of his ethnic background—found it in his heart to purchase baseball gloves for his three sons as they came of age. Robert, the youngest, regularly rubbed neatsfoot oil on his prized possession to keep it in shape for the next game, worked on his curveball in the fields by pitching corncobs to make-believe batters, and in school played real games, though with a rubber ball and a sawed-off broom handle, with Czechs on one side and Germans on the other. His oldest brother, Henry, professed such an undying love for baseball that he organized a Snook team that played games against Fayetteville, New Ulm, New Tabor, Wesley, and other Czech communities on Sunday afternoons. To help pay for equipment, Robert sold soda pop at the games to thirsty fans braving the hot summer sun. John could not help but brag about his sons' exploits on the diamond at SPJST meetings.[22]

The Skrabanek family's enthusiasm for baseball did not signal the decline of Czech ethnic consciousness in Texas. Not until World War II did a host of complex social and technological changes fully expose Texas Czechs to mainstream

America and, in the process, unravel the cohesion of their culture, language, and communities. Texas Czech culture did not remain static from the 1850s to the 1940s, but its main outside influences remained primarily German rather than Anglo. Despite the conflicts that continued to engulf their distant relatives in Europe, Germans and Czechs in Texas eventually learned to live together on relatively good terms and discover cultural affinities with one another. Even second-generation Texas Czechs spoke fluent Czech and German but had only a rudimentary knowledge of English. The fulfillment of religious needs also prompted cooperation between the two ethnic groups. Both Czech Catholics and Protestant Brethren suffered a paucity of Czech-speaking priests and pastors through the late nineteenth century. Rather than wait for an itinerant preacher to arrive on horseback every couple of months or so, community leaders often turned to German missionaries to minister to Czech settlers. In their family structure, farming ethic, and general way of life, Czechs resembled Germans much more than Anglos. And in terms of leisure, even Czechs enjoyed the chance to relax a bit during laid-by time. They could not have helped but notice the excitement of German baseball on Sunday afternoons in July and August. If Germans did not actually teach Czechs how to play the game (which, in all likelihood, they did), they almost certainly taught them the pleasures of the sport. Czech teams began playing German teams in the region as early as 1905. By the time Round Top visited Fayetteville for the doubleheader on the SPJST's fifteenth anniversary in 1911, baseball had become a vital asset in the social life of most Czech communities.[23]

Baseball, it seems, actually complemented, indeed reinforced, the Texas Czech's sense of hospodářství. Behind Czech farmers' performance in the cotton fields and behind Czech players' performance on the baseball field lay the same principles: knowledge of the crop's (or the game's) nuances, reliance on self-help on the one hand and an ethic of cooperation on the other, pride in the execution of duties both great and small, and the capacity to find strength not only in joy and victory but also in suffering and defeat. Just as Czech farmers faced their neighbors' condemnation for allowing weeds to grow in their cultivated land, so too did Czech teams face the wrath of their community for "bad base running," "dummy ball playing," "poor field work," "costly errors," and "struggling batsmen." And heaven help the umpire who did not live up to the high standards of Czech fans: "Oh, ye umpires, ye who hold in your hand the destiny of the game, is it impossible to have a fair game nowadays? Are we so weak that we will take sides and play accordingly? It has been done. The umpire who cannot give a player his just deserts is no umpire and should not be allowed to officiate." If a stranger passed by a baseball game in July or August, so it was said, he would know which team was Czech.[24]

Like German Texans and Czech Texans, contemporary black Texans aspired to landownership, independence, and isolation. Germans and Czechs, however, did not face the same level of external pressures as African Americans. From the early years of emancipation through well into the twentieth century, black farmers in Washington, Fayette, and surrounding counties, while growing the same crops, coping with the relentless heat of Texas summers, and traveling the same muddy roads in winter, lived in a different world from their German, Czech, and Anglo American neighbors. The black proportion of the population in south-central Texas in the late nineteenth and early twentieth centuries ranged from 52 percent in Washington County to less than 25 percent in Fayette, Austin, Burleson, and Lee Counties. But that population, however significant in numbers, was scattered, hidden, and confined to land that white farmers did not want, mostly sandy, heavily wooded creek and river bottoms. Yet even under such adverse conditions, blacks also learned the joys of baseball, so much so that they thought nothing of traveling thirty or forty miles for a game. Here again, baseball became a common denominator among the various ethnic groups of the region. The game did not, however, serve as a bridge between blacks and whites, as it had between Czechs and Germans. Its broad appeal did not break through the Jim Crow mentality and restrictions of the times.[25]

At the end of the Civil War, the quest for land among ex-slaves pervaded the South. Like other nineteenth-century Americans, natives and immigrants alike, freedmen longed for economic independence and deemed economic independence and landownership as synonymous. Without owning land for farming, freedmen believed their freedom incomplete. When the rumor that the federal government intended to provide all ex-slaves with "40 acres and a mule" proved baseless, most blacks, with limited mobility at best, remained in the countryside. In south-central Texas, they had three distinct options: take employment with white landowners as sharecroppers under slavelike conditions on the huge plantations that emerged along the Brazos River on the eastern border of Washington County (thus accounting for the county's large black population); settle in segregated "quarters" at white-approved locations near market towns and county seats; or continue to pursue their dream in small, dispersed "freedmen's settlements," twelve of which emerged in Washington County between 1870 and 1890 (along with several hundred others scattered across the eastern half of the state). The courage to create and maintain these communities came in part from black political participation during the Reconstruction years. In Washington County, blacks and Germans formed a powerful, if unstable, political alliance within the Republican Party. Among former slaves and their children, this experience fostered self-confidence and assertiveness, which sustained them even after southern whites' resumption of power at "Redemption" in the early 1880s.[26]

While no one of these freedmen's settlements epitomized them all, Flat Prairie in western Washington County, the geographical center of this south-central Texas region, illustrates several important characteristics—starting with the community's origins. Flat Prairie was located eight miles northwest of Burton on the south bank of Yegua Creek, a sluggish and muddy stream that today helps fill the reservoir Lake Somerville. As with most freedmen's settlements, its origins are not fully discernible, as county land and tax officials rarely intruded on residents' affairs. Flat Prairie, never incorporated or platted, has rarely appeared on county maps. Written and oral evidence strongly suggests, however, that antebellum landowners in the area, motivated by paternalism and strapped for cash in the wake of the Civil War, either sold or facilitated the sale of this previously uncultivated land to their former slaves for pennies per acre. Gideon Lincecum, the renowned frontier naturalist, for example, owned 2,000 acres in Long Point, halfway between Flat Prairie and Burton. He made no attempt to enter into labor contracts with his twenty former slaves, which would have involved working through the hated Freedman's Bureau. Instead, as he wrote, he "aided them in procuring good places." And sure enough, the 1870 federal census schedules, while recording limited landownership data, identified dozens of blacks in the area as "farmers" (as distinct from the more customary "farm laborers"), including Daniel Lincecum, who had taken the name of his former master. Gideon's son-in-law, James V. Matson, and other nearby plantation owners likely followed suit. Many African Americans, including members of the Coleman, Solomon, Harge, Nickerson, Williams, Taplin, Matson, and Mathis families, surface alongside the Lincecum family in the 1880 census, as well as in every subsequent census through 1930. Names on the pages of the census do not by themselves make a community and, in truth, a casual observer could have passed through Flat Prairie without even noticing it, as the only public buildings were a church and a school. Only residents' collective belief that a community existed put Flat Prairie on the map.[27]

That belief notwithstanding, the hardships of life abounded for Flat Prairie farmers. While Yegua Creek bottomland soils had the potential to produce profusely, they either lay buried in several feet of sand or under forests of virgin hardwoods or, most likely, a combination of both. Clearing the land for agriculture required agonizingly slow and backbreaking work. That work would then go for naught should the creek flood and destroy the crops, which happened every third year or so due to the flatness of the landscape and the region's propensity for heavy rains. Malaria-carrying mosquitoes, poisonous snakes, and algae-ridden water thrived in this environment, as did Johnsongrass, cotton choppers' most formidable foe, with its large roots and rhizomes able to survive winter frosts. "The bottoms attracted the people who had nothing," as one ecologist has observed. Even when farmers did produce a crop, whites cheated them at every opportunity, whether in the fields, at the weigh scale (when picking for other people), or at the closest store, in Burton, by paying them less for their cotton and charging them more for goods. Burton doctors, in addition, did not make house calls to Flat Prairie and often refused to treat blacks when they showed up in town, no matter how serious their illness or injury. Consequently, blacks avoided coming into town as much as possible and pursued subsistence farming to an even greater degree than did Germans or Czechs. Black farmers relied on cotton and corn as cash crops, but their very survival depended much more on home gardens, potato patches, and a wide variety of domestic animals—especially hogs, chickens, and turkeys—raised for food.[28]

Given their options, many blacks preferred these self-segregated communities even with the hardships. On the big plantations, such as Allenfarm on the Brazos River, dozens of black sharecropper families lived and worked much as they had under slavery. They dwelled in run-down, two-room cropper shacks; rose before dawn each morning to the sound of big plantation bells; labored in work gangs under the eyes of pistol-carrying overseers; plowed, chopped, and picked not just their own twenty-acre plots but also on the "through and through" system across the entire plantation; and got paid, in essence, not in shares but in wages, subject to the whims and machinations of landowners and furnishing merchants. The menace of not uncommon beatings, shootings, and lynchings lurked ever present. "They used ta have a little go-by," remembered one sharecropper of his white bosses. "They'd say, 'Kill a mule, buy anothuh. Kill a Negro, hire anothuh.'"[29]

Those who chose to live in black "quarters" on the edge of market towns did not fare much better. Consider, for example, "The Run," a blacks-only neighborhood across the tracks from the main town of Burton (such sections commonly called "Niggertown"). The Run sat close enough for residents to walk into town, where they could sometimes find "public work" to supplement their earnings as farm laborers. But in town, they confronted not only Texas laws requiring segregation of public spaces but the unwritten rules of Jim Crow as well, such as the mandatory use of "Mr.," "Miss," and "Mrs." when referring to whites and avoiding even the hint of physical contact with them, especially black men with white women. To remind blacks of their place, Burton whites maintained an old slave quarters just outside of town. In casual conversation, they called the structure "Lickskillet." The eight to twelve slaves who had lived in the ten-by-ten building, so the common explanation went, "had to lick the skillet to have enough to eat." This sort of humiliation drove some blacks in the area to the wilderness of Yegua Creek. Though burdened with their own difficulties, Flat Prairie farmers chose to withdraw from white authority by living as far away from it as possible. Because Yegua Creek (and creeks and rivers in general in the eastern half of Texas) formed the county line, Flat Prairie was even further removed from the centrally located, and more heavily populated, county seat of Brenham, twelve miles east of Burton.[30]

Flat Prairie offered more than just an escape from white domination. Black farmers in freedmen's settlements took great pride in their ability to grow cotton, corn, and subsistence crops under far-from-optimum conditions. "I like fawmin," recalled Mance Lipscomb, the famous blues musician who spent most of his life as a sharecropper on Allenfarm or as a renter in nearby Mount Falls Settlement. "Cause I understood it, and knowed how ta fawm. . . . If I was able to fawm, that's the happiest life ever I lived in my life, even if I didn't git nothin' outa it. . . . Man, I was at home on a fawm." His longtime friend Bubba Bowser shared Lipscomb's passion. Cotton, Bowser described as "just like humans. Plant it at the wrong time and it won't work—just dry up. Cotton breathes just like a woman breathes. The earth and your plant mate together." Ed Latham, another Mount Falls resident, remembered his days in the cotton fields with fondness as well. He liked the freedom of farming with "no white man walking up and down the rows telling me what to do" but recognized that his autonomy rested on the cooperation of his family and community. Neighbors in freedmen's settlements freely borrowed food, goods, and farming equipment from each other; rushed to each other's aid in times of illness, fire, or flooding; and gave one another excess food from field or garden, knowing that in time the favor would be returned. "Everybody helped everybody," summarized Bowser. "If someone's crop needed chopping, everyone helped—without charging." Whether by blood relation, marriage, or lifelong, face-to-face interactions, ties of familiarity knitted black farm settlements closely and provided them with a powerful sense of will and identity. Though disadvantaged, impoverished, and exploited, farmers in freedmen's settlements clung tenaciously to their land, culture, and social values. In Flat Prairie, longtime resident Grover Williams recalled, prominent community leaders emerged from the Coleman, Solomon, Harge, Nickerson, Williams, Taplin, Matson, Mathis, and Lincecum families and served as role models from one generation to the next.[31]

Members of those same prominent families, Williams added, also played on the Flat Prairie baseball team, though not until the early years of the twentieth century. Baseball caught on with blacks in the region but later than with Germans or Czechs. It was hard for Flat Prairie farmers to get interested in secular amusements because of their incredibly demanding work cycle from predawn to twilight—from "caint see to caint see," as Lipscomb put it. Even during laid-by time, blacks had little chance to relax. While they waited, like everyone else in July and August, for the cotton harvest to begin, Flat Prairie farmers took any odd jobs they could get in town or on white-owned farms—digging wells and postholes, breaking work stock, building chimneys, fixing farm machinery—in addition to tending to their own subsistence crops and resuming the never-ending task of clearing the bottomlands of Yegua Creek for their own agriculture. With the harvest approaching, the wood produced by clearing made an especially valuable commodity to the three steam-powered gins in Burton. Nor did blacks have time for baseball on Sundays. The strict churchgoing Baptist families of Flat Prairie took the Sabbath seriously. No work occurred, even of an emergency nature. If the cows broke free into the cotton fields or the hogs got into the sweet potato patch, true believers faced a profound dilemma. Cooking, fishing, laughing, shouting, whistling, or play of any kind was simply not allowed. Blacks reserved the better part of laid-by time, in fact, for weeklong revivals, which the Zion Hill Baptist Church in Flat Prairie called "Big Sundays." Left to their own devices, blacks might not have discovered baseball at all, let alone embraced it with such fervor.[32]

But Flat Prairie blacks, their yearning for isolation notwithstanding, were not left entirely to their own devices and in fact appeared to follow the pattern set by the other ethnic groups in learning to enjoy baseball. While keeping to themselves within the boundaries of their own community, residents of Flat Prairie were surrounded by Germans—not just in Burton but in the nearby farming settlements of Rehburg, Union Hill, Long Point, and Gay Hill. On the census schedules, one German surname after another literally engulfs the blocks of African American entries. The marketplace necessitated that black community leaders interact with their German neighbors from time to time in the seasonal cycle of the agricultural year, but especially during laid-by time when selling them wood and at harvestime when "settling up" on their cotton. Like the Czechs in Fayette County, blacks in western Washington County could not have missed the

German infatuation with baseball. On diamonds in Burton and throughout the surrounding countryside, Germans liked to "tip up a baseball," as the saying went. When rounding up enough players to field two full teams proved difficult, as often occurred, they had to improvise. "It'd be ten or twelve of us maybe, normally half of them black and half white," recalled one German enthusiast. "But that didn't make any difference. We'd have us a ball game." Having learned from their German neighbors in this manner, blacks gradually took the game back to Flat Prairie where, over time, it caught on. By the turn of the century, schoolchildren played the game regularly, and a baseball field, laid out adjacent to Zion Hill Baptist Church, became part of the settlement's infrastructure. Like Germans and Czechs before them, blacks made time for baseball.[33]

Blacks enhanced baseball's popularity in Flat Prairie all the more by featuring the game in their annual celebration of emancipation—Freedom Day or, more commonly, Juneteenth. The most important secular event of the year, Juneteenth began on June 19, 1865, when Union general Gordon Granger read the Emancipation Proclamation in Galveston, thus belatedly freeing 250,000 slaves in the state of Texas. Former slaves in Galveston rejoiced in the streets that day, and jubilant celebrations began throughout eastern Texas the following year, though not always on June 19. Word of slavery's abolition spread gradually and unevenly across the state in the summer of 1865. Blacks in the Yegua Creek area did not hear the news until August 4 and from that point on chose to commemorate the abolition of slavery on the first weekend of August. With the added advantage of taking place during laid-by time, Juneteenth celebrations in Flat Prairie and Burton often lasted two full days. In the early 1890s, the two black communities combined their efforts into one big celebration held at Mason Park in the Run. Dramatic readings of the Emancipation Proclamation, family reunions, parades, dances, barbecues, music, and the crowning of the Juneteenth Queen became rituals held year after year. At some point in the first decade of the twentieth century, baseball games after the noon meal on Saturday became an integral part of the tradition as well. Though the games were informal, the opposing teams played hard and often well into the evening. Using balls made from rocks wrapped with material from cotton sacks and big sticks for bats, players were known to knock each other's teeth out, or worse. The Juneteenth games in the Run also caught the attention of local white newspapers. As one celebrant put it, "The paper [the *Brenham Banner Press*] gave good coverage on it. 'Bout the only time you see anything for a Negro that wasn't that he stole something was on Freedom Day."[34]

By the 1920s, Flat Prairie had its own team, its own schedule of games, its own rivals, and its own stars—Willie Harge, Lugene Williams, Willie Nickerson, L. V.

Taplin, and Aaron Mathis—from families with deep roots in the community. While the Burton white team continued to play Carmine, La Grange, Somerville, Round Top, and other nearby towns, Flat Prairie took on freedmen's settlements in Lee and Washington Counties, including Antioch, Betts' Chapel, Post Oak, Cross Hogs Branch, and Mount Falls. Separate and unequal conditions prevailed, however. Flat Prairie players wore no uniforms, no gloves, and no protective equipment of any kind. As blacks were not allowed on the railroads and few if any owned automobiles, teams rode horses and buggies or walked to get to the games—forty miles distant in the case of Mount Falls. The diamonds themselves were in poor, even laughable, shape. Of one field in Lee County, Grover Williams remembered, "You might be running after the ball, you might run down in the gully and come up and fall down, all that kind of thing, step in a cow pile or something." Still, added Williams, "they could really play some ball. . . . Those boys knocked them balls out of the park." Even whites, on occasion, took notice and showed up at some of these black baseball games. The Cross Hogs Branch team near Brenham became so popular among whites that they needed "special reservations" for important games. They came primarily to gamble but also, wrote a local correspondent, to admire "the spectacular fielding of the center fielder and second baseman." In moments such as these, few and brief though they were, baseball triumphed over Jim Crow.[35]

Flat Prairie farmers neither sought nor needed white approval to appreciate baseball, however. Residents took great pride in their team, with dozens of them often accompanying the players on road games. Blacks on the big plantation farms on the Brazos River apparently did not share this passion for the game. The freedom to play baseball stemmed directly from the freedom of farming, the freedom of landownership, and the freedom from white authority. The game reinforced black farmers' burning desire for autonomy, rewarded their persistence along strong family lines, and restored their sense of whimsy and innocence.

And what of Texas Anglos? One might surmise that native white southerners played baseball and perhaps played an even more modern, sophisticated version of the game than German, Czech, or African Texans. But in many ways, Anglos stayed on the outside looking in as the game became rooted in the region's rural life. From the early 1880s through the early 1920s, no predominantly Anglo teams existed in Washington, Fayette, and surrounding counties. The many dozens of German and Czech teams in the region might have included an Anglo or two, but only on rare occasions. Only in Brenham, the largest town in the area and with the largest population of Anglos, did four or five regularly play on the community team. The region's demography—sheer numbers and the phenomenon of ethnic clustering—go a long way toward accounting for this discrepancy. Ethnocultural politics also played a big factor. Germans and Czechs became more closely aligned while at the same time remaining apart from Anglos because they both fought prohibition with passion and conviction. Moreover, though neither ethnic group could claim more enlightened racial attitudes than Anglos, they both often found themselves on the same side in politics with blacks. From Reconstruction to the Great Depression, all three communities tended to vote Republican and oppose prohibition. In perhaps the most hotly contested election in twentieth-century Texas history, statewide prohibition lost narrowly in 1911 because of the heavy turnout of Germans, Czechs, and African Americans. In such a climate, most Anglos found the idea of socializing with their opponents repugnant, and many found baseball, for religious and cultural reasons, just as immoral as drinking itself. Baseball in south-central Texas was first and foremost a German, not an Anglo, pastime.[36]

Meanwhile, Germans had troubles of their own. On the eve of World War I, people far and wide knew of their contributions to the agricultural wealth of the region and their instrumental role in spreading the popularity of baseball. Farmers in southern Fayette County, to take just one example, well understood the links between economy, culture, and sport when they cheered the founding of the all-German Schulenburg Giants in 1913, and cheered even louder in 1915 when local merchant Adolf Kehrer constructed a modern new ball field for the team, complete with bleachers and shade overhangs. Yet just two years later, Germans throughout Fayette and Washington Counties found themselves afraid to go into town for any reason, let alone to attend a ball game, even to such predominantly German towns as La Grange, Burton, and Brenham. The United States' entry into the war against Germany generated considerable hysteria among Texas Anglos and considerable stress among Texans of German descent. Many of the latter felt so uncomfortable that they stopped speaking their native language not just in public where Anglos might hear them but also in their schools, churches, and clubs. For the duration of the war, German American citizens cancelled Maifest and other traditional celebrations, disbanded their baseball teams, and displayed Liberty Bond posters in their windows hoping to demonstrate patriotic fervor. Some even denounced their German heritage by changing the spelling of their surnames. Those who chose to speak out more forcefully ran the risk of being tarred and feathered by angry mobs, as happened several times in the Burton area alone.[37]

When word of the armistice came via telegraph on November 11, 1918, Texas Germans rejoiced—though much too early, as it turned out. The nativism and antiforeign sentiment generated by the war persisted into the mid 1920s. Acts of violence and persecution—beatings, boycotts, kidnappings, and more tar and featherings—continued against individuals of German heritage by self-styled "hundred percent Americans," many of whom joined local chapters of the resurgent Ku Klux Klan. The most notorious incident occurred in Brenham on May 19, 1921, the first night of the annual Maifest celebration, which had resumed the previous year. A reported 400 members of the Klan (including multiple reinforcements from Houston) marched in single file through the streets to Firemen's Park, garbed in flowing white robes, high-pointed white caps, and white face masks, with the red-circle, white-cross emblem of the order emblazoned across their chests. At the front of the line, one carried an American flag and another a flaming cross. Many others held large threatening signs such as, "Our fathers were here in '61; their boys are here in '21" and, more to the point, "Speak English or quit talking on Brenham's streets." While no violence occurred at the demonstration, the Klan's show of force made its point loud and clear. A few days later, town leaders, both Anglo and German, called a mass meeting at the Washington County courthouse hoping to achieve stability in the community. After several hours of heated discussion, the assembly of townspeople and farmers announced that it had resolved to use only English at soldiers' funerals, to discontinue teaching the German language in the schools, and to bring local Lutheran ministers into town for intensive instruction in spoken English. The concessions failed to ease tensions, however, and over the next two years, the Klan turned once again to various forms of verbal and physical intimidation to reinforce its anti-German message and reinvigorate anti-German passions.[38]

The Klan's strategy ultimately backfired, however. With the grim specter of the white-robed, masked order hanging over the town, German-American citizens in Brenham and the surrounding countryside became so afraid and full of resentment that they avoided the downtown district altogether and took their business elsewhere. Up to that point, the *Brenham Daily Banner-Press* had willingly published Klan proclamations and reported regularly on the order's "Americanization" efforts. But with the town's several gins, cotton oil mill, farm equipment dealerships, and retail and service establishments suffering noticeably from the sharp drop in German patronage, the paper and the Brenham Chamber of Commerce decided something had to be done. In grand Texas style, leading local merchants spent over $6,000 to throw a massive "Reconciliation Barbeque," held on October 29, 1923. Members of the "barbeque committee" slow-cooked one hundred prime beeves in specially dug meat pits over a thousand feet long, doused each individual serving with plenty of sauce (amounting to hundreds of gallons in all), and provided more than enough pickles, bread, and coffee to go around. A reported 12,000 people (more than half the county) attended the heavily publicized free dinner and, in the spirit of cooperation, sat together at one table over a mile and a half long. While surely no one went home hungry, the *Daily Banner-Press*'s declaration of an "era of good feeling" proved premature once again. When the local chapter of the Klan announced its intent to disband a year later, even the ever-optimistic Brenham paper warned that "each and everyone, Klan and Anti-Klan, needs to join hands and work for the upbuilding of Brenham and Washington County."[39]

While the barbeque helped start the healing process, the sensational baseball season of 1925 supplied the key impetus. The mastermind behind the Brenham Wildcats was its player-manager, Dick Hooper, a war veteran who returned from Europe with only one arm. Undeterred, Hooper played outfield by catching the ball, tossing it up in the air in front of him, putting his glove under the stump of his missing arm, catching the ball again, and throwing it—in the blink of an eye. He was also considered one of the best hitters on the team. Hooper did not approach the 1925 season with reuniting the community in mind. He cared only about a player's ability, not his ethnic background, position on prohibition, religion, or political party. With his sole objective "to place Brenham on the baseball map," he organized the Brenham Baseball Association, composed of the leading merchants in town, to raise funds for the team. Its four officers included three of German heritage and the other of Czech. He then recruited the twelve "most seasoned" ballplayers in the area to open the season. The ethnic breakdown of the team reflected that of the white population of Washington County as well as that of Brenham teams since the turn of the century: five German players, five Anglo, and two Czech. Hooper could no doubt have strengthened his team even more with stars from Flat Prairie or Cross Hogs Branch, but such an approach remained unthinkable given the deeply entrenched customs and laws of segregation of the times. The 1925 season was for whites only.[40]

Hooper began the season arranging games with nearby community teams on an ad hoc basis. Led by the pitching of "flamethrower" Al Artz and the clutch hitting of centerfielder Pier Wendt and first baseman Joe Clauss, the team got off to a fast start with wins against old rivals New Ulm (still predominantly Czech), Burton (all German), Somerville (mostly Germans and Czechs), and Bellville (predominantly German). Upward of 1,000 fans attended the home games at Fireman's Park, prompting Brenham Maifest organizers to reincorporate baseball into the three-day celebration of Texas German culture with the hopes of drawing more visitors—just as the Germania Verein had done back in 1884. The strategy worked again. The "largest crowds to ever witness ballgames" in Washington County watched Brenham beat Bellville twice, extending the team's winning streak to seven. And between games on the night of the 22nd, more citizens witnessed the coronation ceremony of the Maifest queen than ever before. Organizers announced that profits from the festivities totaled $704, $627 of which came from gate receipts from the ball games. "Never has Maifest been more popular," the queen declared.[41]

With the added publicity from Maifest, news of the team's success began to reach beyond Washington, Austin, and Fayette Counties. As a result, Hooper could schedule games with Houston, Conroe, and Rosenberg—the latter resulting in the Wildcat's first loss of the season. Then came the break Hooper had hoped for from the start. In mid June, the Wildcats received an invitation to participate in the Austin American Cup Race, a league, sponsored by the capital city newspaper, composed of the nine best community teams in central Texas—Georgetown, Elgin, Bertram, Austin, Hutto, Smithville, Llano, Lytton Springs, and now Brenham. To the delight of its ever-increasing fan base, Brenham passed its first test, sweeping previously undefeated Elgin in a three-game series at the end of June behind the pitching of Artz and Otto Krenek and the "brilliant fielding" of Clauss and outfielder Max Bleberstein. On the fourth of July, before an estimated 1,500 packed-in fans at Fireman's Park, Artz shut out Bellville, 2 to 0, on just five hits. That week, energized fans donated $615 to the Brenham Baseball Association for new uniforms and equipment for their beloved Wildcats. As the season progressed, the *Daily Banner-Press* extended its coverage of the team, printing players' batting averages on a regular basis, adding a "baseball gossip" column, and moving its lively and detailed accounts of the games from the back page to the front page. "Delegations" of as many as 300 fans joined the team on road trips to away games, and businesses in Brenham closed their doors early on game days "so that all who can attend will attend." Three times over the course of the remaining season additional bleachers were added to Fireman's Park to accommodate the "overflowing crowds." "Wildcat fever," the *Daily Banner-Press* proclaimed, "has hit the entire county."[42]

So too had a terrible drought—one of the worst in the state's history. The rains stopped in February and held off all through the spring and summer. In the midst of the Wildcats' success, the crops and cotton economy failed in south-central Texas. One of the main reasons that the *Daily Banner-Press* expanded its coverage of baseball was that it had nothing much to print about cotton. Farmers could not remember another year when the lack of rain forced them to import hay from outside the region just to feed their stock. Then, when the drought did finally break in late October, sixteen inches fell in just a couple of days, washing out roads, carrying away bridges, drowning cattle, and eroding the parched cotton fields. Across the drought-stricken region, farmers struggled to get by. For many, following the Wildcats win victory after victory provided a welcome, if not magical, distraction from grasshopper invasions, dust storms, and their dead-in-the-ground corn and cotton.[43]

The fairy-tale baseball season then came to a fitting end. With Artz "holding the opposition at his mercy the entire route," Brenham beat Austin 14 to 0 on July 26 to capture the Austin American Cup, finishing the league season with eight wins and two losses. Hooper then put together the Little Dixie Series—five games with Crockett, the "champions of East Texas." After losing the first game 2 to 1 in eleven innings, Brenham roared back to sweep the remaining four games to "cop the flag." In the decisive fourth game, billed as "the battle of the ages" by the *Daily Banner-Press*, hundreds of fans who could not make the trip to Crockett gathered in and around Citizens Drug Store in downtown Brenham, "waiting impatiently for news of the game [via telephone] and cheering wildly when it came in such welcome form." Hooper, still not satisfied, then organized a three-game set in Brenham with China Spring (near Waco) for "the undisputed independent baseball championship of Texas." In "gripping baseball drama," Brenham once again lost the first game but took the final two in thrilling fashion to win the title. Many hundreds of fans from throughout Washington County—Germans, Anglos, and Czechs alike—gathered on the streets around the courthouse "to vent their feelings by shouting themselves hoarse" and staging an impromptu parade to honor their team. "Their joy," wrote the *Daily Banner-Press*, "was unconfined."[44]

It seemed almost as though the Klan's march through those same streets just four years earlier had never happened. Hooper achieved his original objective of putting Brenham baseball on the map, but in the process, the Wildcats accomplished something of far greater significance. Winning ball games with Germans, Anglos, and Czechs on the field greatly enhanced efforts to reconcile Germans, Anglos, and Czechs off the field. The storied 1925 season did not put an end to anti-German hostilities or to cultural conflicts in south-central Texas more generally, but it did signal a turning point in the region's complex ethnic relations. The war and its aftermath brought a disruption rather than an elimination of German (and, to a lesser extent, Czech) traditions and institutions. Prior to the war, the relationship between the three major white ethnic groups in the region was marked by a patronizing attitude on the part of Texas Anglos and an aloofness on the part of Texas Germans and Texas Czechs, both of whom asked nothing of their neighbors except to be left alone in order that they might acquire economic independence and preserve the language and customs of their homelands. After the Wildcats' run to the championship, Germans and Czechs resumed their major roles in the south-central Texas economy and continued to assert their ethnicity through social and cultural means—including, if not especially, baseball. So too did Texas blacks, but largely in the isolation of their communities in the remote countryside.[45]

CHAPTER FOUR

The Making of Bob Feller and the Modern American Farmer

"Without knowing the town of Van Meter, Iowa, it is impossible to understand the miracle of Bob Feller." So began Kyle Crichton in a feature article for *Collier's*, which appeared March 6, 1937. A member of the New York literary set, Crichton had published many an interview with screen, stage, and radio celebrities. This particular assignment, however, took him to "nowhere," as he characterized his destination, to interview a farmer, school principal, filling station attendant, and county newspaper reporter—in the dead of winter, no less. Crichton's portrayal of the town reflected his displeasure and big city pretensions: "You could have wandered around with your eyes closed and have been in no danger of death from collision. One look was enough to reveal that a good active walker could touch every house in town in fifteen minutes. There was a main street looking like a movie set for a Buck Jones Western and almost no activity. There is no bus service into Van Meter, no movie house, no drugstore, no pool hall. . . . One train [comes] west every day at 8:36 in the morning; one east at 7:37 in the evening, stopping only when flagged." Writers from the *Saturday Evening Post*, *Time*, *New York Herald Tribune*, *New York Daily Mirror*, *Cleveland Plain Dealer*, *Cleveland Press*, and *Chicago Herald-Examiner* also made the trek to Van Meter that winter to observe Feller "in his native setting," as one called the town of 410 residents.[1]

The "miracle" to which Crichton referred occurred the previous summer. Having just completed his junior year at Van Meter Consolidated High School, Bob Feller burst upon the national scene as a rookie pitching sensation for the Cleveland Indians. On July 6, 1936, four months before his eighteenth birthday, he struck out eight of the twelve batters he faced in an exhibition game against the St. Louis Cardinals' fabled Gashouse Gang. In his first official start, on August 23 against the St. Louis Browns, he struck out fifteen, one short of the American League record. Then, three weeks later, he broke that mark, fanning seventeen Philadelphia Athletics to tie Dizzy Dean's major league record. Batters could barely see his blazing fastball—since estimated at more than 100 miles per hour—let alone hit it. As New York Yankee pitcher Lefty Gomez remarked to an umpire after three Feller pitches blew by him, "That last one sounded a bit low." When Feller returned to Van Meter for his senior year that fall, ten thousand people, including the governor of Iowa, jammed the town on Bob Feller Day trying to get a look at the new star. Later that spring, he made the cover of *Time* magazine and the front of the Wheaties box. And when "Master Bob," as the press liked to call him, graduated in May 1937 along with eighteen classmates, NBC radio broadcast the ceremony live, in its entirety. Newspapers across the country covered the event on the front page, right alongside the crash of the Hindenburg and the coronation of King George VI.[2]

Feller's feats mesmerized the nation, baseball fans and nonfans alike. Everyone wanted to know his life story, and Crichton and the others gave it to them in considerable detail. Feller himself produced an "autobiography"—a fifteen-part series entitled "My Own Story," run that April in the *Chicago Herald-Examiner* and other major newspapers under Bob's byline (though ghostwritten by a *Des Moines Tribune* staff writer). Photographs of young Bob at the typewriter, with sleeves rolled up and pencil behind his ear, lent the series an air of authenticity. "I would feel more at home with my foot on the slab, getting my sign from my catcher, than I do starting this story of my life, but here goes!" he began with modest exclamation. There followed a winsome, farm-boy-makes-good narrative, truthful in some parts, fanciful in others, nostalgic and sentimental throughout—the perfect counterpart to Crichton's urbane and cynical version. "As far back as I can remember," Master Bob wrote, "I was walking around the barnyard behind dad, lugging a ball and a couple of mitts, waiting for him to finish his chores. I usually hurried through mine so we'd have a longer time to play catch." Who could resist?[3]

In both its sentimental and cynical forms (or, as in many renditions, a combination of the two), the Feller narrative captured the public's imagination. Bob's rise from poor farm boy to big city star allowed Americans to celebrate their rags to riches ideals (even though the Fellers were by no means poor). His story resonated deeply in a society itself moving physically and culturally from the countryside to the city. Both versions used generally the same details—toddler Bob rolling a ball across the living room floor; child prodigy Bob breaking two of dad's ribs playing catch in the barn; adolescent Bob striking out batters twice his age on the field his dad built right on the farm. Both versions had the same omissions, avoiding references to the outside world and often not meshing with his true life story. While no one person controlled the storyline, one person did provide the details. Bob's father, William, often portrayed as "Pa Feller" amid a background of rural simplicity, was no stranger to big city condescension.[4] Neither hick nor hayseed but a modern, sophisticated farmer, Will knew how to capitalize on Americans' emotional attachment to the agrarian ideal. Under his tutelage, young Bob became as much a cultural curiosity as a baseball star, an image that "the heater from Van Meter" exploited for all it was worth through the end of his Hall of Fame career and beyond. Bob hustled on the field and off, a behavior consistent with four generations of Feller farmers in Iowa since the 1850s. Indeed, without knowing the *history* of Van Meter, to rephrase Crichton's lead, it is impossible to understand the *phenomenon* of Bob Feller.

At some point in the mid 1850s, Henri and Marie Feller, both in their late forties, made the decision to leave their farm in France and migrate to America. Along with their four sons and two daughters, ranging in age from six to twenty, they arrived in New York on the passenger ship *Mercury* on November 13, 1856, and headed straight for Jackson County, Iowa, just west of the Mississippi River. The Fellers typified migrants to the West (the Midwest in today's parlance) in that they were older, came as a family unit, and had experience with farming—clearing and planting ground, harvesting crops, and building their own home. They differed in that most contemporary Iowans were native-born, having moved from the Ohio Valley, Northeast, or Upper South. A small percentage came from western Europe, but even then almost entirely from Germany, Ireland, and England. Their minority status may explain why the Fellers chose to Americanize their first names almost immediately upon arrival (Henri to Henry, Marie to Mary, Andre to Andrew, Jacques to Jacob, and Jean to John). The decisiveness with which they moved coupled with large numbers of settlers with the surname Feller already in the region suggest chain migration at work. Henri and Marie probably followed other family members who had provided glowing accounts of Iowa's many physical features. Henry and Mary sought a better life than they had had in Europe and arrived intent on acquiring land and planting bountiful crops.[5]

Their expectations proved well founded. The Fellers arrived toward the end of an era long regarded as "the farmer's age," the period 1815–1860. If ever farmers took center stage in American history, this was the time. As the American population spread westward at a rapid pace, farmers (particularly in the North) adopted labor-saving equipment, improved their techniques, produced surplus crops, and experienced a significantly higher standard of living. Expansion seemed to permeate everything, from transportation networks, to markets, to people's very horizon of experience. New canals (the Erie, most prominently), improved roads, and—by the 1840s and 1850s—railroads broke down old geographical barriers and provided routes for an increasing flow of farm products to the East. They also opened up the Midwestern prairies to settlement in a remarkable manner. The process of farm making on the level, rich land gathered tremendous speed and momentum. Farmers could bring their acres into cultivation without the old restrictive requirement of a lifetime devoted to clearing trees, though the lack of timber on the prairies for buildings, fences, and fuel presented a problem of its own. In the decade of the 1850s alone, an astounding 2.2 million people swelled the population of Illinois, Indiana, Iowa, and Missouri. This constituted 25 percent of the total population increase of the forty-one states and territories. Not all the newcomers were farmers (a considerable portion concentrated in urban centers such as Chicago and St. Louis), but the vast majority resided in rural areas.

Farmers in the countryside and businessmen in cities actually had much in common. For much of the nineteenth century, Americans held two competing conceptions of the West. According to Jeffersonian intellectual tradition, each family in America's new heartland would form an island unto itself—producing for its own needs on a modest piece of land and practicing bucolic virtues, free of the corrupt influences of the marketplace and rude intrusions of industrialization. The second idea, usually associated with Alexander Hamilton and Henry Clay, envisioned an aggressive, expanding commercialized agriculture, in which a farmer produced not only for himself but also for the nation and the world. For farmers themselves, the two conceptions were not necessarily mutually exclusive. Many who crossed the Appalachians to new settlements saw themselves as chosen people carving out an agrarian paradise in the wilderness. Despite what they may have thought, farmers swiftly found themselves locked into an advancing market economy. To this day, we tend to think that this country evolved naturally from frontier settlement to industrialization in two distinct historical phases. In fact, each drove the other.

This gradual change in outlook reflected the extraordinary faith among Midwestern farmers in new technology and their vigorous response to market opportunities—so extraordinary and so vigorous that historians often refer to this period (the 1840s and 1850s) as the First Agricultural Revolution. Technological innovation—steel plows, cultivators, threshers, and especially reapers—broke down production and cultural barriers by midcentury. Cutting grain with a sickle or cradle and grass with a scythe were backbreaking jobs and expensive in terms of manhours. The reapers introduced by Cyrus McCormick, Obed Hussey, and others harvested grains more thoroughly and seven times more rapidly than the cradle, with half the labor force. Put another way, a man could cut one-half to three-quarters of an acre of wheat a day with a sickle, two to three acres with a cradle, or ten to twelve acres with a reaper.

In practical terms, this meant that farmers no longer had to limit their fields to the amount their families (and hirelings, if they could afford them) could harvest, a development that proved downright seductive. The breaking of the production bottleneck dramatically altered farmers' perception of the marketplace even more. Supply, they now believed, created its own demand; the more they produced, the better off they would become. That fundamental assumption—an expression of extreme confidence and optimism—both motivated and haunted farmers for the rest of the century and beyond.[6]

The Fellers wasted little time reaping the benefits of "the farmer's age." Early on, they discovered that available land in Jackson County was scarce and expensive, as settlement in eastern Iowa had flourished for two decades. Like many later arrivals, the Feller family found it necessary to move farther into the central part of the state, which had already begun to demonstrate its potential as a major agricultural region. In the summer of 1858, they rented a sixty-eight-acre farm a mile north of the Raccoon River in Boone Township, Dallas County, eighteen miles west of Fort Des Moines, the state capital. Just five years later, on April 25, 1863, the Fellers realized their dream of landownership when Henry purchased 140 acres not far from their tenant farm for $1,000. With the help of the Stumps, Wrights, Stags, Claytons, Browns, and other neighbors, the newcomers built a two-room farmhouse and several other structures on a bluff atop the river. Though located squarely in the center of Iowa's tall-grass prairie lands, the Feller farm, with its proximity to the river, contained forty acres of oak timberland, two steep ravines, and gently rolling hills. At the time, the Fellers believed the land provided the best of both worlds—the advantages of wood and water along with more than eighty acres of rich farmland and pasture. The varied landscape also resembled conditions back home in France. They learned in time that the bumpy terrain would be less accommodating to mechanization than the more level prairie.[7]

Drawing upon the experience of older settlers in the township and following the conventional wisdom of the times, Henry and his sons diversified their operations, planting corn, buckwheat, rye, and wheat, with the latter their principal cash crop. They utilized all the latest plows, cultivators, threshers, and reapers, borrowing them from neighbors at first but gradually purchasing their own. They also raised a few head of cattle and a dozen or so hogs. When they first arrived, they found two mills and two general stores within hauling distance of five to ten miles, and by 1868, the new town of Van Meter, just three and a half miles southwest of the Feller farm on the south bank of the Raccoon River, became the main retail and service center for the surrounding farm community. When the Rock Island Railroad came through town in 1869, making it possible to send Dallas County products, via Chicago, to East Coast markets, crop prices climbed even higher. A productive coal mine a couple of miles down the river gave Henry and his sons additional opportunities for short-term work during the winter months. By 1870, the move to Iowa had truly paid off. The Feller farm rose in value to $5,000 and contained personal property worth another $2,000. Four years earlier, Henry's eldest son, Andrew, had purchased 160 acres of his own adjacent to the family homestead and shortly thereafter had married Elizabeth Brotchi of Adel, the Dallas County seat. His small start-up farm was valued at $2,400 in 1870. The future looked promising indeed.[8]

The Fellers' good fortune in their first decade of settlement stemmed in part from federal policy during the Civil War. The economic measures passed after the Republican victory of 1860 were designed, in no uncertain terms, to stimulate production. Midwestern farmers had virtually all of their major demands satisfied: a homestead act that gave 160 acres of free public land to settlers who would live and labor on it (though not much unclaimed land remained in central Iowa by the time the Fellers arrived); a series of grants to railroad companies to provide still more transportation for moving crops and opening settlements; and a federal Department of Agriculture to offer government services. Aid of this magnitude strengthened farmers' commitment to unrestrained expansion, heightened their commercial identity, assured the continued rapid exploitation of the country's farming resources, and strengthened the link between agricultural and industrial sectors.[9]

Even before 1870, however, clear signs indicated that the great age of American farming was drawing to a close. Indeed, the latter third of the nineteenth century might well be called the age of paradox in American agricultural history. Farm output, after doubling between 1840 and 1860, more than tripled from 1860 to 1900, yet for farmers themselves, this productivity led to deep agricultural discontent. Farmers received less and less for their efforts. The laws of supply and demand worked against them, as they did against virtually all producers during this time. In this long, drawn-out period of deflation, commodity prices fell precipitously across the board. Unable to face the possibility that their fundamental assumption—that the Midwest could not overproduce—might be fallacious, farmers tried to fight back and find someone to blame. Largely through the Grange, originally a social-educational organization, they denounced railroads for discriminatory freight rates, banks for inadequate credit, grain elevators for excessive charges, state and federal governments for insufficient regulatory legislation, and implement manufacturers for gouging them mercilessly. To Midwestern farmers, something basically wrong undergirded a system that enabled giant corporations to flourish while the men who supplied them with basic goods could hardly make a living. Farmers vented their frustrations even louder during the Populist revolt at the end of the century, but in the end it had no more success. While Iowa farmers complained of financial distress, they showed little enthusiasm for independent politics. Unlike Nebraska, Kansas, Minnesota, and the Dakotas, the state of Iowa had a competitive-party system that, in response to farmers' demands, produced enough moderate reforms to discourage third-party formation.[10]

Andrew Feller struggled much of his adult life to come to terms with the age of paradox. With the deaths of his parents in the 1870s and subsequent relocations of his three brothers to the prairie region of western Dallas County, Andrew became the principal operator of the Feller farmstead. Faced with falling commodity prices, Andrew tried to produce his way out of financial hardship. He took on considerable debt to add another 340 acres, thus more than doubling the size of his farm to 640 acres (80 of them wooded) and making it four times the size of the average Iowa farm (roughly 160 acres). He continued to practice "sit down" farming by buying an array of new implements—sulky gangplows, check-row planters, and riding cultivators pulled across the fields by teams of fine horses. While continuing to diversify farm operations, he gradually replaced wheat with corn as his staple crop. Along with a generation of Iowa farmers, Andrew learned that the best financial returns could be realized by feeding most of the corn to hogs, for which a strong market flourished in eastern cities. In the mid-1870s, Andrew joined the Dallas County Grange, which provided him and his neighbors with enjoyable social gatherings but little in the way of economic relief. In 1886, he built a large, cavernous barn from native lumber and wooden pegs where he could store his crops when markets were particularly tight. Even his children proved burdensome in terms of farm production. He and Elizabeth had four, but the first two were girls, the third was a son who died of pneumonia at the age of five, and the fourth, William Andrew, was not born until 1886. Consequently, the Fellers had to rely heavily on hired labor to run the farm. When Andrew died suddenly in 1898 at the age of fifty-eight, leaving his wife, two daughters, and nine-year-old son heavily in debt, the Feller farm appeared in grave danger of failing. His brothers John and Jacob helped Elizabeth find tenants to make ends meet, but only to bide time for William Andrew to come of age.[11]

In the rural America that young William inherited, the competition between Jeffersonian and Hamiltonian intellectual traditions now seemed hopelessly antiquated. By 1900, four clear signs showed that farmers had firmly embraced the market. The first was the increasing specialization of cash crops. The so-called belts of American agriculture—corn, wheat, dairy, and cotton—were firmly entrenched, perhaps the surest indication of all of how few farmers still raised crops primarily for home consumption. Second, farmers actually showed little passion for the land they cultivated; they stood ready to pick up and leave whenever their acreage appreciated substantially—as Andrew's three brothers had done. Third, when feeling prosperous, farmers rushed into debt to buy more land and more farm equipment—just as Andrew himself did. And fourth, they clearly relished the innovations of the industrial age, especially the railroad and new advances in labor-saving farm machinery. Production costs for the leading crops dropped by half between 1850 and 1900.[12]

Farmers such as the Fellers now stood at the center of a vast complex network of trade and industry. A highly sophisticated array of commodity exchanges, run by brokers wearing shirts and ties in Chicago and other big cities, determined prices and found buyers throughout the country and overseas. Great processing industries turned wheat into flour, livestock into packaged meat, and fruits and vegetables into canned goods. Entire rail systems, port facilities, and fleets of ships focused on moving the products of American farmers. Farming, in other words, had irrevocably become a business. Jefferson has spun in his grave ever since.[13]

Or so it would seem. Despite all the evidence to the contrary, agrarianism simply would not die. Although up-and-coming businessmen, farmers still seemed of two minds about themselves at the turn of the twentieth century. They still saw themselves as independent, self-reliant, even virtuous tillers of the soil, yet they understood all too well that they had become fully integrated into the modern economic order. This dual self-image got reinforced by the great majority of urban Americans who still believed, if largely in the abstract, something basically good about farmers and farming. These two ironies were compounded by yet another: even while Americans continued to have a romantic faith in the agrarian ideal of the independent yeoman living in bucolic abundance, millions of them in fact deserted this idyllic condition for greener pastures in the city. In simple truth, rural people found it increasingly difficult to swallow the widening discrepancy in the quality of life between farm and city. Farming did not pay as well as nonfarm employment; it required harder work and longer hours; electricity, indoor plumbing, and paved roads had not yet come to the farm; and in terms of cultural opportunities and social amenities, the rural lifestyle could not compete with the attractions of urban living. By the opening of the twentieth century, farmers no longer constituted the majority of the population. It took many years for Americans, rural and urban alike, to grasp the social, cultural, and political implications of this fundamental and far-reaching change. The disjuncture between statistical reality and the lag in the popular consciousness shaped rural-urban relations for the first four decades of the twentieth century and, as such, greatly affected Will Feller's life.[14]

In 1904, Will Feller, only sixteen years old, found himself in charge of the farm his family had owned for forty years. Though his mother, in accordance with his father's will, owned the property, Will assumed full responsibility for its operations, his uncles having decided that the time had come for them to step aside. Living only with his mother and sister Ida, Will faced the daunting challenge of farming 650 acres with no help from male family members. He leased roughly one-third of the acreage to tenants but took on the rest by himself, along with two full-time hired hands and, at harvesttime, several additional workers.[15]

On the whole, economic conditions among farmers, after a generation of hard times, had finally taken a turn for the better—much for the better. The years between 1897 and 1918 marked a period of sustained economic growth in American agriculture. Farm prices rose steadily, and sometimes dramatically, every year during that period and often at a rate slightly faster than nonfarm prices—the result primarily of a favorable world market for agricultural commodities. In this "golden age of American agriculture," gross farm income more than doubled, and the value of the average farm more than tripled. In just ten years after taking over the farm, Will Feller saw the value of his land increase from thirty-five to eighty dollars per acre. He resisted the lure of these sensational developments, however. While many of his neighbors purchased additional land, machinery, and purebred livestock on credit, Will managed the farm conservatively—even during World War I, when the opportunity for still greater profits beckoned. Under his mother's guidance, Will's point of reference remained the hard times of the late nineteenth century. He bought no additional land, kept investments in new machinery to a minimum, and in general hesitated to plow money back into the farm.[16]

Will did allow himself a few modern conveniences. He remodeled the modest home his grandfather had built in the early 1860s into a nine-room, two-story white frame farmhouse, complete with more furnishings, a hand pump in the kitchen connected to a cistern, screened doors and windows, and a battery-powered telephone shared with seventeen families on a party line. He also added several new outbuildings, including a smokehouse, icehouse, hoghouse, and machine shed. Along with a thousand other residents in Dallas County by 1914, Will could not resist buying a Model T Ford, which Henry Ford, a farm boy himself, had shrewdly designed and marketed with rural budgets and problems in mind. At $240, many farmers could afford it, and its simple engine allowed them to repair it themselves cheaply. The car widened Will's world considerably, allowing him (and his mother) to go beyond local towns and villages for shopping, medical attention, and recreation, including to Des Moines, now just an hour's drive away.[17]

The Model T also came in handy to accommodate Will's new passion, baseball. No less so than in New York, California, or Texas, "baseball burst splendidly upon the scene" across Iowa in the last quarter of the nineteenth century, as one observer put it. Though his responsibilities on the farm limited his playing time, Will became well known in the county for his skills on the diamond. The Van Meter town team often relied on him not only for his pitching and hitting but also for driving players to and from ball fields across the region on Sunday afternoons. One of those fields sat in a nearby pasture on the farm of Edward Forret, a local baseball legend in his own right during his playing days in the 1880s. Back in the day, locals liked to recall Forret as "the best durned pitcher in Ioway." More importantly for the moment, Will began courting Forret's daughter Lena at one of these games and married her not long thereafter, on January 16, 1918. More importantly for the future, Will and Lena had their first child, Robert William Andrew Feller, on November 3 of that year.[18]

Even before Bob was born, both Will and Lena had committed themselves to improving education in their community. Three generations of Fellers and Forrets had attended the same school, a classic one-room country schoolhouse less than a mile from the Feller farm. All that time, a small neighborhood district had administered the school in the same manner as a dozen other such schools scattered about Van Meter Township. In the prosperous times of the early twentieth century, the Fellers, Forrets, and other farm families taxed themselves to upgrade their school, painting the building, installing new privies, purchasing new blackboards and desks, and hiring fully trained teachers, including Lena. Shortly after getting married, both Will and Lena were elected to the school board, which traditionally had determined the curriculum, scheduled the school term around the peak periods of the corn production cycle, and decided how to spend the local property tax assessed to support the school. But in recent years, educational reformers in Des Moines had circulated petitions for the consolidation of one-room school districts. They argued that centralized districts, with their wider tax bases, offered rural youth a broader, more efficient education grounded in progressive theories and practices, thus better preparing them for full participation in modern society. One such petition circulated in Van Meter Township in 1916. But a large majority, led by Will and Lena, had little enthusiasm for reshaping their schools in accordance with reformers' desires and rejected the initiative. They refused to defer to outside expertise and authority—especially urban expertise and authority—and in doing so reaffirmed the primacy of their communities and the virtues of self-reliance. Their schools did what they had always done, and that was what the patrons wanted. Rural schools were being contested in this manner across much of America at the time.[19]

Meanwhile, the agricultural economy approached another sharp turn—this time for the worst. With the tremendous wartime demand, prices for farm commodities rose to levels that intoxicated most farmers. Given the rare opportunity to produce to their heart's content *and* receive higher prices, farmers thought nothing of taking out second mortgages at high interest rates to buy more land and better farm equipment. The boom did not last long, however. A severe recession began in the latter half of 1920 and continued through 1921. For most Americans, the sharp downturn lasted only a short time. By 1922, the economy started to recover, and the recovery continued virtually uninterrupted until 1929. The farm population, however, found itself largely excluded from the benefits of recovery. At war's end, European countries resumed agricultural production just as American farmers were harvesting large crops. The world market became glutted, and prices plummeted. American farmers, having borrowed heavily in inflationary times, now had far fewer real dollars to pay off those debts. The war had also transformed the United States into a creditor nation. Britain and other U.S. debtor nations found it to their benefit, as a result, to buy their wheat, beef, and pork from other suppliers like Argentina, Canada, and Australia. Lower prices, high debts, and few buyers, in short, made it impossible for American farmers to dig their way out of the recession and share in the prosperity of their urban counterparts.[20]

The most crushing price crisis that American agriculture had ever experienced hit hard in Van Meter and surrounding communities. Nationwide, from July to December 1920, the average price of the ten leading crops fell 57 percent, and by

May 1921, prices declined to but one-third of the preceding June's. The statistic that mattered most to central Iowans, the price of corn, fell from $1.73 a bushel on July 1, 1920, to $0.69 by the end of the year. For the year 1921, corn plunged to an average of $0.41, and for the entire decade of the 1920s, it averaged only $0.68. Pork prices followed a similar devastating pattern, and farm income declined precipitously. For much of the decade, farm foreclosures, bank failures, and commercial bankruptcies filled the pages of the *Dallas County News*.[21]

The consequences affected everyone, but Will Feller was far less afflicted than most. Having not participated in the speculative frenzy of the previous decade, Will came through the recession and its aftermath in a much stronger position than his neighbors. He owned all his land outright, continued receiving a steady income from his farm tenants, and avoided the widespread financial and emotional hardship suffered by those who had spread themselves too thin. Over the course of the decade, he could afford a number of luxury items, including a $500 Delco battery-powered generator that provided heating and lighting for the house and outbuildings on the farm; a 1922 Dodge truck priced at $985; the Feller family's first tractor, a $2,000 J. I. Case crossmotor; and a $5,000 four-door Rickenbacker Brougham sedan, one of only three registered in the county in 1927. He also purchased several town lots, both commercial and residential, in Van Meter. Around the county, people referred to Will as "a well-off farmer," a prominent member of the region's rural middle class.[22]

As severe decline in the agricultural economy set in, the one-room country schoolhouse became an issue in Van Meter Township once again. Resistance to school reform gradually dwindled as locals found it increasingly difficult to support education on their own. In 1921, when the state legislature provided special financial inducements for rural school consolidation, including funding for new buildings, buses, and teachers, residents of Van Meter Township, by a bare majority, voted to centralize education into a single school district. While the town of Van Meter overwhelmingly approved the measure, most farmers in the surrounding countryside, including Will Feller, rejected it. Shortly after the initiative passed, Will filed suit in the District Court of Dallas County against the Consolidated Independent School District of Van Meter, initially seeking a temporary injunction to prevent the school board from proceeding with its plans. But in the long term, Will made clear, he sought to "dissolve said school district." He based his argument largely on moral and jurisdictional grounds. The consolidated school, Will maintained in the suit, would be so large and so distant that neighborhood patrons would have little or no influence in its operation. What right, he asked, did the town of Van Meter, much less the city of Des Moines, have to dictate the education of rural children? Such an approach would "do irreparable injury to the rights of this plaintiff and other taxpayers." The judge granted the injunction, but Will could not secure enough signatures to overturn the original vote. Economic hardship made consolidation too attractive an option. Will had fought for his agrarian principles and, despite the defeat, continued to remain true to them. But he became increasingly defensive of his values and cynical toward outside influence.[23]

The agricultural depression of the 1920s changed Will and many farmers throughout the Midwest in other ways as well. It raised their political consciousness and emphasized the need for more effective organization. While some aggrieved farmers turned to radical political solutions espoused by the Socialist Party, the Nonpartisan League and, in the early 1930s, the Farmers Holiday Association, the majority favored a more conservative approach. They sought not to change the capitalist system in any dramatic fashion but to secure a larger slice of the pie from the existing economy—in other words, to act as an organized interest group. The American Farm Bureau Federation took center stage in this effort. The Farm Bureau evolved directly from the Smith-Lever Act of 1914—the key figure in the legislation being the county extension agent; the key technique, demonstration work among local farmers; and the key organization, the county farm bureaus. From 1915 onward, county farm bureaus began to join together in state bureaus, and these state bureaus in turn set up the national organization in 1920. In Van Meter and elsewhere across much of rural America, county agents held regular meetings and picnics where they discussed the latest scientific knowledge and agricultural techniques, but farmers—fiercely individualistic and self-reliant—often resented the implication that they did not know how to farm.[24]

Farmers' resistance to government intervention gradually changed with the downturn in the economy. When the depression of 1920-1921 hit, the Farm Bureau moved quickly. It organized a bipartisan group of congressmen known as the "farm bloc," which pushed through an impressive program of legislation benefiting farmers, including laws regulating stockyard and grain exchanges and laws improving credit facilities. But the new laws did not begin to pull farmers out of their doldrums. Indeed, the Farm Bureau exhausted its agenda in 1922 without solving the basic problem of depressed commodity prices. Subsequent efforts in Congress took that challenge head-on, most notably through a series of bills, sponsored by Republican senators Charles McNary and Gilbert Haugen, proposing a system of federal price supports for the major crops, wheat, corn, cotton, rice, and tobacco. Farmers would receive a "parity price"—fair equivalent value between what they received for what they produced and what they paid for what they consumed. The Republican Party declined to embrace McNary-Haugenism. The two bills never made it out of Congress in 1924 and 1926, and President Calvin Coolidge vetoed two others in 1927 and 1928. For farmers themselves, the solution seemed increasingly clear. They would turn directly to the federal government to solve the problems they could not solve themselves. The defeats notwithstanding, a new political course opened up over the course of the 1920s. Federal government support of farmer interests entered the realm of legitimate political debate. It became increasingly a question not of whether the government should interfere and support farmers but of what forms that support would take.[25]

It took the Great Depression and a new president to answer that question decisively. The depression triggered a downturn in the already depressed agricultural sector. From the high point of the decade before the stock market crash in 1929 to the depths of the depression in 1933, the price of corn fell from $0.81 to $0.33 a bushel, to cite the statistic closest to Iowans' hearts and wallets. Overall, farm income in the United States fell from $12 billion to only $5 billion. When Franklin Roosevelt took office in March 1933, the entire economy lay in shambles. But from the very beginning, agriculture was at the forefront of his mind. Strongly influenced by his secretary of agriculture, Iowan Henry C. Wallace, Roosevelt believed that if the government could get farm prices to rise, those prices might spur a more general recovery. Wallace also strongly supported the Farm Bureau, which once again moved decisively, determined to make good on its claim that it was "the voice of the farmer." Other FDR advisors included George Peek, the father of McNary-Haugenism, and Rexford Tugwell, a Columbia University economist who believed in national economic planning and sympathized with the plight of American farmers. The Farm Bureau, Wallace, Peek, and Tugwell all shared Roosevelt's pragmatic political style, enthusiasm for experimentation, and hope of prying Midwestern farmers away from the Republican party.[26]

Their efforts produced the Agricultural Adjustment Act (AAA), which Roosevelt signed into law on May 12, 1933, just two months after he came into office. The AAA grew out of the same spirit as McNary-Haugenism and kept the concept of parity, but its authors knew they needed to avoid the pitfalls of the failed bills of the 1920s. Agriculture's problem they diagnosed as simple and straightforward: overproduction. They then presented a twofold solution. First, the bill authorized the federal government to pay farmers to limit the production of seven basic commodities—wheat, cotton, corn, hogs, rice, tobacco, and dairy products—in order to end the great surplus choking the economy. Upon the approval of a county AAA committee, farmers who removed the prescribed number of acres from production would receive direct cash payments from the federal government—the number of acres and how much cash based on a formula tied directly to parity. Second, some agency had to administer the AAA somehow—a seemingly massive undertaking. But a structure already existed: the Farm Bureau. Local administration of the AAA passed to the county agents of the Extension Service, invariably collaborators of the local farm bureaus. The American Farm Bureau Federation, through its already existing state and county committees, brought together farmers from around the country and implemented the commodity-reduction programs. The Farm Bureau's state and county structure essentially became the structure of the federal price-support program.[27]

In Van Meter and Dallas County in 1933, Donald Fish, the county agent, followed the same strategy that farm bureaus adopted in the 1910s. Back then, the county agents submerged themselves in a community, identified farmers willing to cooperate, demonstrated new skills or innovations to them, and then retreated into the background to allow neighbors to take part on their own. Gradually, the strategy presumed, farmers in the community would learn to trust their agent and then volunteer their assistance by forming a farm "bureau"—what one agent described as "a sort of giant experiment station with several hundred community observers who hold monthly caucuses to compare results." Farm bureaus thus hoped to disseminate scientific knowledge and advanced techniques to farmers but to make it seem like the farmers were disseminating it themselves. In 1933, under desperate conditions, Fish employed the same method with a different objective: to convince farmers to ignore their instincts and limit their production. In Van Meter Township, Fish turned to Will Feller.[28]

Three years earlier, Will had taken an enormous gamble. With corn prices plummeting and production ever on the rise, he decided to plow up most of his corn and replant his fields with wheat, the cash crop of his grandfather's generation. Wheat prices were falling as well, but at least he would have far less competition in Dallas County, where farmers produced fifteen times more corn than wheat. Any hope of clearing a profit, Will knew, required expensive machinery. In August 1930, Will decided to roll the dice. For $3,500, he purchased a new Caterpillar Cat Twenty tractor teamed with a twelve-foot combine, becoming only the second person in the county and one of the first east of the Missouri River to do so. The crawler treads worked especially well on the hilly surface of Will's land, and the combine reduced his labor costs considerably. Much smaller than the huge, unwieldy combines used in the wheat fields of the Great Plains and

Will Feller (on the hood of his Caterpillar Cat Twenty tractor), young Bob (in the driver's seat), two farmhands, and family members posing on the Feller combine in the early 1930s.
Bob Feller Museum, Van Meter, Iowa.

Pacific Northwest, Will's new implement eliminated the need for additional harvesters or threshing crews. At most, he now required one man to drive the tractor; another to ride the combine, operate the cutter bar, and monitor the gasoline engine; and one or two others to haul the threshed wheat to the grain elevator in nearby Booneville. Combines (as opposed to binders) could cut two to three times as much wheat per day, thus greatly reducing the risk of bad weather at harvesttime. When corn production skyrocketed the following year, Will looked like a genius. His boldness made a strong impression on his young son as well. "He ran ahead of the crowd," said Bob many years later. "If everyone planted corn, he planted wheat. He knew what to plant and when to plant it. We didn't get hurt as bad as some during the depression."[29]

Will made a strong impression on Donald Fish as well. Long known as a community leader and, more recently, an active member of the Van Meter farm bureau, Will became a local celebrity for his Caterpillar tractor and combine. Who better, thought Fish in July 1933, to help organize the 400 wheat farmers of Dallas County under Roosevelt's new Farm Act? Fish held a series of township meetings to explain the allotment plan to farmers, identify leaders within their ranks, and conduct elections for directors who would serve on the Dallas County Wheat Production Control Association. Those directors then elected officers from among themselves. In August, farmers interested in joining the program could sign contracts with the federal government to reduce their acreage for the 1934 season by an amount (not to exceed 20 percent) to be specified by Secretary of Agriculture Henry A. Wallace. Throughout the process, Will distinguished himself at both the township and county levels—so much so that he emerged not only as director of Van Meter Township but also, by the end of the summer, as president of the county wheat acreage adjustment association. Under his leadership, the local AAA campaign convinced fully 75 percent of the county's wheat farmers to sign up that first year. Checks were distributed in December, and as the largest landowner, Will received the largest, for $246.40. He remained president through 1936. By necessity, in the world of big business and big government, Will had become both a bureaucrat and a dependent, not what his father, grandfather, or even Will himself a decade earlier would have liked.[30]

Yet urban Americans still commonly regarded farmers like Will Feller in contradictory ways—in the abstract, as carriers of Jefferson's agrarian tradition and, in reality, as backward and retrograde elements in an increasingly sophisticated society. In the 1920s and 1930s, city people commonly joked that running water on farms depended on how fast someone could carry it from the pump to the house. Such attempts at humor at rural peoples' expense angered Will and cut to the core of the deep sense of inferiority he felt as a farmer, even with all his success. Every time he drove to Des Moines, where electricity, running water, and paved roads had long been the norm, he vowed—like so many other rural Americans of his generation—to give his son a chance at a better life. In Will's mind, this meant working hard, seizing every opportunity that presented itself, and beating city people at their own game.[31]

Henry Feller, Andrew Feller, and William Andrew Feller all knew first hand the meaning of hard work on the farm; so too did Robert William Andrew Feller as he came of age in the 1920s and 1930s. The labor-saving implements of the twentieth century did not ease the burden shouldered by this typical Iowa farm boy. At the age of eight, he began helping his father plow, cultivate, and harvest the crop. When Will bought his Caterpillar in 1930, Bob, at age eleven, drove the tractor while his father manned the combine. Bob also shucked corn, fed the hogs, pumped water into the tank for livestock, lifted hay bales, cleaned the barn, and helped his mother tend the family vegetable garden, make soap, and feed the chickens. During the arid conditions of the mid-1930s (Iowans were not in the Dust Bowl but suffered through drought nonetheless), Bob helped his father carry water for cattle from the Raccoon River when ponds in the pasture went dry. Unable to get the truck closer than 200 yards from the river without getting mired in mud, father and son together transported upwards of 2,000 gallons per trip with nothing but muscle and seven-gallon buckets. Even a chore seemingly as simple as milking the cows put considerable pressure on Bob. Someone—usually him—had to show up every morning and every evening, seven days a week, 365 days a year. "I was working all the time," he later recalled without exaggeration. Like most children throughout the rural Midwest, Bob left most of his boyhood behind by age thirteen, if not earlier.[32]

The Fellers played hard, too. Bob thrived under his father's work ethic, whether in the corn field, wheat field, or baseball field. Will and Grandpa Forret played catch with Bob as soon as he was big enough—though after awhile, catch became something much more than "play." The work of the farm had hindered their own baseball ambitions, so Will and Ed made baseball part of Bob's work routine. One of them (or one of the hired hands) threw to him at the noon hour and at dusk after chores. Gradually, batting and fielding practice were added to the regimen. In the winter, practice moved inside the barn, where Will hung lights powered by the Delco generator. When Bob turned eleven, Will built him a batting cage and a pitcher's mound behind the barn to better simulate game conditions. And one year later, Will cut down an acre of oak trees with nothing but an old crosscut saw and built Bob a complete baseball field—diamond, outfield with a fence, scoreboard, backstop, and grandstand. Will scheduled games at "Oak View Park" all summer long, managed the team (the "Oak Views") on and off the field, and, in addition, signed Bob up to play even more games on the American Legion junior baseball teams in Adel and Des Moines. At age fourteen, Bob also pitched high school ball, though by then he threw so hard and struck out so many batters that teams stopped scheduling Van Meter Consolidated. And at age 16, Bob pitched for the semi-pro Farmers' Union Insurance team of Des Moines, starting more than thirty games. All along, Will saw to it that Bob had the best equipment, including regulation balls, not the homespun variety that farm boys typically made themselves. Baseball was a serious matter on the Feller farm, demanding strenuous work and dedication—no less so than for getting in the crops or milking the cows.[33]

Will taught Bob not only to work hard but also to seize the moment. From a very early age, Bob learned the value of money and how to make a buck. He took advantage, for example, of the fact that the main road in those days from Van Meter to Des Moines ran right past the Feller farm. During the spring thaw, when drivers often got stuck in mud holes, Bob and the neighbor boys made a small business out of coming to their rescue. They would ride to the scene with a team of horses and chains and pull the cars to dry ground for, as he later put it, the "extremely reasonable price" of two dollars. In a similar vein, young Bob made a killing in Dallas County's never-ending battle against pocket gophers. When the damage to the crops these stalk-chewing varmints could inflict got out of hand, the Farm Bureau established cash bounties of ten cents per scalp (or, sometimes, per pair of front claws). A spirited competition would ensue that not only helped bring the problem under control (if only temporarily) but also gave "young gopher chasers" like Bob a chance to earn good money. Another chance came when Will purchased his Caterpillar tractor and combine in 1930. He and Bob offered custom harvesting services for their neighbors at two dollars an acre, with Bob getting half the proceeds.[34]

Baseball soon became Bob's best way of pocketing cash, with his father once again showing the way. From 1932 through 1935, fierce competition ensued at Oak View Park as teams played not just for fun but for gate receipts on a winner-take-all basis. Tickets selling for 25 cents (35 cents for a doubleheader) and crowds of several hundred spectators filling the grandstand and lining the foul lines each week meant high stakes indeed. Manager Feller pulled out all the stops to win. On one occasion, in the rubber match of a three-game tournament against the Van Meter town team, he substituted six ringers from Des Moines in the seventh inning with the Oak Views down 3 to 1, but they lost anyway. On the weekends when his team played road games, Will rented Oak View Park to other community teams. He also did not hesitate to recruit players from Des Moines' small African American population, some of whom doubled as laborers on the Feller farm, or schedule games against all-black teams from the capital city. Bob himself became the main draw by the time he turned fourteen. In the larger parks in Des Moines, 2,000 people often packed the stands to watch the "youthful mound sensation" pitch. By fifteen, Bob became a ringer himself, pitching semi-pro ball on a pay-by-game basis in towns one hundred miles around for $100 a game and a tank of gas. To stay eligible for high school sports (he also played basketball), he used an assumed name, Bill Burton. So anxious were the Farmers' Union Insurance team promoters to secure Bob's services that they put him on the company payroll as a clerk. That summer (1935), Bob won twenty-five games, lost only four, and averaged 19.4 strikeouts per game. His electrifying performance caught the attention of long-time Cleveland Indians scout C. C. Slapnicka, who signed Bob at the age of sixteen to his first professional contract. Like his father, grandfather, and great-grandfather before him, Bob was always on the alert for a chance to make a shrewd deal. This one, all of them would have agreed, capped them all.[35]

The chance to make an even shrewder deal—more lucrative and of more lasting consequence—presented itself just a few months later. The day after Bob struck out fifteen bewildered St. Louis Browns, one short of the American League record, in his first official start for the Indians on August 23, 1936, *Des Moines Tribune* sportswriter Frank Brody drove out to the Feller farm to interview the family for a feature story. Sitting in the living room of the farmhouse, Will reminisced about Bob's childhood—playing catch with Grandpa Forret, adjourning to the barn on winter days, and whiffing twenty-three batters in a memorable game against Waukee at Oak View Park. While they talked, Lena and Bob's young sister, Marguerite, brought in a family scrapbook with the penciled-in title "From Sandlots to the Majors." In the text of his article, which the *Tribune* ran the next day, Brody relied heavily on Will's stories and several quotations from the likes of Dizzy Dean, Pepper Martin, and Mickey Cochrane describing the meteoric start of Bob's career. But what stole the show were the several photographs from the scrapbook: Bob at age ten in full uniform playing catch behind the barn; Bob at bat in front of the hog pen one year later; Will, "the catcher," posing next to the farmhouse. "It was here on the farm," Brody emphasized, "where Bob inherited his great love for the diamond game."[36]

When the Brody article hit the wires, several other newspapers quickly picked it up, including the two dailies in Cleveland, the *New York World Telegram*, and, a week later, the *Sporting News*. Then, when Bob struck out seventeen Philadelphia Athletics to break the record on September 13, the excitement "hit the newspapers like thunder and lightning," as he later recalled. Requests for more interviews, stories, and photographs from newspapers and magazines across the country filled the mailbox in front of the Feller farm. At that point, Kyle Crichton of *Collier's*, J. Roy Stockton of the *Saturday Evening Post*, and other high-profile writers began making their way to Van Meter. By January, so many had sat down with the Fellers in their living room that the neighbors barely noticed anymore. "More fame for Bob," as the local newspaper put it, became a commonplace occurrence.[37]

Will enjoyed the attention but was neither starstruck nor surprised. The main theme of these articles—farm boy makes big leagues—was not new to him. As an avid reader of several farm and popular periodicals, he knew that for much of the 1920s and 1930s, writers often had stressed the rural origins of most players, expressed the rural resentment of the growing urban dominance, praised rural simplicity and virtue, and condemned the corrupting forces of urban decadence. Long before Bob Feller, farm boys Walter Johnson, Grover Cleveland Alexander, and Dazzy Vance, the *Sporting News* maintained, stood as proof positive that the "mightiest pitchers" and "best players" more often came from Kansas or Iowa than from cities on either coast. Later studies showed that no more than two-fifths of the players at any one time in the first half of the twentieth century came from rural areas, and many of them actually grew up in cities. But the facts did not concern Will. Though he regarded much of the literature as condescending to modern, sophisticated farmers like himself, he understood that the "farm boys in baseball" theme resonated deeply among Americans, rural and urban alike. All the living room chats and resulting publications led him to realize that he could take advantage of the aw shucks rural boy image and indeed profit by it. The best way to do this, he came to believe by January or February, was to have Bob write his own "autobiography."[38]

"My Own Story" was not Will's idea alone. The Indians, a middling team in the 1920s and 1930s (they had not won the pennant since 1920), regarded Bob as their main drawing card and welcomed any chance to shine the spotlight on their star pitcher. Slapnicka, whom the Indians had promoted from scout to "special assistant" to the president, had a special knack for publicity and helped Will cultivate the idea. And the *Des Moines Tribune* never scoffed at a chance to sell more newspapers. But only Will knew the details. "My Own Story," ghostwritten by Frank Brody, appeared daily in fifteen parts from April 5 to April 20, 1937. The first segment set the tone for the series. It began with the headline "From Corn Shuckin' to Baseball Chuckin'" and was adorned by two photographs from the Feller family scrapbook: one, a baby picture with the caption, "That right arm which sends the ball in a white streak over the plate is quickly discernible even when Bob Feller was but nine months old"; the other, an action shot of Bob, age eleven, at shortstop for the American Legion team in Adel. "I love the farm," concluded the young scribe at end of his debut. "The hard work on the farm built up the muscles which get most of the work when I pitch. I depend almost entirely on a fast ball."[39]

Will, Brody, and Slapnicka knew they had a romping good tale. What followed over the next two weeks milked the farm-boy-makes-good angle for all it was worth. And if they had to expand the truth to liven things up just a bit, then they did. Seemingly all the main events of Bob's childhood centered, in one way or another, on baseball. Gopher bounties, to cite just one example, gave nine-year-old Bob the chance to earn five dollars, just the amount he needed for a baseball autographed by Babe Ruth and Lou Gehrig, who barnstormed their way through Des Moines late in October 1928. He did, in fact, kill fifty gophers to buy the ball, but "My Own Story" credits Bob (not the Farm Bureau) for the idea and baseball (not money) for his motivation. Young Bob, the story insisted, carried water from the Raccoon River not just to the truck but all the way up the hill to the house (a superhuman feat given the distance and steep climb), and not because of drought but to strengthen

Bob Feller, age eighteen, posing at the typewriter for the *Des Moines Tribune* in April 1937. His "autobiography"—a fifteen-part series entitled "My Own Story"—launched a farm-boy-makes-good narrative that has been retold in several biographies, dozens of magazine articles, and hundreds of newspapers stories ever since.
©1937, The Des Moines Register and Tribune Company. Reprinted with permission.

his pitching arm. His father switched from corn to wheat not because of overproduction and low prices in hard times but because wheat supposedly required less labor and thus freed up more time for baseball. In reality, the wheat-harvesting season brought the baseball season to a screeching halt for three weeks every July. The failure to cut wheat at the right time endangered the quality and quantity of the crop. Time mattered less for corn, however. The ears could remain in the stalks for several months with little danger of damage or loss in value. For sheer drama, however, having Will change crops to advance Bob's baseball career seemed the ultimate agrarian sacrifice. Photographs continued to enhance the desired effect: young Bob driving the Caterpillar tractor; the barn "where Feller learned to play"; and Oak View Park, "where Dad built me a real baseball diamond." These three parts of the story, even more than the others, made "My Own Story" a hit.[40]

The photograph of Bob on the Caterpillar spoke volumes by itself. It gave the reader direct access to life on the Feller farm and showed Bob as a *real* farmer, overalls and all. Readers knew Bob well on the pitcher's mound but now saw him for the first time in the wheat fields, and the implicit contrast made the rookie pitching sensation all the more fascinating. Will and Brody then took that image and wove it into the climactic moment of Bob's transformation from farm boy to ball player, said to have occurred on July 21, 1935: "We were in the fields that day, combining wheat, and I was driving the tractor. As the tractor climbed a slight rise, I could see the figure of a man coming toward us, threading his way through the wheat. Like my father, he was tall and thin. As he came closer, I decided that they looked a great deal alike. 'Howdy,' he said, and my father nodded. 'I'm Cyril Slapnicka,' he continued, 'of the Cleveland Indians. That the boy they tell me is quite a pitcher?'"

Slapnicka found out for himself the next day, watching Bob pitch another shutout for the Farmers Union team. He signed him to a contract (scribbled on the stationary of a Des Moines hotel) on the spot, the story went. The image of Slapnicka's godlike emergence from the wheat fields into Bob's life was so compelling that few (if any) observers, then or since, have questioned it, though the chances of "threading through" 500 acres of wheat and finding Bob and Will ran from slim to none. Their meeting more than likely took place in the Feller living room like all the others. Nor did Slapnicka find Bob by himself. Some of the umpires in American Legion ball, who often served as so-called birddog scouts for major league teams, tipped him off.[41]

One of the more intriguing shots featured neither Bob nor Will but a landscape photograph of the Feller farmstead. Standing majestically on a stone foundation, the big red barn built by Bob's grandfather Andrew in 1886 dominates the forefront. In the background stands the Feller's white frame farmhouse, whose first two rooms Bob's great-grandparents Henry and Mary had built by in the early 1860s. An outhouse, still in use at the time, sits between the two structures. The image also gives one a sense of the hilly terrain of the Feller farm. But readers on April 6, 1937, when the photograph first appeared in "My Own Story," saw only one thing: the place where "Bullitt Bob" Feller learned to play baseball. Intentional or not, the angle of the shot (taken from below) gives the barn the appearance of a rural cathedral, and the exclusion of people in the context of the story allows one's imagination to run wild. One can easily envision young Bob playing catch with his dad, practicing his windmill windup, and developing his blazing fastball on the patch of grass barely visible between the barn and the house or

The Feller farmstead, 1937, featuring the barn built by Bob's grandfather, Andrew, in 1886. The photograph first appeared in the *Des Moines Tribune* on April 6, 1937, with the caption, "On rainy days, Bob Feller pitched in this barn on the family farm in Van Meter, Iowa." It has been reprinted dozens of times thereafter for its agrarian symbolism and hidden, yet vivid, baseball imagery.

inside the barn itself in the winter. Though half a century old, the exceptionally well-preserved barn offers a testimony to Andrew's and Will's dedication to the farm, which itself stemmed from their deeply ingrained belief that farmers work hand-in-hand with the Creator to supply people's physical needs. This agrarian symbolism coupled with the hidden yet vivid baseball imagery makes for a powerful scene, one reprinted numerous times over the years.[42]

Readers also found the story and photograph of Oak View Park irresistible. Here again, young Bob—in fact, Will and Brody—combined baseball and farm life in compelling, if sometimes misleading, fashion:

> So, next spring, that was in 1932, we cleared and rolled the field. Dad bought a lot of chicken wire and some lumber. We built a wire backstop and a chicken wire fence that extended 150 feet along the thirdbase line and 150 feet along the firstbase line.
>
> We found a heavy plank behind the barn and made a home plate and a pitcher's rubber. I sure worked fast. Couldn't wait until we got the field ready to play. Every once and a while I had to shag one or more of our horses or cows out of that nice flat infield. A cow certainly can ruin an infield, or an outfield, for that matter.
>
> Once I looked out and saw about 10 of our turkeys assembled in deep short. They seemed to be holding an indignation meeting of some sort. It used to be their favorite browsing ground, you see. Evidently they came to some decision, because the next time I looked over that way they were heading out toward rightfield.

The down-home, folksy approach had no room for one of the main reasons for building Oak View Park: to make money. While the story describes some of young Bob's best pitching performances for the Oak Views, it pays little notice to the fierce, winner-take-all competition that characterized those community games. Scribe Bob also stresses the uniqueness of Oak View Park, even though ball fields in cow pastures had mottled rural America for decades—including one on Grandfather Forret's farm and another where the Van Meter town team played. Much later, in the 1980s, when *The Natural* and *Field of Dreams* became big hits, Feller described his upbringing as a "real life" version of both films and claimed that his father had built the first "field of dreams." The popularity of the two movies reinvigorated the wholesome, if not magical, image of baseball on the Feller farm fifty years after "My Own Story" first appeared.[43]

With the 1937 publication of Bob's "autobiography" in the *Des Moines Tribune*, Will Feller and Frank Brody planted the seed for the Feller narrative. Halfway through the fifteen-part series, the *Chicago Herald-Examiner*, *Cleveland Press*, and other major newspapers around the country picked up "My Own Story" and ran it in its entirety, word-for-word, photograph-for-photograph.[44] For years thereafter, writers then drew upon and added to the narrative at every milestone in Bob's life. For example, when Feller was elected to the

Hall of Fame in 1962—after a career that included 266 wins, 2,581 strikeouts, three no-hitters, and twelve one-hitters (despite missing four seasons during his service in World War II)—the press had a field day. "From the Cornfields to Cooperstown," crowed the *Cleveland Plain Dealer.* "Iowa Farm Boy—to the Hall of Fame," chimed in the *Sporting News.* In a feature story published in 2005, the generally sophisticated *Sports Illustrated* swallowed the Feller narrative hook, line, and sinker, recounting all the old tales of his childhood. "It sounds almost as if Ma and Pa Kettle were down the road a piece," the article quipped. Even upon his death, few could resist the allure of the farm-boy-makes-good narrative. The obituary in the *Plain Dealer,* for example, included another famous photograph from "My Own Story" of Bob posing in overalls and a Cleveland Indians cap in front of the red barn with a bushel of corn balanced on his right shoulder.[45] Three biographies, dozens of magazine articles, and hundreds of newspaper stories over the decades have repeated the details of the Feller narrative over and over again.[46]

No one, however, promoted Bob Feller and the Feller narrative better than Bob Feller himself. Will taught his son to hustle both on and off the field, and Bob took that knowledge and ran with it. Just as he had capitalized on stuck-in-the-mud cars, gopher bounties, custom harvesting, and pitching-for-hire opportunities while growing up, so too did he seize every opportunity as a professional ballplayer. Feller became famous not only for his high base salary (he was the best paid pitcher in the majors for most of his eighteen-year career) but also for the bonus clause in his contract based on attendance (he was also the game's top drawing card) and for the additional money he made from his weekly radio show, daily newspaper column, personal appearances, and commercial endorsements for sporting goods, ice cream, peanut butter, breakfast foods, and shaving cream. His barnstorming tours with the legendary Satchel Paige in the late 1930s and 1940s, financed and planned by Feller himself, added handsomely to his income. When asked about playing with blacks, he said, simply, "We were interested in one thing, making money."[47] Still more money spun off his specious life story. Over the years, Feller published three full-length autobiographies and countless "in-his-own-words" articles in newspapers, magazines, and book chapters, all of them repeating the ever-popular anecdotes from "My Own Story."[48] On the farm in Iowa, he insisted, he led "a Norman Rockwell life, where every day could have been one of his *Saturday Evening Post* covers. . . . Abner Doubleday could have related to my life in those years, and Tom Sawyer could have too." Feller's rise from "once naïve farm boy" to "self-made sports capitalist" puzzled many a writer over the years, including one from the *Saturday Evening Post*. But Bob knew better, as would have Will, Andrew, and Henry before him. It was all part of being a farmer in the modern age.[49]

Did agrarianism in the Feller family, the question remains, die out completely with Bob? It certainly seems so. Feller lived in a Cleveland suburb for most of his adult life and frequently expressed his disdain for farming ("I grew up on one, but the work held no great fascination for me") and for Van Meter itself ("a jerk town," he once called it). Like his father, he enjoyed the good things in life. In the late 1940s, he owned his own Beechcraft Bonanza airplane, Cadillac, motorcycle, and, in his wife's words, "every gadget imaginable." In 1940, for the then outrageous sum of $75,000, Bob built his parents a spacious English-style brick home on the Feller farmstead next to the big red barn and the old white frame house. Designed by a *Better Homes and Gardens* architect, it came equipped with all the modern conveniences including copper piping, walnut woodwork, air conditioning, dishwasher, garbage disposal, and three bathrooms finished in color glazed tile. While Eastern writers called the home "a perfect haven," the neighbors, many of whom still had neither running water nor electricity, found it extravagant and ostentatious. Later, in the 1980s, Feller was among the first ex-ballplayers to realize that their signatures had more than sentimental value. He sold so many autographs (more than any other ballplayer, he boasted in 2005) that he became the butt of a memorabilia industry joke: What's more valuable than a ball autographed by Bob Feller? A ball not signed by Bob Feller.[50]

Yet, to paraphrase another common expression, you can't take all the farm out of the boy. Late in life, Feller became an avid collector of vintage Caterpillar tractors. "Despite my achievements on the baseball diamond, a big part of my heart still belongs to the farm fields of my youth," he wrote in a history of North American tractors that features a full-page photograph of Feller on a Caterpillar Cat Twenty, the same model he drove as a boy on his father's farm. Though no longer owned by the family, the Feller barn still stands and, as of 1999, is listed on the National Register of Historic Places—thanks in large part to Bob's efforts. In 1995, Feller established a small museum in Van Meter stocked with artifacts from his baseball career—primarily as a means to sell more autographs but also as an excuse to return to his home town every few months. Van Meter, by then, though just a few minutes drive down Interstate 80 from the sprawl of West Des Moines, remained small (about 1,000 residents) and isolated. Feller delighted in taking small groups up to the old farmstead and especially to the site a quarter mile down the road (still gravel) where Oak View Park stood. He liked to stand at the edge of the now empty field and point out where home plate, the pitching rubber, and the outfield fence once sat. The stories he told certainly perpetuated the old Feller narrative. But as one writer observed after one of these tours, "He is quite happy because the 'heater from Van Meter' is home."[51]

CHAPTER FIVE

The Milroy Yankees and the Decline of Southwest Minnesota

"Don't plan on buying a loaf of bread, a sack of flour, or a yard of percale in Milroy Monday afternoon," warned the *Redwood Gazette* on September 11, 1947. "The village is closing shop and going to a ball game." The *Gazette* reporter meant what he said. Just as they had the previous month for a game against archrival Wanda for the Redwood County League championship, members of the Milroy Commercial Club agreed to "lock up the town" for the game on Monday against Carlos in Mankato—a first-round matchup in the Twenty-Fourth Annual Minnesota State Amateur Tournament. The schools were also dismissed so the buses could be used to transfer fans to the game, ninety miles away to the east. More than 350 from the town and surrounding countryside (the population of the town itself was only 261) made the trip and saw their beloved Yankees edge Carlos, 7 to 6. Third baseman Joe Dolan had the key hit—a triple off the left-field wall in the bottom of the seventh inning—and the key play—a spectacular unassisted triple play in the top of that same inning. With runners on second and third, no outs, and the game hanging in the balance, Dolan snared a screaming line drive off the bat of the hitter, tagged the runner coming down from second, and stepped on third just in time to get the runner trying to get back. Though Milroy's 7-to-1 loss to Rochester the following Thursday eliminated the Yankees from the tournament, players and fans alike cherished the memories of the Carlos game for years, indeed decades, to come.[1]

The excitement that baseball generated in Milroy exemplified the emergence, from the 1880s through the 1950s, of the small-town team as an institution in rural

America every bit as much as the little red schoolhouse and the old-fashioned Fourth of July celebration. Diamonds dotted the countryside right alongside grain elevators, water towers, courthouse squares, and churches. "Everywhere in all this land the sunny spring afternoons resound to the well-known and eagerly-awaited 'Play ball!'" wrote novelist Zane Grey in 1909. "There is no village, far from the maddening crowd, that does not boast of its nine." The psychologist Hugo Münsterberg, trying to explain the magnitude of the game's popularity in small-town America to his German readers in 1914, estimated that on any given Sunday afternoon in the summer, "base-ball matches are played in more than thirty thousand places." Both Grey and Münsterberg well understood that every small town in rural America that considered itself a "progressive, modern place" had its own baseball team.[2]

We do not normally think of small rural towns as progressive, modern places. After all, the great paradox of supply and demand in agriculture became even more pronounced in the twentieth century. Despite—and sometimes because of—unimaginable gains in production spurred by machines, chemicals, and improved plant and animal breeds, the twentieth century was not kind to farmers. One crisis followed another: economic crises, particularly in the 1920s, 1930s, 1950s, and 1980s, and resulting demographic crises. In 1900, more than 50 percent of the labor force in the United States still earned a living from the soil. That proportion shrank in each succeeding census until at present less than 2 percent of the labor force remains engaged in agriculture. Even in the 1920s and 1950s, decades normally associated with prosperity, good times on the farm were few and far between. The resulting exodus from the countryside made rural-to-urban migrations in the nineteenth century pale in comparison.[3]

How then to explain this fundamental restructuring of American agriculture juxtaposed against this progressive image of rural life? Literature does not provide much help. Two recurring themes have prevailed: doom and gloom, as in the works of Hamlin Garland, Sinclair Lewis, and Jane Smiley, and the deep nostalgia conveyed by novelists from Laura Ingalls Wilder to Garrison Keillor.[4] History has locked itself into a similar dichotomy, from Richard Hofstadter's culturally deprived and socially regressive farmers to Wendell Berry's glorification of them as the epitome of American individualism, independence, and democracy.[5] Either way, farmers come across as traditionalists—backward-looking, predictable, with little or no agency or initiative. Such a portrayal cannot explain why 350 fans closed shop and hopped buses to Mankato to watch their Yankees beat Carlos. Perhaps novelists and historians have looked in the wrong places. For farmers and residents of small towns, even in this prolonged period of decline, the ball field functioned as a progressive, modern place.

At first glance, Milroy, Minnesota, looks right out of a Sinclair Lewis novel. It was (and is) much smaller and more isolated than Lewis's Gopher Prairie, the fictionalized version of Sauk Centre, Minnesota, Lewis's hometown, made famous in his novel *Main Street* (1920). Urbanite Carol Kennicot, its principal character, would have looked out at the endless fields of corn and oats that engulfed Milroy and declared it even uglier and more mundane than Gopher Prairie, 120 miles to the north. Located in the southwest corner of the state, 150 miles from Minneapolis and St. Paul, Milroy does appear, by all indications, to sit in the proverbial middle of nowhere. But beauty, of course, is in the eye of the beholder. Southwest Minnesota's great snows, diverse ecosystems, birds and other wildlife, and long, empty distances have inspired a rich array of art, literature, and poetry over the decades. Locals have surely looked askance at Lewis's biting satire. Several towns banned the book in the 1920s, and more recently, one critic referred to the novelist as "but another alienated nineteenth- and twentieth-century Western intellectual." Some have retained a sense of humor and perspective. "This region has more writers *per capita* than anywhere else in the country," a local scholar observed. "But we have not many *capitas*."[6]

Nor does Lewis's portrayal of Gopher Prairie begin to capture the complexity of the region's history—Milroy's in particular. Minnesota was one of the many new territories opened in the latter third of the nineteenth century, when railroads initiated a new era of commerce and industry. Settlers from more established eastern states, as well as Iowa, Illinois, and Ohio, moved in, gradually spreading westward across the tall grass prairie. They were lured by the prospects of securing two 160-acre plots—one a homestead, the other a tree claim (free for promising to plant at least a dozen trees)—and cultivating an abundance of wheat and small grains. Westline Township in Redwood County, Milroy's eventual location, attracted only a few dozen hearty farmers, isolated as it was from the nearest village, Walnut Grove, ten miles away. Thirty miles distant, the largest town in the county, Redwood Falls, consisted primarily of a government land office, post office, school, and stockade. Canvas-covered bobsleds conveyed children from the outer regions, and with the sheriff visiting the township only twice a year, the law had little relevance. "Why did you bring us to such a God-forsaken place?" one woman remembered asking her husband after seeing for the first time their homestead, a mass of mud and thistle.[7]

The region's slow development all but stopped in the 1890s, due to drought and a depressed economy, but resumed with a vengeance around the turn of the century. With the promise of renewed prosperity and visions of great profits generated from prairie farms supplying food to the nation's industrial cities, the Chicago & Northwestern Railway Company constructed dozens of lines crisscrossing southwest Minnesota. With the new roads came new town sites, laid out by officials every five or six miles so that any given station and accompanying grain elevator required no more than a half day's trip by wagon from any farm in the region. Milroy, as one of these towns, was born in 1902 on a drafting board of the Western Town Lot Company, a subsidiary of the railroad, put on a fixed grid of five blocks by five blocks, and given standard street names (Railroad, Cherry, Cedar, etc.) before its first inhabitants arrived. Some of the business lots sold for more than $1,000 at open-air auctions before the railroad arrived. Virtually overnight, the town had three general stores, a saloon, hotel, harness shop, barber shop, implement dealership, livery barn and dray line, lumber company, weekly newspaper, and three grain elevators. Further indicative of its sterile and nondescript beginnings, the town was named for Maj. Gen. Robert H. Milroy, "a gallant Union soldier" with no apparent connection to Minnesota, who, according to one less-than-glowing account, "had been promoted beyond his capabilities."[8]

Though Milroy started with a bang, it sputtered thereafter—almost immediately and continuously thereafter. Newly founded towns like Milroy got little chance to enjoy their prosperity before they had to share it with even newer towns. By design, railroad officials left these towns to compete with each other for settlers and profits, knowing that only a few would eventually emerge as substantial retail and service centers. In its first two years of existence, Milroy seemed ahead of the game, at least when compared to its neighbor to the east, Wanda, established by the same railroad by the same process in 1899. In its first two years of existence, Wanda had also looked like a winner. Thus the pattern, with local business leaders not soon forgetting that one town's gain made for another's loss. Over the years, Milroy lost much more than it won. It lost to Marshall, fifteen miles to the northwest, in the race to become the region's principal economic center; Redwood Falls beat out Milroy for the county seat; and Laura Ingalls Wilder chose Walnut Grove, not Milroy, as the setting for the *Little House on the Prairie*. Milroy's population has never surpassed 300; Main Street never exceeded two blocks; and to this day, the five-by-five grid has neither expanded nor filled in completely. In 1905, local officials seemed already to know that Milroy had reached its demographic apex when they petitioned county commissioners to reduce the incorporation limits of the village from two full sections (1,280 acres) to just one quarter section (160 acres). Milroy, like many towns in southwest Minnesota, began to die as soon as it was born.[9]

Yet from the very outset, baseball was all the rage in Milroy, popular among the region's settlers even before the railroad came through. While no town teams existed before towns, farmers played informal games in pastures with their families and neighbors. Joe Dolan's father, John, whose grandparents homesteaded in 1873 about three miles southwest of Milroy's eventual location, fondly remembered playing ball every day on the farm, weather permitting, even during the threshing season. "At noon hour you played ball, whenever the ground was dry. That was our pastime and it stayed with us through the years." Teams of neighbors gradually formed, and though they did not maintain regular schedules, they gathered for games in Walnut Grove or Redwood Falls on market days, Decoration Day, and the Fourth of July and on occasion held three-day tournaments at the close of the summer season.[10]

The atmosphere changed considerably when Milroy's first team formed in 1903, shortly after the town's incorporation. Playing ball did little to cement goodwill among competing teams—just the opposite, in fact. The winner-take-all attitude among town officials and merchants translated directly into a winner-take-all attitude on the field. Towns accused one another of playing ringers, of engaging in unfair noisemaking to rattle opponents at crucial moments, and of employing crooked umpires. The home team often fired an umpire in the middle of the game and replaced him with a more sympathetic arbiter. Life for team managers, as one player remembered, could get particularly rough. "If a team kept losing and you had to get rid of the manager, it became a community crisis. The manager couldn't leave town or go to another league. He just had to suffer in disgrace, and his whole family with him." The ball parks themselves, usually on the edge of town, were primitive. The town of New Munich, for example, had a graveyard in left field. "If you hit a good one," the same player recalled, "the fielders were reluctant to chase the balls as they caromed off the tombstones of their ancestors." In Milroy, the right field foul line ran straight alongside the highway, and left field was right next to a row of elevators on the north side of town. In the late afternoon, the sun shone off the bins and blinded the fielders. And in medium-deep right field stood a utility building that made for rather unconventional caroms and collisions. The field boasted no outfield fence and only a crude set of bleachers. Milroy apparently fielded good teams in the first decade of settlement and even better in the 1920s. The games came to a stop, however, with the onset of the

Great Depression, when players had neither the time nor the resources to play ball. World War II then took many of them far away from home. "It looked for all the world like Milroy's love affair with baseball was over," remembered one resident.[11]

At war's end, farmers and town residents, along with the rest of the country, anxiously looked forward to better days ahead. Good economic times provided an aura of optimism and confidence not seen in Milroy for decades. Town businesses boomed, jobs were plentiful, agricultural commodity prices remained high, and baseball became more popular than ever. Two long-term residents, John Dolan and a young second-generation Milroy farmer named Bob Zwach, put together a ragtag team of farmers and store clerks whose collective enthusiasm outran their collective ballplaying skills. In 1946, the Milroy Yankees finished dead last in the newly formed Redwood County League. One telling incident stuck in Zwach's mind for years thereafter: "Shorty Royer was our manager, an' his signal for a bunt, from third base, was to take a pinch of snoose. Well, he took out 3 *chews*, an' this batter *still* was swingin', an' just as he struck out, Shorty threw that damned box of snuff right at the batter's head, sailed right on over him. Well, that was our 1946 season."[12]

Embarrassed, but more determined, Zwach and Dolan combed the countryside for better players, many of them just returning from the service. Largely on the basis of their efforts, the core of the team for years to come came together in 1947: the all-Dolan infield, cheered on by their father, featuring Jack at first, Louie at second, Spike at short, and Joe at third; outfielders Rich Kramer, Paul Lodges, and Ed Wurscher; Zwach at catcher; and pitchers Boob Penke, Slim Klein, and Ed Uchansky. The Yankees started the season hot and never cooled off, sending their fans into a frenzy. By the middle of the season, 400 to 500 attended each home game, filling the grandstand and lining the foul lines and outfield, many of them in their cars, honking for key hits and good defensive plays. For farmers and townspeople alike, home games became the highlight of the weekly social calendar. "We had a great spirit here in Milroy," recalled Spike Dolan. "Saturday night was always a big night in the small towns. Farmers would come to town and bring their families, buy their groceries, and visit. And I can recall just about every Saturday night groups of people talking about the ball game that was going to be on Sunday. And as soon as they saw some of us players they had to come and ask us how's our chances tomorrow. And that was really the conversation on Saturday night in town."[13]

That summer, Milroy won the Redwood County League championship and regional playoffs, which gave the team a berth in the state tournament. No greater honor existed for these teams than to play in the four-tiered, single-elimination extravaganza sponsored by the Minnesota Amateur Baseball Association (MABA). Though the tournament was created in 1924, it remained a small affair until the postwar boom, when total attendance for the September games regularly surpassed an astounding 30,000. Hundreds of teams from around the state, playing in two different divisions (Class A and Class B) started each season in their county leagues with dreams of reaching the tournament, but only two to three dozen (depending on the year) actually made it. (Some years also featured a Class AA division.) Big city newspapers covered the two-weekend event extensively and carried the box scores of all the games. "Seeing your name in the *Minneapolis Tribune*—that was the Big Time," recalled one of the Milroy players. After beating Carlos and then losing in the second round in 1947, Milroy kept its winning ways, reaching the tournament in 1948, 1949, and 1950, though never advancing past the first round. Proud but frustrated, the team wanted nothing more than to bring a Class B (small-town) championship back to its community of loyal, devoted families and neighbors.[14]

Baseball had long been a family and community affair in Milroy. The majority of the players were second- or third-generation residents, and the Dolan family went back four generations to the area's first homesteaders. Like most rural activities, baseball required considerable cooperation. The players in large part were farmers who worked long and hard, six days a week, all summer, and the farm had to come first. Louie Dolan would have missed the 1947 tournament game against Carlos had twenty-five neighbors not dropped everything to help him finish his oat harvest. Nor did baseball on Sundays preempt church. Players attended their chosen house of worship—Catholic, Lutheran, Methodist, or Presbyterian—in the morning, with ministers often speeding up their sermons to finish in time for the first pitch, or even excusing players midway through for road games. For decades, Milroy teams, dominated by German, Norwegian, and Irish players (reflecting the population of Redwood County and southwest Minnesota more generally), crossed ethnic and religious boundaries for players who could pitch, catch, and hit the long ball. "Baseball, church, and farming—that's what we were," recalled Rich Kramer, the team's best hitter, summarizing the importance of custom and heritage in shaping players' lives.[15]

There was also a strong defensive strain in Milroy's passion for baseball that was rooted in the region's fierce economic rivalries. The towns in the Redwood County League—Milroy, Wanda, Sanborn, Wabasso, Lamberton, Tracy, Walnut Grove, and Balaton, all within twenty-five miles of one another—had competed against each other since the turn of the century. The sheer number of possible settlers a town could attract depended on the size of farms and amount of surrounding farmland. As a result, it bears repeating, one town's gain most often constituted another town's loss. The steady decline of a region blessed with fertile soil, abundant water, and hardworking citizens then made for all the more contentious relations between towns. These underlying rivalries and winner-take-all mentalities played out in Sunday afternoon games. The crowds became increasingly large and competition for bragging rights all the more heated.[16]

No games were more heated and more bitterly contested than those between longtime rivals Milroy and Wanda, perennial contenders for the Redwood County League title in the postwar years. Wanda had the edge early on. Zwach remembered playing Wanda one afternoon when "they laughed us out of the place. I was catching and I had an old mitt that wouldn't stick, I couldn't hold it with two hands. Leiter the banker and Bordy, Oh, they made fun of Milroy. Spike made an error at shortstop and they told him to lower his apron. They beat the hell out of us! That determined us in '46 and '47, we'll get Wanda." And get Wanda they did, though not until 1948. That year Milroy and Wanda met for three crucial games in August, the first for the Redwood County League pennant, with both teams tied for first place with eleven wins and three losses. Milroy got off to a fast start with three runs in the first inning, but Wanda came back to scratch out a 4-to-3 lead in the sixth. With two outs in the eighth inning, Joe Dolan blasted a three-run homer to give Milroy back the lead and provide the final margin for the Yankees' 6-to-4 victory. Two weeks later, the teams met again, this time in the Redwood County League playoffs for a best-out-of-three series. Behind the pitching of Big Ed Uchansky, who limited Wanda to just five hits, Milroy edged their rival 4 to 3 in the first game. The even bigger story that day was the attendance—2,300 fans crowded the Milroy field, according to the *Marshall Messenger*, more than five times the combined population of the two towns. A few days later, Milroy then closed out Wanda, 6 to 2, for the league championship, led by the fine defensive play of the Dolan infield and the steady hurling of Uchansky. So important were these games that two years later Zwach missed the birth of his first child, which conflicted with an away game against his team's archrival. "We'll get Wanda," he had promised his teammates, and he meant it.[17]

Gradually, a new rivalry on the diamond emerged that fueled equal, if not greater, emotions in Milroy players and fans. Marshall, fifteen miles to the northwest, had long since become the economic hub of southwest Minnesota. Though Milroy residents depended on Marshall for valuable goods and services, they nonetheless harbored deep-seated resentment of their neighbor's elevated status. With a population of 6,000 in 1950, Marshall fielded a baseball team that belonged to Class A in the MABA rankings. In addition to its much greater population base from which to draw players, Marshall also benefited from two key differences in the class structure of amateur baseball in Minnesota. Class A teams could field two "outside" players, defined generally by a fifteen-mile radius from the town, while no outside players could play for Class B teams (Class AA could have three). And while no restrictions applied to salaries for Class A (and AA) teams, Class B teams could not pay their players. Consequently, through the 1940s, Marshall rarely played Milroy. With its newfound success, however, Milroy wanted to try its luck against Marshall and, in the early 1950s, the two teams scheduled an annual home-and-home series that drew tremendous crowds and generated fierce excitement. Play on the field was rough, and out-and-out brawls not uncommon. Even the chatter from the dugouts could be unmerciful. One would not hear "Hum battah, hum battah" or "let's go boys," but more likely, "stick it in his ear" or "who was that I saw with your wife last night?" Zwach liked to tell the story of the time when he heard two men talking on the streets of St. Paul shortly after one of the few games in which Milroy had beaten Marshall: "Said one to the other: 'Where in the hell is Marshall, Minnesota?' And the other one, quicker'n a flash, said: 'That's the town west of Milroy.'" By 1954, when asked what they enjoyed most about playing baseball for Milroy, the players invariably responded, beating Marshall. "Milroy has tradition," one added. "Marshall don't."[18]

Baseball did provide Milroy tradition, along with a powerful community identity. But it also revealed the innovative and, indeed, progressive aspects of players' ideas and actions. Under the leadership of Zwach, who became the team's player-manager in 1950, the Yankees did everything they could to win, including watering down the baselines to slow down fast opposing base runners, freezing balls to take the bounce out of them, and riveting bottle caps to pitchers' belts so they could scuff balls to embellish their sliders. If home attendance started to wane, Zwach would "liven up the game," as he liked to put it. "I'd talk with the other manager before the game and say, 'I'm going to raise a little hell with you, an' I might even shove you around a little. An' you can chase me a little bit.' If you aren't drawin' too good an' you put on a little exhibition an' you look as if you mean business, you'll get a better crowd the next time." In terms of game strategy, Zwach earned a reputation as a master. To encourage his players to be aggressive, he frequently put on the hit-and-run, flashed the steal sign, gave them the green light on 3-0 pitches, and demanded that they run the bases with abandon (especially from first to third on hits to the outfield). His favorite call was for the suicide squeeze, a bold and thrilling play in which the runner on third takes off for home before the pitcher releases the ball and the batter squares to bunt. If the batter puts the ball in play on the ground, the run scores easily, but if he misses the ball or pops it up, the runner coming home has no chance. This high-risk, high-reward tactic epitomized the Yankees' approach to the game. They *competed* on the field, sometimes even recklessly, with a deeply ingrained desire to win—"as though our lives depended on it," one player put it.[19]

Zwach continued to build the team with cunning and persistence. His greatest coup was recruiting a farm boy, Reed Lovsness, who returned home to nearby Cottonwood in 1952 after pitching three years in the minors in the Pittsburgh Pirates organization and serving two years in Korea. Just how nearby became an issue of much controversy. The rules clearly prohibited Class B teams from signing players who lived more than fifteen miles away. Cottonwood was a good twenty-mile drive, but Zwach determined with a plat map and a compass that it was exactly fifteen miles, as the crow flies, from the outer edge of Milroy to the outer edge of Lovsness's farm. The lanky right-hander accepted Zwach's offer because while having made $250 a month in pro ball and entertaining similar offers to pitch for Marshall, he eventually raked in twice that much playing for Milroy. The money came not from salary, because that was against the rules, but from shares of the team's income left over at the end of the season after all expenses were paid, as Zwach explained it to MABA officials. Several teams in the Redwood County League suspected Lovsness from the start and filed a protest alleging that Milroy paid salaries in violation of Class B rules. But the rules did not specifically prohibit paying shares, and Zwach did not disclose just how many shares he planned to pay his new recruit. By securing Lovsness, Milroy not only got a "super-duper" pitcher but also "stuck it to Marshall" in the process, Zwach later noted with glee.[20]

Then, to the sheer delight of their fans, the Yankees put it all together in 1954. In the regular season, the team went 33 and 3, including an electrifying seventeen-game winning streak in August. They stormed through their Redwood County League schedule, finishing 13 and 1, whipping Wanda twice and outscoring their opponents by an average of 11 to 3. Lovsness more than proved his worth, finishing the year with a sparkling 18-and-0 record. His sailing fastball, devastating curve, and pinpoint control made him virtually unhittable. Outfielder Rich Kramer, already an accomplished batsman, became "the best hitter in the state," according to the *Redwood Gazette*. The left-handed slugger had learned his trade, he later recalled, by batting stones for hours on end as a boy on the farm. In the league championship game on August 25, Kramer not only went five for six with three booming home runs; he also pitched the Yankees to a resounding 17-to-8 victory over Balaton. In the first game of the double-elimination regional playoffs, Milroy roared past Searles, champions of the Tomahawk League, 15 to 0, with Lovsness pitching a three-hitter and, for good measure, slugging a two-run blast of his own. After beating Searles a second time, 7 to 0, on September 2, the Yankees proceeded to knock off Franklin, 7 to 2, four days later in a game that featured a mammoth shot by Kramer onto the railroad tracks well beyond the center-field fence. Milroy then secured a spot in the Class B state amateur tournament, held in St. Cloud that year, by downing Franklin again, this time at the Yankees' home park before 1,500 delirious fans. The only blemish on the game occurred during a publicity stunt in the seventh inning, billed as "the highest fly ball of the season"; a "bombardier" dropped a ball from an airplane flying over the field but missed his intended target, the Milroy catcher, by fifty feet. Zwach hoped the "misplay" was not an omen. "We haven't done so well in other state tournaments," he warned after the game. "But," he quickly added, "we've got a pretty fair chance this time."[21]

Zwach need not have worried, if indeed he had been worried at all. Milroy left little doubt in anyone's mind that it had the best Class B team in the state. On September 15, 1954, in the first game of the tournament against Perham, the odds-on favorite to win in all, Milroy scored two runs in the first inning and then handed the game over to Lovsness. The Yankees' ace responded with a three-hit shutout, striking out fourteen and walking no one in the 2-to-0 victory, a performance so dominant that not one Perham runner got beyond first base, and the only one who tried was thrown out on an attempted steal. A columnist for the *Redwood Gazette* called it "the greatest pitching performance in state tournament history." Heavy rains delayed the game for two days and led to the unusual starting time of 9:30 in the morning, but that did not stop a large contingent of Yankee fans from leaving Milroy at 5:00 a.m. to make the first pitch. Two convincing wins followed over the weekend, 9 to 5 over Hibbing and 19 to 3 against Warroad, all of Milroy's runs scoring without the benefit of a home run. A ten-run explosion in the fourth inning in the Warroad game, highlighted by two three-run triples off the bats of Kramer and Joe Dolan, "put the game into the realm of the ridiculous," according to the *Gazette*. Only St. Joseph stood between Milroy and the Class B title, but the champions of the Great Sioux League proved no match for the Yankees. On September 21, Lovsness once again rose to the occasion, pitching a five-hitter and fanning a tournament record twenty batters, including striking out the side in the first, third, fourth, and sixth innings. Milroy scored all of its runs in the first four innings and won 11 to 2. For the tournament, seven of Milroy's fourteen-man squad hit over .300, with veteran

Joe Dolan leading the way with ten hits in fifteen at bats and ten runs batted in. After the game, a high-ranking MABA official presented the Yankees with the coveted championship trophy, and the next day headlines in newspapers across the state declared, "Milroy Wins State B Title." Milroy had won its "bragging rights," as Lovsness later put it—not just over Wanda, not just over Marshall, but over all of small-town Minnesota.[22]

One last game remained that season: the "Mythical State Amateur Championship" between the winners of the Class A and Class B divisions, held the following Sunday in Madison before a crowd of 4,000. "Mythical" simply because the winner received no trophy or prize—strictly pride and glory. No lower-class team had won since 1945, and Milroy's chances did not look good. Class A champion Benson had won the West Central League with ease, breezed through its regional playoffs, and swept five consecutive tournament games—all against teams from cities many times the size of Milroy. No one picked the Yankees over the Chiefs, not even the Yankee players or fans themselves. To make matters all the more grim, Zwach announced just before game time that Lovsness had developed a stiff arm and could not pitch. Benson jumped on his replacement, the little-used Pat Sanborn, for three runs in the top of the second inning to take what appeared an insurmountable lead, with the Chiefs' star right-hander, Bud Eicker, on the mound. Milroy scored an unearned run in the third, but Eicker seemed in full control through six. In their most dramatic rally of the season, the Yankees burst ahead with three runs in the seventh. Spike Dolan's two-run single, his third hit of the afternoon, tied the score and knocked Eicker out of the game. After a walk to Kramer, Joe Dolan then executed the suicide squeeze to perfection to give Milroy the lead, to the utter delight of the Milroy fans and the shock of those rooting for Benson. Despite walking ten, Sanborn finished off the Chiefs, 4 to 3, with a seven-hit complete game victory. The Yankees had achieved the unthinkable. In all, more than 700 teams in the two divisions competed in Minnesota amateur baseball in 1954 with only one left standing, tiny little Milroy.[23]

Shortly after the champs returned home, Milroy merchants and dignitaries honored the team with a community banquet at St. Michael's Church, where the Zwach and Dolan families had worshipped since 1904. With tickets going for two dollars a plate, families, neighbors, and fans jammed the spacious parlor—"taxing it to capacity," as one newspaper described it—for the gala celebration on October 12. Six trophies significant of the team's accomplishments decorated the tables—those commemorating the 1947, 1948, 1949, 1950, and 1954 Redwood County League pennants and, towering over the others in the center of the room, the 1954 Class B championship trophy. At the end of the "splendid" three-course dinner, the village baker presented the team with a victory cake bearing the inscription, "Milroy State B Baseball Champions," which was served for dessert and enjoyed by all. A series of speakers then took the podium, including the mayor, two local ministers, two umpires, and the president of the MABA all the way from St. Paul, each receiving warm applause. Zwach, the last speaker on the program, brought down the house. He attributed the Yankees' success to teamwork and the loyalty of the fans. "Six months we play baseball and the other six months we promote it," Zwach said. "Whether on the field or off the field, we act as a unit." Zwach did not disclose that just prior to the dinner, the players had met privately to divide the team's leftover income. They unanimously agreed to pay Lovsness *all* the shares for his spectacular performance—an amount totaling more than $600 a month that season, the star right-hander revealed years later. "We gave Reed the whole damn thing that year," confirmed his manager.[24]

The team had that kind of money because the players were such good fundraisers and because the fans were such generous donors. The largest share of the team's income came from the games themselves on Sunday afternoons, with tickets costing one dollar. Since rainouts were, in essence, lost revenue, only the most severe downpours caused cancellations. If a storm came through in the morning, the teams played in damp, muddy conditions that afternoon. Supporting the local ball club required more than gate receipts, however. Teams not only paid big bucks for stars like Lovsness; they also had to buy uniforms and equipment, maintain the field, pay the umpires, and transport themselves to away games. This was a private effort, except for the special permit the team obtained from the village council to sell beer on Sunday, itself a lucrative fundraising activity. For every hundred fans at a game, the team sold at least fifty dollars worth of beer, Zwach later estimated. Few towns the size of Milroy even sold beer, except in saloons, and beer was hard to come by anywhere on Sundays. When beer sales began in 1947, attendance climbed substantially. On especially hot afternoons, Zwach added, they relied on "some of our more faithful fans" to drive to Marshall to get ice "to keep the beer cold."[25]

With pride overflowing after the championship season, the community of faithful fans decided to build a new, state-of-the-art ball field for their beloved Yankees. Over the years, players and fans increasingly regarded the quirks of the old field adjacent to the elevator bins less as amusing and more as unbecoming of a team of Milroy's stature. The unenclosed field presented problems for ticket takers trying to collect from many hundreds of people wandering in from all directions. And its location right next to the highway made parking difficult as well.

Shortly after the banquet at St. Michael's church, community leaders identified a five-and-a-half-acre plot of land on the eastern edge of town suitable for a new field and began soliciting donations. In all, seventy-five families pledged ten to one hundred dollars. An implement dealer in town lent the necessary equipment to level the ground, and a farmer donated the sod for the field from his pasture. Dozens of volunteers, many of them working in the evenings after farming all day, then scraped the infield, laid the outfield turf, built the grandstand, and enclosed the field with a wooden fence—all in time for the 1955 season to begin. "It was a community thing," summed up one of the players.[26]

With expectations from the community now higher than ever, the pressure to win mounted. Winning became that much more difficult when the MABA, filled with suspicion about the Lovsness deal and the Yankees' success, forced small Milroy into the ranks of Class A. Zwach made a formal protest to league officials at a state board meeting in St. Paul, but to no avail. As a result, the Yankees moved out of the Redwood County League and into the much more competitive First Night League. The other teams—Marshall, Worthington, Fulda, Pipestone, and Lismore—had much larger populations (ranging from Lismore's 1,000 to Worthington's 8,000), were located as far as seventy miles away from Milroy, and, as the name indicates, had had lights installed in recent years at their ballparks. This meant that every team in the league except Milroy could schedule weekday evening games. Under these conditions, not surprisingly, the Yankees struggled. They went 14 and 14 during the regular season and 9 and 10 in league play. In six games against hated Marshall (four league and two exhibition), Milroy lost four, including a 10-to-4 blowout in July when the Tigers knocked Lovsness out of the box in the fourth inning. As the First Night League round-robin playoffs got under way the first week of August, Marshall—14 and 4 in league, 23 and 4 for the year—was the clear favorite, while Milroy seemed all but out of the running for the championship.[27]

The Yankees had not lost all their magic, however. The team did not get off to a rousing start, losing to Marshall in the opening round, 4 to 3, at the new park in Milroy. Tiger ace Paul Ebert not only outdueled Lovsness, but he also belted the game-winning homer in the top of the eleventh inning. Two days later, Milroy got back to even by beating Lismore, 5 to 4, behind Spike Dolan's three run-scoring doubles. But the Yankees then lost to Pipestone on August 12 and to Worthington the following Sunday, leaving them one loss away from elimination. In the next game against Fulda on August 16—described by the *Marshall Messenger* as "a grim battle for survival"—Rich Kramer kept Milroy alive by lashing a two-out, two-run single in the top of the eighth inning for a 2-to-1 Yankee victory. Over the

Aerial view of Milroy from the southwest, 1969. The town's original five-by-five grid remains intact. "The new field" on the east side of town dominates the landscape; "the old field" sat opposite the grain elevators on the other side of town.
Vincent H. Mart Photograph Collection, Minnesota Historical Society Library, St. Paul.

course of the game, Milroy outfielders threw out three Giant runners at the plate—all on very close plays. The win gave Milroy a berth in the semifinals, but with a 2-and-3 record, one more loss would still seal their fate. They beat Worthington twice in two tough road games to set up a decisive series against their longtime nemesis, the Tigers. In the first game, on August 25, in jam-packed Legion Field in Marshall, Milroy avenged its opening round loss, winning by the same score, 4 to 3, and pinning the loss on Ebert. Kramer's third hit of the game put the Yankees ahead in the seventh inning, and in the ninth, the Tigers got the tying run just ninety feet from home plate with one out but did not score. Three days later, on a sweltering-hot Sunday in Milroy, the Yankees "squeezed Marshall to death," the *Messenger* quipped, beating their rivals 14 to 12 in dramatic fashion. With the game, the season, and the league title on the line in the bottom of the eighth inning, Milroy pulled off a mind-boggling three consecutive suicide squeeze bunts against the bewildered Tigers to seize the victory. Asked after the game to explain his team's audacity in such a close and important game, Zwach replied simply, "We get fired up against Marshall."[28]

With another MABA championship suddenly within their grasp, Milroy entered the regional playoffs confident and determined. Once again, however, the Yankees found themselves with their backs against the wall after an opening round loss to Winnebago, the champions of the Faribault County League. This time, Milroy's aggressiveness backfired. Trailing 5 to 4 in the last of the ninth with runners on first and third and one out, Zwach put on the suicide squeeze once again, but when the batter failed to get wood on the ball, the runner was a dead duck. Now, only a sweep of the remaining two games in the series would send Milroy to the state tournament. Following their postseason pattern, the Yankees rose to the occasion, routing Winnebago twice by the identical scores of 15 to 2. In the clinching game, Lovsness went the distance, striking out fourteen and limiting the Indians to just three hits. Milroy, wrote the *Marshall Messenger*, "doesn't know when it is beaten. . . . When the chips are stacked against them, the team has picked themselves off the floor repeatedly."[29]

The Yankees took that attitude with them to Chaska, the site of the Thirty-Second Annual MABA Tournament. As though continuing to follow the script, Milroy lost a heartbreaker to St. Paul Briteway, 3 to 2. The Cleaners stole a page out of the Yankees' playbook, scoring the winning run in the top of the twelfth inning on a single and three consecutive bunts, the third a successful suicide squeeze. Hanging on the brink of disaster in this double-elimination Class A tournament, Milroy then took on the Hutchinson Hornets on September 13. With two on, two outs, and a 3-to-1 lead in the bottom of the ninth, Milroy appeared in control of the game and poised to move on to the semifinals. Lovsness, already with eighteen strikeouts, two shy of his own tournament record, threw a 2-2 fastball right down the middle, but the umpire missed the call (later apologizing with tears in his eyes). On the next pitch, Jiggs Westergaard, the Hornets' manager and occasional relief pitcher, slugged a three-run homer to win the game. So stunned were the Milroy players that they could not move from the field for what seemed to them like an eternity. After the game, Zwach, uncharacteristically speechless, could only mutter, "You win some, you lose some, and the rest get rained out."[30]

Though the players and fans could not have known it at the time, that frustrating finish foretold the end of the glory days of Milroy. In 1955, we can see in retrospect, farmers and townspeople faced a future that offered little hope and considerable despair. Even as the national economy enjoyed one of its greatest periods of growth, small rural towns like Milroy trudged through a long period of stagnation. The rural economy had in fact declined since the 1920s, with the brief post–World War II boom proving just a blip in the downward curve. The root cause inhabitants of southwest Minnesota often called "the new style of farming," by which they meant the advances in agricultural technology and science. Tractors, combines, and sophisticated power equipment along with new hybrid seeds, improved pesticides and fertilizers, and advances in animal science and veterinary medicine dramatically increased production levels but at the same time dramatically reduced the demand for farm labor. Through the mid 1950s, local residents barely perceived these slowly developing trends. In the two decades thereafter, however, "the new style of farming" took hold at an accelerating rate, and the sagging fortunes of the region became conspicuous. Between 1939 and 1964, the number of farms in southwest Minnesota dropped by almost 25 percent; the region's total population declined by almost 10 percent, and more than twice that in outlying areas (while statewide the number of inhabitants grew steadily); the region became increasingly populated by old people as the young migrated to Mankato, St. Cloud, or the Twin Cities to find jobs; and of those families who stayed put, fully one-fourth lived in poverty.[31]

A region of fewer, older, and poorer residents had dire consequences. Milroy's population remained steady at about 250, but the majority of its residents commuted to industrial and service jobs in Marshall. With the smaller farm population, local merchants began to suffer from reduced sales. Kagel's Grocery, Outsky's Hardware, Nylen's Café, and all the other long-established businesses housed in the once thriving Milroy Block, the largest building on Main Street, closed their doors one by one over the course of the 1970s. The building remained empty for years thereafter, deteriorated from lack of use, and was demolished in 1997. By then, the town had one bar, a beauty salon, and a small engine shop, but no restaurants, groceries, farm supply stores, or gas stations. The railroad, once the lifeblood of the town and region, met a similar fate. Through the 1920s, Milroy enjoyed daily freight and passenger service, with several scheduled stops per day. By the early 1950s, service had declined to one freight train per day (not including Saturday and Sunday), which stopped only when flagged. The Chicago & Northwestern Railway Company then tore down the poorly maintained depot in 1963 before discontinuing the line altogether and removing the tracks in 1979. Created by the railroad eight decades earlier, Milroy now seemed literally and symbolically stripped of its identity.[32]

Baseball was not immune to the town's decay. As the regional economy slumped, and as the younger generation moved on, local baseball declined in participation and popularity. By the late 1950s, the outburst of community enthusiasm for the local team that had developed during the postwar boom had run its course. Farmers and townspeople found it difficult to support the team in the manner to which they had become accustomed. No longer could they donate twenty-five dollars to the Yankees to help maintain the field or spend their hard-earned money on tickets and beer on Sunday afternoons without thinking twice about it. Merchants and other residents, in fact, learned to turn the other way when ballplayers approached them with fundraising ideas. The advent of television and the arrival of the Minnesota Twins in 1961 also hurt town team baseball. Going to the ball field to watch a game on a hot Sunday afternoon no longer seemed preferable to watching Mickey Mantle, Ted Williams, and Willie Mays—or even bowling or professional wrestling—on TV in the comfort of one's air-conditioned living room. Milroy continued to field a team over the years, but the era of passion and prosperity had gone. The Yankees no longer carried the hopes and pride of the community on their shoulders.[33]

While Milroy residents lost interest in the game on the field, they did not abandon baseball altogether. To the contrary, memories of past Yankee magic gave them a means to console each other, lighten their minds of difficult times, and feel good about themselves. Over the decades, the town took every opportunity to celebrate its heroes of yesteryear. In the 1960s, Rich Kramer Day, John Dolan Day, Spike Dolan Day, and Bob Zwach Day drew hundreds of people from the town and surrounding countryside to commemorate the accomplishments of the former Yankee greats. When John Dolan was inducted into the Minnesota Amateur Baseball Hall of Fame in 1967, two hundred locals made the long drive to St. Paul to participate in the festivities and honor "the father of Milroy baseball." During the town's "diamond jubilee" in 1977, more than 2,000 fans jammed Milroy's ballpark to watch the aging champions of 1954 beat an all-star team of former Redwood County League players by a score of 10 to 0. Kramer, one observer remembered, hit the first pitch he saw off the right field fence.[34] And when General Mills ran a "Wheaties Search for Champions" contest in 1984, Milroy campaigned furiously to have its own Bob Zwach pictured on the front of the cereal box. Voters had to purchase a large-size box, cut out their ballots on the back, mark them, and mail them. Only the top six vote-getters nationwide won the grand prize. Milroy's 250 residents bought a lot of cereal during the two-month contest as Zwach received an astounding 2,200 votes. Though not enough to get his picture on the box, Zwach made the top fifty, which won him a consolation prize of $2,200 (one dollar per vote). Local newspapers ran story after story on the contest, with photographs of the 1954 team and detailed accounts of the championship season. Asked what he missed most about the game, Zwach responded, without missing a beat, "razzing the umpires" and "beating Marshall."[35]

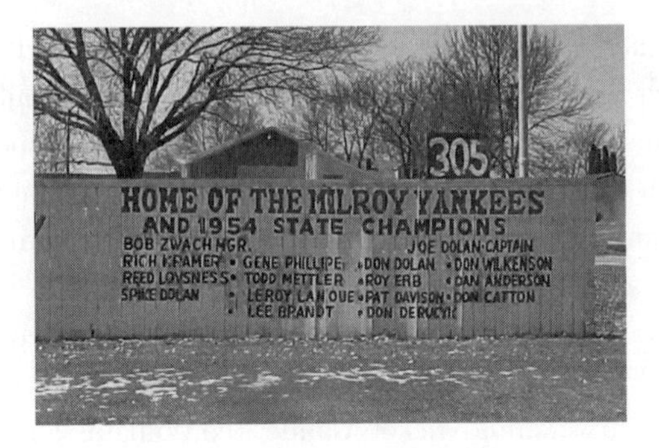

The town still honors the Milroy Yankees' championship season of 1954 with this sign on the right field fence of "the new field."
Photograph by C. J. Molitor.

Nearly twenty-five years later, not much had changed—as revealed, with special clarity, in an interview with Spike Dolan in April 2007. Several years earlier, Spike and his wife had moved off the farm to a house in town—and not just any house but one right next to the new park (as he still called the 1955 field), just behind home plate. He could watch the games from his front porch and field an occasional foul ball. While a couple of blocks away on Main Street many of the buildings were boarded up, and the town in general seemed all but abandoned, the ball field was immaculate, as though ready to host Wanda or Marshall any time (or the current high school team). Clearly visible on the right field fence, a hand-painted sign read, "Home of the Milroy Yankees and 1954 State Champions," followed by the names of all the players from that team. One question—"Tell me about the Yankees"—would release a flood of memories: his brother Joe's unassisted triple play against Carlos in the first round of the 1947 state tournament; beating Wanda for the league championship in 1948; Lovsness's dominant pitching and Kramer's booming homeruns in 1954; winning the mythical state championship that year on a suicide squeeze; the heartbreaking loss to Hutchinson in the 1955 tournament. All along, the smile and energy of the seventy-five-year-old former shortstop filled the room. Other interviews that day produced similar responses. And later that evening, a gathering of 200 enthusiasts at the nearby state university—including Spike, Lovsness, Kramer, and other teammates—fueled an outpouring of reminiscing on Milroy's storied past. The atmosphere was neither nostalgic nor sentimental; it was electric, with everyone enjoying the moment to the utmost.[36]

Rural decline in southwest Minnesota has not stopped people from feeling good about themselves. But they derive much of their joy from the past. For this, there has been no better tonic than baseball. For decades, farmers and townspeople of Milroy, whether on the field or in memories, have expressed themselves through baseball—not with a sense of fatalism but with passion, ingenuity, and a burning desire to beat their rivals one way or another.

CHAPTER SIX

Gaylord Perry, the Spitter, and Farm Life in Eastern North Carolina

Gaylord Perry threw a spitter for the first, but hardly the last, time in his career on the night of May 31, 1964. The circumstances were dire. The Giants and the Mets, in the second game of the longest doubleheader in major league history (nearly ten full hours of playing time), were locked in a 6-to-6 tie in the bottom of the thirteenth inning. Giants manager Alvin Dark waved Perry in from the bullpen with little confidence. He was the eleventh pitcher on the Giants' eleven-man pitching staff and the only option left. With six years in and out of the minors, an ordinary fastball and inconsistent curve, and an earned run average of 4.77 in just seven appearances so far that year, the twenty-five-year-old Perry had every reason to believe that his career hung in the balance. So too did his catcher, Tom Haller, who upon greeting Perry on the mound said simply, "Gaylord, it's time to try it out." They both knew what he meant. Under the tutelage of veteran spitballer Bob Shaw, Perry had been diligently working on his special (and illegal) pitch for over a year—how to load it up, how big a load the ball would carry, where to drop the load, how to grip the ball, how to release it, how to control it, and how to hide it from the four umpires and the entire opposing team. "We're not high school boys anymore," Shaw had told him in no uncertain terms. "Hitters are taking the bread out of your mouth."[1]

Bread had always been an issue for Perry. The son of a sharecropper in the heart of the eastern North Carolina tobacco belt, Perry learned to survive by whatever means necessary. As he came of age in the 1940s and '50s, tobacco farming remained premodern—unmechanized, labor-intensive, and poverty-stricken. The Perry family's yearly routine demanded hard, unrelenting work and afforded few pleasures, baseball chief among them. Throughout his major league career, Perry again learned to survive by whatever means necessary. "In this game," he said in a rare moment of candor, "you gotta do what it takes. If it takes being mean, you be mean. If it takes brushin' a hitter back, you brush 'im back. If it takes bein' wet, you moisten up." And sure enough, with his spitter splashing in Haller's mitt, Perry pitched ten scoreless innings to beat the Mets that night, finished the 1964 season with twelve victories as a starter, and went on to become one of the premier pitchers of his generation. Perry returned to his farming roots and southern way of life even before retiring from the game in 1983, but this time his survival skills met with disaster. Overextended and deeply in debt, he could not prevent his 410-acre farm from failing in 1986 during the decade's devastating agricultural crisis. Baseball had offered Perry an outlet for the tensions of rural life and a means of translating a core set of values into action. But prosperity on the farm, he learned, depended on a much more cruel reality. It rested not just on hard work, determination, and resiliency, but on favorable market conditions, over which—unlike the spitter—he had no control.[2]

Perry's experience—his innovative ascent from rural poverty to baseball stardom and subsequent descent to failure on the farm—raises new and important questions not only about his own life and career but also, more broadly, about links between rural southern culture and American popular culture.[3] Inborn talent in large part propelled Perry to the National Baseball Hall of Fame. But what about his rural background, values, and character nurtured that talent before major league scouts recognized his potential? How, in turn, did his storied baseball career—his mastery of the spitter, in particular—repeat and reinforce his grounding in rural southern culture, so much so that he chose to return to the farm after becoming a national sports hero? What role did race play in Perry's approach to baseball and farming? And finally, what larger meanings can we extract from Perry's odyssey concerning race, popular culture, and the vast social and economic changes in the rural South from the 1940s to the later part of the century? A more comprehensive, systematic study of these issues, complete with an extensive historiographical overview, a comparative analysis of players from within and outside the rural South, and a more detailed account of Perry's twenty-two years in the big leagues, awaits a full-length biography. A fresh starting point, however, can begin here through an intensive, if suggestive, case study of a quintessentially southern, authentically rural icon of popular culture.

Gaylord Jackson Perry, born September 15, 1938, grew up in Farm Life, a cluster of tenant farms, appropriately named, ten miles south of the town of Williamston (population 6,500) and 100 miles from the nearest major city, Raleigh to the west or Norfolk, Virginia, to the north. Like other tobacco communities in the northeast quadrant of North Carolina, Farm Life was not only isolated but underdeveloped, sparsely populated, and plagued with poor interior and external communications. Farm Life had no downtown of any sort to serve its 1,200 residents, only the occasional crossroads store, schoolhouse, or church, most of them Baptist or Methodist. Families furnished at least three-fourths of the food they ate—vegetables, milk and butter, poultry and eggs, and home-raised pork—and walked much more than they drove or rode. Little seemed to change. As in most, if not all, rural communities across much of the South, the Farm Life that Perry knew in the 1940s and '50s differed little from the Farm Life of the 1920s or, for that matter, from the Farm Life of the 1880s.[4]

Farming itself was primitive. Some farming practices—plowing, for example—had also changed little since the first families began to settle the area under a grant from King George in 1774. Many of their descendants—the Griffins, Robersons, Mannings, Peeles, and Biggs—still owned much of the land.[5] The Perry family had no such lineage, however. Gaylord's father, Evan, orphaned in infancy, toiled as a sharecropper— "cropper," in the terminology of the U.S. Bureau of the Census—and as such occupied the bottom rung on the agricultural ladder in a system of labor that had not changed since the Civil War. His landlord, Asa Roberson, provided Evan and his wife, Ruby, with a house, two mules, some farming equipment, and twenty-five acres. Evan and Ruby, in turn, furnished the house inside, grew the crops, and kept up the farm. Landlord and tenant split the cost of seed and fertilizers and then split the proceeds evenly at the end of each harvest. The terms of their agreement echoed those that evolved from the Reconstruction era between landowners and former slaves.[6]

Tobacco was the Perry family's money crop. With nothing but their hands, ingenuity, and the two mules, family members provided all the labor. From start to finish, raising a crop was so demanding—350 man-hours for one acre of tobacco, as compared to just three for an acre of corn—that farmers often joked that the production process required a thirteenth month in their calendar called "Tobaccuary." From the time they were seven years old, Gaylord and his older brother, Jim, worked all day, six days a week, sewing, tending, harvesting, and curing the crop, plowing the fields, pulling out tree stumps, and cutting wood. Evan and Ruby, just eighteen when Jim was born and twenty when Gaylord came along, were thankful for their two strong sons, but when their third child, Carolyn, was born seven years after Gaylord, they decided they had to stop there. "We couldn't take the chance on having another girl," Evan recalled, "not with the bills we had to meet." In a good year, the Perrys might clear $3,000, but their fortunes fluctuated with the price of tobacco and the luck of the growing season. In 1959, the median income for Martin County men who were farmers and farm managers was $1,261, well below the statewide median figure for families of $3,956.[7]

Beyond the long hot hours in the fields were additional hardships to endure. The Perry farm had no electricity until Gaylord turned twelve, and neither he nor his brother knew indoor plumbing until they went to high school. Gaylord and Jim grew up sleeping in the same bed and sharing the same tub of bath water on the back porch on Saturday nights. Their century-old farmhouse had a second floor, kept locked because they could not afford to heat it in the winter or furnish it any time of year. They had a community telephone with their own ring, and except for church on Sundays and an occasional revival meeting, hog killing, or trip to Noah Roberson's general store, they had no other contact with the neighbors. The nearest ones lived a mile away. "Hard" was the operative word: hard work, hard conditions, hard times. But hard did not evoke self-pity. "Daddy, Jim, and I never looked at a day of farm work with dread," Gaylord recalled. "It was something you had to do to eat. Dirt farming taught you to think about what you were doing right then, never ahead to all the work waiting for you that day, that week, or for the rest of your life." Each chore or routine—every aspect of making a crop—was important, necessary, and thus rewarding because it contributed to the family's livelihood.[8]

The Perry men played hard, too. Using balls they made with rocks, tape, and rolled-up stockings, oak roots for bats, and one worn-out fielder's glove between them, Evan, Jim, and Gaylord played baseball whenever they could find the time—for an hour at lunch, before nightfall, and on Sunday afternoons after church. "From the time they could throw a ball they were playing," Evan said. "When we weren't working, we was playing ball." When it was just the three of them, they had to improvise. Evan usually pitched, with Gaylord and Jim alternating between hitting and fielding. They used the potato barn as a backstop and devised their own rules: the batter was out when the ball was caught on a fly and score was kept by how far the ball was hit. Evan drove the boys just as hard on the baseball field as in the tobacco field. "Being poor, they knew how to apply themselves to work," he added. "They knew it was important to learn the right way to do a job before you got chewed out for doing it the wrong way. They approached baseball the same way." The boys thrived under their father's work ethic. "Baseball was everything when Jim and I were growing up," Gaylord remembered vividly. "It was work in the fields, go to church on Sunday, and play ball. Baseball stirred the soul, like a religion."[9]

The Perrys' devotion to the game, it should be stressed, was home grown. "Down in North Carolina," as Gaylord put it, "the big leagues seemed a long way away." His heroes were not Bob Feller or Stan Musial but local legends Jimmy Brown, Slim Gardner, and his own father, Evan Perry. "Little Jimmy" Brown of Jamesville, just up the road from Farm Life, played in the short-lived Coastal Plains League in the early 1930s—short-lived because during the Great Depression the players could not afford gloves, shoes, uniforms, and transportation. The 139-pound Brown caught lightning in a bottle, however, signing on with the St. Louis Cardinals as a utility infielder in the late 1930s and playing for several years. Slim Gardner—six-foot-six, strong as a mule, and toothless—pitched for the Farm Life community team in the Beaufort County League for thirty years, until he was forty-five. Legend has it that his fastball "could match a bolt of lightning" and that his spitter (or "tobacco ball," as he called it) once broke so sharply that it split his catcher's toenail in two. In 1941, the folks around Farm Life chatted not about Joe DiMaggio's fifty-six-game hitting streak or Ted Williams's .406 batting average but about the superhuman feat performed by Slim's teammate, Evan Perry. On the hottest day in local history, over 110 degrees, and with Slim laid up, Perry pitched Farm Life to a 4-to-1 victory over White Post in the first game of a doubleheader and came right back with another complete-game win in the second, 9 to 3. Big league scouts approached Slim and Evan on different occasions, but both had no choice but to turn them down. Neither could afford to leave his family and farm work behind for anything so risky as a career in professional sports. Nor could many from Gaylord's own generation pursue their dreams, though as many as twenty-five in the county, he later estimated, had the talent to play pro ball, most notably Simon Hardeson, a left-handed slugger who "had a reputation around here for being one of the greatest hitters ever in any league." One can only guess how many others life in the rural South, as Evan put it, "kept down" from playing.[10]

Farm Life was money poor but rich in talent—and even richer, perhaps, in oral tradition. Baseball in the area and the fantastic stories the game produced rarely made headlines but instead traveled down through the generations via word of mouth. The tradition of the game produced the community pitcher—Slim Gardner and Evan Perry, two cases in point—an institution "comparable to the town parson, the corner druggist, and the community Confederate veteran," as one local put it. When Jim and Gaylord turned fourteen, they joined their father on the Farm Life team, each adding his own chapter to Beaufort County League lore. Often, so it was said, they played in front of "two, three thousand people at a game, all up and down the foul lines and in the outfield, all over."[11]

Only Ruby Perry seemed to balk at baseball. When Evan, Jim, and Gaylord practiced at lunchtime, she would shake her head and holler: "Evan? Evan, you and the boys are blamed fools playin' ball in this awful heat when you should be restin'." At best, she thought baseball "kind of a silly waste"; at worst, she believed it a mortal sin. A devout fundamentalist, whose family were charter members of Maple Grove (First Christian) Church where the Perrys worshipped on Sunday mornings, Ruby was suspicious of play and recreation and took to heart a common saying across the rural South, "An idle brain and a playground are the devil's workshop." The bible, she had long since internalized, gave hope for eternal happiness to people who had few worldly joys, which made playing on Sundays even more blasphemous. The more the boys played baseball, moreover, the less time they had to help their mother with chores around the house. And for a wife and mother on a tobacco farm, Ruby's work, both in the house and in the fields, never ended.[12]

But Evan had made up his mind that Jim and Gaylord would have time for baseball, no matter how much work they had. He could not have dreamed how good they would become. At six-foot-three and two hundred pounds, they both distinguished themselves in high school ball and in football and basketball as well.[13] In 1955, Jim's last year and Gaylord's first at Williamston High, the brothers won the state championship, one playing third base while the other pitched. In the last five games of the tournament, all shutouts, Gaylord won two and Jim three, limiting Williamston's opponents to just twelve total hits and not allowing even one runner to reach third base. When Jim went on to junior college the next year, major league scouts flocked to eastern North Carolina to watch him pitch. One of them, Tim Murchison of the Giants, found Jim's kid brother even more impressive, calling him "the best seventeen-year-old in the country." Jim signed with the Cleveland Indians in 1956 for a $4,000 bonus, the maximum allowed, at the time, for players not on the big league roster. "Not since Jimmy Brown moved up into the big time has a ball player of potential major league caliber been signed out of this section of the woods with so much promise," declared the *Williamston Enterprise*.[14]

"The Perry Era," as the *Enterprise* labeled these years, had just begun. As a junior, Gaylord opened the season with a perfect game, pitched five no hitters, averaged better than two strikeouts an inning, and did not allow a single earned run the entire year. When his senior year proved not quite as spectacular, a local merchant arranged an exhibition game against a team of selected semipro stars to showcase Perry for major league scouts, including Murchison and Giants chief scout, Tom Sheehan, who flew out all the way from San Francisco. After walking the first three hitters, Perry struck out the next seventeen in a row and won the game 5 to 1. "Make arrangements to sign that boy," Sheehan told Murchison. For a week after Gaylord's graduation, scouts from thirteen major league teams descended on the Perry farm to bid for his services. He signed with the Giants for an astounding $73,500, the bonus rule having been dropped the previous year, and gave half of it to his father. For the first time in his life, Evan Perry found himself free of debt and with peace of mind.[15]

Despite all the time and energy needed to operate the farm, baseball played a major role in the lives of the Perrys and, indeed, was deeply ingrained in the region's rural culture. In sharecropper communities in eastern North Carolina and across the South, farmers devoted almost as much (and often more) of their spare time to the sport as they did to church. They saw baseball not as a sanctuary from their real world but as very much part of their real world. Moreover, and this cannot be emphasized enough, baseball was a local, not a national, pastime in the South. The closest major league teams played hundreds of miles away in the Northeast and Midwest and might as well have been thousands of miles away. Competition on the diamond was a matter of local pride reinforced by an uncompromising rural work ethic. For Gaylord, life on a tobacco farm not only helped improve his physical and athletic capabilities but also taught him self-discipline, perseverance, and the value of teamwork. His raw talent for the game gave him opportunities open to relatively few in the rural South, but at the same time, the hardness he took from the farm into baseball set him apart from most other professional athletes right from the start. Without the lessons learned on the farm, from his family, and in Farm Life, there would have been, in all likelihood, no scouts, no major league career, no Cooperstown.

With the stroke of the pen that made Gaylord a "bonus baby," the Perrys gained immediate entry into the lifestyle of the middle class. The parents bought a new bed for the first time in twenty years, a new oil heater, an oil stove to replace their wood-burning model, new curtains, and a rug; Evan purchased a new truck and Gaylord himself a new Plymouth. Even Ruby allowed herself two dresses and a new hat. One year later, Gaylord moved still higher up the social scale by marrying Blanche Manning from Farm Life's most prominent family. Unlike the Perrys, the Mannings had what was called "breeding" in the South. They not only owned lots of land but also attended college, had preachers, merchants, and newspaper editors in the family; played prominent roles in religion and education in the community; and even had their own private family cemetery. They were, as Gaylord put it, "well-known folk." Before attending Duke University, Blanche starred on the Williamston High basketball team, which gave Gaylord and her common ground. They did most of their courting on the team bus. Blanche's father worried less about their class differences than about Gaylord's baseball future. "Don't ruin that boy's career," he would say, not allowing Blanche to date him the night before a game. Gaylord, however, did worry about the class difference. "If he hadn't got that big bonus to play baseball," Blanche maintained, "Gaylord might never have overcome his hang up over the differences in our lifestyles and his relative poverty." The couple seemed to find a happy medium right away. Their lavish wedding splashed across the *Enterprise* society page, but they honeymooned at the Dixie Classic Basketball Tournament in Raleigh.[16]

As Perry made his way through the minor leagues—St. Cloud, Minnesota; Corpus Christi, Texas; Harlington, Texas; Tacoma, Washington—and on to San Francisco, a whole new life opened up for him. Pitching in professional baseball meant that he could save money, buy homes (one in San Carlos, south of San Francisco, and one in Williamston), and start college funds for the four Perry children (born between 1963 and 1968). In 1962, with the half-share of World Series money he received in his rookie year with the Giants, he put a down payment on a seventy-acre spread in Farm Life for his father and declared himself "no longer the son of a sharecropper." The stark contrast between the National League and the Beaufort County League, moreover—the finely manicured fields, plush locker rooms, and fancy hotels, for example—marked the change in his life and circumstances. But it did not really hit him until his first start of the 1967 season in front of more than 50,000 fans at Dodger Stadium. The loudspeakers blared the starting lineups before the game: "and on the mound for the Giants will be Gaylord Perry of Williamston, North Carolina." At that moment, he realized just how far he had come. Little did he know that his name would continue to echo in stadiums around the country for another sixteen seasons and, starting with his trade to Cleveland prior to the 1972 season, with seven more teams—the Indians, Texas Rangers, San Diego Padres, New York Yankees, Atlanta Braves, Seattle Mariners, and Kansas City Royals.[17]

Yet all along, Perry cleaved to the values and approach to life that Farm Life instilled in him. Pitching for Perry became another form of work, nothing more—like hammering down a fence post halfway into the ground with one swing or picking tobacco from dawn to dark. He built his career as a pitcher of remarkable strength, energy, durability, and focus. "The only goals I set for myself," he said toward the end of his twenty-two-year career, "are to be ready to pitch when the manager calls on me and to keep my team in the game. It's hard work. I grew up like that. You've gotta fight and work for it." His 314 wins, 3,524 strikeouts, and two

Cy Young awards (one in each league) got him into the Hall of Fame, but perhaps most striking, he pitched 5,352 innings (6,244, including the minor leagues), with at least 200 innings in seventeen different seasons and more than 300 six times. Over his long career on the mound, he missed only two scheduled starts and never suffered a sore arm. The proverbial workhorse and a competitor second to none, he stressed, "You pay attention and learn. You study the hitters. You try to master new pitches. You take care of your arm. You run to keep your legs in shape. You aim to stay on top of your game mentally, to believe in your ability. You keep looking for anything that will give you an edge."[18]

Perry's biggest find, of course, was the spitter. His spectacular achievements notwithstanding, the spitter made Perry famous—or infamous, depending on one's perspective. Though many have tried the spitter, relatively few have mastered it. To throw one, a pitcher moistens the first two fingers of his hand, keeps the thumb dry, and avoids contact with the seams. He then throws the ball like a fastball, but the moisture lessens the friction at the point of release and reduces the spin—like "squirting a wet watermelon seed from your fingers," quipped Perry. A sphere so thrown tends, when tossed overhand, to take a sudden drop near the plate. Thrown sidearm, it veers sharply right or left. Its slippery release and abrupt movement make it a tricky pitch to throw consistently well. It took Perry months of practice to control it and even longer to believe that he could conceal it. According to the rules of the game (Rule 8.02, implemented after the 1920 season, to be precise) pitchers may not apply any "foreign substance" to the ball—specifically including spit—on penalty of ten days' suspension. They could, when Perry first started throwing the pitch, wet their fingers on the mound so long as they wiped them dry on their uniforms. Perry spent hours in front of the mirror at home faking his dry moves and bouncing the rosin bag around his pitching hand (using his daughter Amy's bean bag for practice) without touching his wet fingers. To keep up his saliva level up during a game, he sucked on Thayers Slippery Elm lozenges, like an opera singer with a dry throat—a technique passed down through generations of spitballers since the turn of the twentieth century.[19]

The spitter has a long and inglorious history. The pitch, invented by Fort Wayne, Indiana's Bobby Matthews in 1871, according to baseball lore, was legal until the Black Sox scandal of 1919, when several of the Chicago White Sox admitted to throwing games in the World Series. In his attempts to clean up the image of the game, the new commissioner, Judge Kenesaw Mountain Landis, upheld the decision of a joint rules committee to ban the spitball and all other doctored deliveries. In addition, in 1919, Babe Ruth made his conversion from pitching to the outfield and hit a record twenty-nine home runs, which demonstrated to Landis and the team owners that they could make more money on the long ball than on pitching. The new rule looked even better in 1920, when Ruth clouted fifty-four homers and, tragically, his teammate, Carl Mays, a notoriously wild spitballer, threw one that hit Ray Chapman in the head, killing him in the batter's box. Rule 8.02 proved a dead letter from the start, however. Try as they might, umpires have never managed to enforce it. Said one, "I know when I see it. The ball takes a funny break and really down deep in your heart you know it's a spitter, but it's too late to prove it. The rule is clear, but it is unenforceable, because how can you *prove* that a guy threw it?" Cheating, moreover, is a time-honored tradition among ballplayers. Corking bats to quicken one's bat speed, watering down the baselines to slow down fast opposing baserunners, freezing balls to take the bounce out of them, stealing catcher's signs with binoculars from inside outfield scoreboards, and other such antics have filled the game's history. "If you ain't cheatin', you ain't tryin'," many a player has summed it up.[20]

Perry was certainly "tryin'." But just as he had perfected his craft, Rule 8.02 was amended prior to the 1968 season to prevent pitchers from going to their mouths. The change seemed not only to give umpires more tangible evidence for enforcing the rule but also to favor the hitter to add more excitement to the game—along with, over the next few years, lowering the mound, installing artificial turf, and creating the designated hitter. Undeterred, Perry wasted no time switching from spit to grease that winter. He tried several different lubricants—Vaseline (too greasy), K-Y jelly prescribed by his wife's gynecologist (dried too quickly), baby oil, hair tonic, moustache wax—before settling on a generic petroleum jelly that mixed "just right" with his sweat. The only safe place to store it, he learned through trial and error, was somewhere on his exposed skin, where he could wipe it away in an instant, before a suspicious umpire could make his way to the mound. With the right lubricant in hand, he got back in front of the mirror to perfect an elaborate series of decoys—hand to the cap, to the brim, to the cheek, the neck, the shirt, the belt—as many as fifteen rapid-fire moves before every pitch, all to keep the umpires from detecting "the spot." And to keep his sweat level up over the course of a game, even on the coldest of nights at Candlestick Park in San Francisco, Perry's trainer rubbed his entire upper body with capsolin, a strong-scented ointment derived from red chili peppers grown in China that burned so hot his entire body would turn scarlet. "He smells like a drugstore," combative manager Billy Martin once remarked. After practicing his new routine with Blanche in their backyard for hours on end, he went on to win sixteen games that season, including a no-hitter, 1 to 0, against Bob Gibson and the St. Louis Cardinals, in which all but four of his pitches were, reportedly, greasers.[21]

Over time, Perry learned to control not only the pitch but the behavior of opposing hitters and managers. They became fixated on Perry's antics on the mound, much to his delight. "Hitters were coming back to the dugout and saying, 'Today he's got it on his hat, no it's his belt, no it's his neck,'" Perry observed. "They'd be worried more about where I was touching than looking for the ball. And it really upset them." Did it ever, as epitomized in a game against the Yankees in 1973. When outfielder Bobby Murcer struck out on two pitches that bounced fifteen feet in front of home plate, he cursed Perry, who ignored him, cursed the umpire, who threw him out of the game, and cursed Commissioner Bowie Kuhn, who fined and suspended him. A couple of innings later, manager Ralph Houk lost it so completely that he exploded from the dugout to the mound, jerked Perry's cap from his head, stomped on it, and kicked it around the infield until the umpires led him away. Perry, as usual, walked away uncharged, unfined, and unflappable. In his entire career, in fact, he was ejected from a game only once for allegedly throwing the controversial pitch, but even then not until 1982, a few days shy of his forty-fourth birthday in his next to last season.[22]

Never one to rest on his laurels, Perry seized the opportunity provided by the success of the illegal pitch to develop two new legal pitches, the forkball and split-fingered fastball. Both broke sharply downward at the last instant, much like the greaser, so that umpires and opposing players found all three difficult to tell apart. By the mid-1970s, with his arsenal complete, Perry no longer had to rely on the greaser to get batters out. If his other pitches worked well in a game, he might not throw one at all. But if he needed it, he always had it. Greaser or no greaser, Perry continued to run through his series of decoys before every delivery to maintain his psychological edge. He then fanned the controversy by admitting his past crimes to the world in his "autobiographical confession," *Me and the Spitter*, written with sportswriter Bob Sudyk in 1974. "I reckon I tried everything on the old apple but salt and pepper and chocolate sauce toppin'," he boasted. He then quickly added, "Of course, I'm reformed now. I'm a pure, law-abiding citizen." The book elevated the stature of Perry's lawless image all the more, infuriating Murcer, Houk, and pretty much everyone else in the American League.[23]

More zingers followed—in the book, with reporters in the locker room, and with opposing players on the field. When Hank Aaron once complained to the umpire, "Why don't you just let him carry a bucket of water out there?" Perry responded, "That pitch was as dry as a Baptist wedding." When a foul ball once

In a game against the Detroit Tigers on June 1, 1972, Perry enjoys confounding yet another umpire at the mound in search of "the spot" where he (may have) hid the grease. Perry's sleight-of-hand artistry, outlaw status, and the spitter itself, wrote one insightful sportswriter, were "part of his country boy savvy."
The Plain Dealer/Landov. Reprinted with permission.

came back into the press box with an oily blemish on it, Perry, then a Ranger, told reporters, "It must have splattered a mosquito on the way up there. They grow 'em pretty big here in Texas, you know." And after his milestone victory in 1983, he wore a T-shirt to the press conference that read, "300 wins Ain't Nothin' to Spit At." All the "I reckons," "yonders," "y'alls," and "fixin' tos" in his soft North Carolina drawl were certainly genuine—farm boys from Farm Life talk that way. But Perry, no country bumpkin, chose his words as part of the con, calculated to exploit his country-boy, aw-shucks, too-innocent-to-be-bad demeanor. The whole spitter phenomenon, as one sportswriter put it, "was part of Perry's country boy savvy." Even his five-year-old daughter, Allison, got into the act. "Does your daddy throw a grease ball, honey?" a television reporter asked her on camera during a game. "It's a hard slider," she responded, without missing a beat. Slim Gardner could not have said it better himself.[24]

The "hard slider" was not strictly southern, per se. Many other accused practitioners used it during the 1960s and 1970s—Don Drysdale, Phil Regan, Bill Singer, Jim Maloney, for example—none of them from the South, and by the same token, many contemporary southerners—Catfish Hunter, Hoyt Wilhelm, even Perry's brother, Jim—remained above the law (or rule). No one, however, threw the spitter (or greaser) as well, or for as long, as Gaylord Perry. The creativity, drive, and persistence that it took for him to perfect the pitch and subvert authority stemmed directly from his southern rural background. That background, moreover, not only shaped Perry's approach to his career but also added a new and exciting dimension to the game. On the days when Perry pitched, he was *the* story. Where, the fans buzzed, does he hide the grease? Why don't the umpires stop him? Did you see what that pitch just *did*? Above and beyond his natural talent, Perry's sleight-of hand artistry, his outlaw status, and the circus atmosphere that surrounded his starts made him one of the most entertaining players in the game in the last half of the twentieth century. He brought fun and intrigue to an occupation that was otherwise monotonous, repetitious, and appreciated mostly by wins and losses, strikeouts and walks, and earned run averages. As Perry himself put it, "I gave the fans somethin' else to look at besides pitchin' stats. I brought more fun to the park than any gimmick or promotion baseball ever came up with." Added one sportswriter succinctly, "Gaylord was Broadway box office." Though few fans realized it, when they cheered (or booed) Perry in stadiums across the country they, in essence, celebrated southern rural values and character. Farm Life, through Perry, made its mark on popular culture.[25]

Perry was not fully satisfied, however. It was not enough for him to think, talk, or pitch like a farmer. He wanted to *be* a farmer. After his trade to Cleveland, where, as the team's only star player, both his salary and endorsement income increased substantially, Perry purchased a 410-acre farm within spitting distance from where he grew up. He started growing tobacco, peanuts, soybeans, and corn, though this time with tractors, not mules. He hired a manager to oversee operations during the baseball season but spent his off seasons working the land himself. As many curious reporters discovered, he was anything but a "gentleman farmer," a term he abhorred. Rural children who make good and move to the city rarely come back to the farm—witness again his brother, law-abiding Jim, who after a fine career of his own (215 wins, most of them with the Twins), preferred to remain with his family in Minneapolis. The irony of his return did not escape Perry, and he clearly enjoyed the attention. "The idea of farming made me become a pitcher, but now I pitch so I can farm," he told the press.[26]

The move back to the farm allowed Gaylord and Blanche to raise their four kids where they felt, as he put it, "comfortable." Comfortable meant back home with family members and friends—over 1,000 of whom had turned out on a fall day in 1970 to celebrate "Perry Brothers' Day" at the Roanoke Country Club in Williamston. It meant living in a small town, where "you know everybody, you know you can count on everybody, and you get to depend on people," and where people pronounced his name the right way—"GAY-lerd." It implied a certain aesthetic, even agrarian, quality. "City boys," Perry wrote, "never get to know the gentleness of a mill creek, or the beauty of deer sniffing around the barns in winter looking for food." And similarly, "I wanted my children to share some of the experiences with nature that I had, like sleeping in a barn to nurse a sick cow and waking up with a deer nuzzling me through a window." The Perrys themselves felt like "animals in a pen" in the suburbs of San Francisco, even after moving to a three-acre ranch home in Portola Valley in 1969. And comfortable meant the immense satisfaction of returning as a landowner "after not having things early in life."[27]

Comfortable also meant southern, particularly with regard to race. The South, when Gaylord and Blanche grew up, had strict segregation laws, though such laws more effectively separated races in cities and towns than in rural areas. In Farm Life, whites and blacks, in roughly a two-to-one ratio in population, lived and labored in close proximity as fellow tenants, bosses and hands, and neighbors. They also shared country stores, tobacco warehouses, roads, creditors, and poverty. Nonetheless, schools remained separate, as did churches, social clubs, and cemeteries. Pick-up games of basketball or baseball between integrated teams were not unusual, but organized sports—the Beaufort County League, for example—existed for whites only. Over a hundred Farm Life families took great pride in having ancestors who fought in the Civil War, and the Mannings thought it a badge of honor to have had a Confederate judge (Blanche's great-grandfather) in the family. One of the Manning's prize possessions, handed down through the generations, was a large silver watch taken from the body of a dead Yankee soldier. Francis Manning, longtime editor of the *Williamston Enterprise*, filled the paper, especially its expanded annual "tobacco edition," with epic stories of "our heroes" defending the South during and after the war.[28]

In nearby Williamston, decidedly separate and unequal conditions prevailed. "Colored" and "White" signs hung over restrooms and drinking fountains in most public buildings, including the municipal library, county hospital, and courthouse. Segregation prevailed in restaurants, motels, theaters, department stores, Laundromats, funeral parlors, and the Roanoke Country Club. Most black residents lived "Down the Hill," as the saying went, where property values, living conditions, income levels, and the quality of education dropped along with the elevation.[29] Though whites prided themselves on their "cordial" relations with blacks, as editor Manning's *Enterprise* often asserted, Williamston was dangerous for its African American population. Lynchings in the area occurred as late as 1957 and, in one particularly gruesome case, a jury of twelve white men took less than fifteen minutes to acquit one of their own on trial, much to the horror of the spectators seated in the "Colored" section of the courtroom.[30] In response to the racial violence and injustice, a full-fledged freedom movement, centered on voting rights and school integration, led by the Southern Christian Leadership Conference, and avidly opposed by a revived Ku Klux Klan, captured the regional and, for a time, national spotlight in the fall of 1963. For several weeks, African Americans held nightly meetings, formulated sweeping demands, participated in dozens of marches and sit-ins, and staged an economic boycott of white-owned businesses. While leaders of the movement called Williamston the "segregated-est town in the U.S.," local whites compared the "invasion" of "Yankee sympathizers" in 1963 to a raid on Williamston led by Union cavalry during the Civil War.[31]

In this environment, Gaylord and Blanche had adhered to the laws and customs of segregation as a matter of course when growing up. "Down home, that's where we had separate schools for the blacks, separate toilets, separate sides of the street, and front-and-back buses," he wrote matter-of-factly. The Perrys and the Mannings belonged to the Farm Life Ruritan Club, which, along with hundreds of other local chapters in rural areas across the South, aimed to achieve "Fellowship, Goodwill and Community Service"—but only for whites. Every spring, the Ruritans put on a minstrel show, billed as "the Big Night at Farm Life." In 1954, young Gaylord, then in the eighth grade, felt honored to make the cast, which put on a two-act musical comedy lampooning *Uncle Tom's Cabin*, featuring such characters as Harriet Beecher Stowe, Uncle Tom, Simon Legree, Little Eva, and Miss Ophelia, all in blackface.[32] In contrast to the minstrel show, the U.S. Supreme Court's historic decision in the *Brown* school desegregation case, announced just one month later, went virtually unnoticed in Farm Life and surrounding areas. Residents knew that the ruling concerned them, but they trusted that the leading public figures in the state and region would find a viable way to circumvent, as the *Enterprise* put it, "this stinging blow to the Southern way of life." Any alternative narrative seemed unimaginable to them.[33]

Despite race relations far from "cordial," the capricious nature of southern segregation allowed, and even encouraged, whites in Farm Life to develop friendships across racial boundaries. In his autobiography, Perry insisted that he held no animosity toward blacks, and to demonstrate his sincerity he described, at some length, his friendship of many years with a farmhand named Annox Peale. Peale, said Perry, "was a wonderful man, a hard worker, and a happy man." All that seemed missing from his life, from Perry's perspective, was that "he'd never really known a vacation in his life." Several of Perry's friends in the area regularly organized bus trips to northern cities to watch him pitch, and in 1968, Peale made the trip with them. Perry went out of his way to show Peale the time of his life, including introducing him to his idol, Willie Mays, who autographed a photograph of the two of them on the field. In this episode, Perry doubtless displayed a genuine heartfelt affection, but in the context of his life experience, it also, in all likelihood, manifested southern-bred paternalism.[34]

By 1960, the sports world had achieved more integration than society at large, especially in Horace Stoneham's Giants baseball club, whose scouts prowled Latin America for prospects just as they had the Negro Leagues in years past. Perry expressed genuine fondness for his black teammates, enjoyed their company, and respected them as persons. He bragged about living next door to Bobby Bonds in San Carlos, and later named the family dog Tito, after "my old second-basemen" (Tito Fuentes). But Perry nevertheless sounded patronizing at times. "A lot of folks down home believe the blacks had it better when things were segregated," he wrote. " I don't buy that. I'm a southerner, but I sure believe in integration. I ought to. I don't know what I'd have done later on without Willie Mays and Willie McCovey behind me." Like many of his Giant teammates, Perry singled out Mays for teaching him more about the game than anyone else. Winning, Mays preached, required first and foremost putting aside racial differences. "Everyone [regardless of race] likes money . . . and money goes with winning," he said. "Ain't nothing wrong with that." Thus, when the opposing pitcher knocked Mays down with an high-inside fastball, for example, Perry well understood that he had to retaliate by throwing at the other team even harder and more viciously—regardless of the color of the target.[35]

Under certain circumstances, however, Perry's deep-seated racial assumptions could resurface. The most notable instance came in 1975, when the Cleveland Indians named Frank Robinson the major league's first black manager. Perry and Robinson, both proud and stubborn men, clashed almost immediately, ostensibly over salary and conditioning techniques. Perry, the team's star player the previous three years, was furious that Robinson's starting salary was considerably higher than his own. And while Perry preferred his own pregame regimen of running sprints and taking grounders at third base, Robinson wanted all his pitchers to take long runs in the outfield, back and forth fifteen times from foul-line to foul-line. "I'm nobody's slave," Perry told reporters defiantly. "I'm not training for a marathon race, and I'm not about to let some superstar who never pitched a game in his life tell me how to get ready to pitch." The more the two traded barbs as the season wore on, the more Perry revealed his disdain for Robinson's leadership. It was one thing to have African American teammates but quite another to have a black man in such a visible position of authority. In Perry's mind, deeply ingrained since childhood, blacks were intellectually inferior to whites, plain and simple, and thus unfit to administer organizations or institutions successfully. Not surprisingly, the conflict proved irreconcilable, with the two nearly coming to blows on more than one occasion. Despite having won twenty-one games for the Indians the previous year, the Cy Young Award two years before that, and 39 percent of all the team's victories over three years, Perry was traded to the Texas Rangers in June. "Things just didn't work out," he said.[36]

Perry had wanted to avoid just this sort of uncomfortable situation by moving his family back home, where he found the rules, regulations, and conventions of life much more congenial than in San Francisco or Cleveland. But much had changed since Perry had left in 1958. The public schools had implemented a "total integration plan" after losing federal funding in 1969 for failure to comply with the Civil Rights Act. His old haunts, such as Griffin's Quick Lunch and the Shamrock Restaurant, no longer seated whites only. The physical walls of segregation, in fact, had been knocked down all over town. Barriers to racial equality remained, however, in large part due to the unrelenting resolve of resentful white residents. Those families who could afford it, the Perrys among them, sent their children to Martin Academy just outside of town, one of hundreds of private "seg-academies" that sprouted up across the South in defiance of integration. Martin Academy emphasized saluting the flag, in-class prayer, personal discipline, and strength of community. Such "white flight," however, inevitably resulted in diminishing community support and the overall quality of the local public schools.[37]

Defiance of this sort fueled the "new conservatism" of Senator Jesse Helms, whom Perry staunchly supported over the years. Helms's popularity stemmed from his ability to capitalize on the frustrations of white rural North Carolinians, who deeply resented the rapid changes in the 1950s and '60s. He fashioned a strong populist appeal that rejected the civil rights revolution, the growth of the federal government at the expense of state and local power, rising taxes, and campus unrest and bohemian counterculture. Perry found hippies particularly offensive and, in many ways, had more outward difficulty dealing with the new long-haired breed of white ballplayers and journalists in the '60s and '70s than he did with blacks. When Helms championed hard work, self-reliance, and moral behavior, he struck a chord with Perry and, ultimately, millions of likeminded southerners. So motivated, Perry appeared numerous times in campaign commercials on television for Helms, served as co-chairman of the Farmers for Helms organization, and briefly contemplated, with Helms urging him on, a bid for Congress himself in the mid 1980s. Around Williamston, longtime residents praised Perry, with the utmost of respect, for having "stayed loyal."[38]

By 1980, Perry seemed not only "comfortable" with his life; he seemed to have it all. Veteran sportswriter Ron Fimrite certainly thought so when he visited Farm Life to do a story on Perry for *Sports Illustrated* on the occasion of Perry's 295th career victory, five shy of one of baseball's most hallowed milestones. But Fimrite became more intrigued by Perry the farmer than Perry the pitcher, especially after an all-day tour in Perry's pickup truck over the dusty roads that twisted through his farm, Farm Life, and Williamston. "People like him here," Fimrite discovered. "He's a good farmer." Though portraying Perry as "the archetypal rural Southerner," Fimrite did not engage him on the issue of race other than a brief mention of the Frank Robinson affair. Such an omission did not differentiate this story from most other accounts of contemporary white southern ballplayers, popular and scholarly alike. Though racism reigned in the rural South and the major leagues for much of the twentieth century, the penchant among writers to romanticize the southern country boy, not only in baseball but in American popular culture more broadly, has shielded star players from such scrutiny. Fimrite focused instead on Perry's fiercely competitive nature, both on the mound and on the farm, ending the story with his own words: "I don't ever go out there figuring to lose. I'm not made that way." Perry was indeed "bound for glory" in baseball, but "made that way" or not, disaster loomed on the farm.[39]

Perry's generation was the last to come of age in the segregated South and also the last generation of sharecroppers. Farming, as with race relations, had changed dramatically since Perry left Farm Life in 1958. Mechanization transformed production and, in the process, made farming a large-scale, expensive enterprise, tenants a vanishing breed, and mules an endangered species. Powerful diesel tractors (sound-proofed and air-conditioned) pulled massive eight-row plows, harrows, and planters with ease, cultivating up to seventy-five acres per day. The tobacco harvester, every bit as revolutionary as the cotton gin in a much earlier era, brought sweeping changes in the production of the golden leaf. Instead of the 350 man-hours per acre that an all-hand-labor operation required, the harvester and accompanying machines performed the task in a mere fifty-eight hours. Or, put another way, while it previously would have taken sixteen tenant families to farm Perry's 410 acres (at the standard twenty-five acres per family), he now could get along fine with just three or four hands. The immense savings in field labor produced a mass exodus of sharecroppers, including more than a few of Perry's old neighbors, most of whom pulled up stakes and moved to southern cities for low-paying industrial jobs.[40]

Perry, however, reaped the benefits of the new "push-button" agriculture. Every year, the farm took up more of his life, and when he retired from the game in 1983, it became his life, consuming not only his time and energy but much of his savings as well. The nationwide agricultural boom of the 1970s prompted farmers to rush into debt to buy more land and more farm equipment, and Perry followed the trend. Not a year went by when he did not borrow money against the rising value of his land to add to his acreage and increase production. By the end of the decade, his farm had grown twice as large. Farm equipment dealers from miles around recognized Perry's pickup truck by sight and beamed with anticipation when he walked into their showrooms. No more extravagant than most of his peers, Perry, like the vast majority, believed that rising commodity prices and lower interest rates would carry over into the next decade. As late as 1981, his wife could quip, "That's the third tractor he's bought in a month. Why, that man can't afford to farm."[41]

Even before then, however, the situation was no joke. As early as 1977, favorable market conditions began to turn for the worse. That year, and for several thereafter, farmers produced at record levels, causing a sharp drop in commodity prices. The resulting loss of farm income from overproduction alone made it difficult for farm debtors to make their loan payments. That competition among optimistic farmers for more cropland had driven the cost of farm real estate sky-high made it even more difficult. That the Federal Reserve Board began raising interest rates in 1979 as a means of curbing inflation, the debtor's best friend, made it still more difficult. The addition of a lethal combination of developments—Jimmy Carter's embargo on selling grain to the Soviets, which cost farmers a big chunk of the world market; Ronald Reagan's tax cuts, which kept interest rates high; and farmers' penchant for trying to produce their way out of debt—then sent agriculture spiraling into a devastating economic crisis. In North Carolina, two bad crop years in the 1980s did not help. In 1986, the *Charlotte Observer* went so far as to declare "a southern rural depression," and for good reason. At that point, farm prices had fallen to their lowest levels relative to the cost of production and the cost of living since the early 1930s.[42]

Perry had never walked away from a challenge in baseball, and he did not give up his farm without a fight. But he could not will his way to win against prevailing market forces. In eight of the ten seasons between 1977 and 1986, the Perry farm lost at least $100,000. Each year, he tried to predict which crop—tobacco, corn, soybeans, peanuts—would bring the highest market value, not wanting to acknowledge that all commodity prices remained on a steep downward swing. Neither his investments nor his stubbornness brought much return. "Three years ago, I thought corn was going to be $4 a bushel and beans would go for $9 a bushel," he said in 1985. "This year, corn is going for $1.50 a bushel and beans are selling for $4. All farmers want is a fair price for their product. But we're not getting that now. It's just arithmetic, and it's catching up with us." The arithmetic finally overtook Perry in 1986; he planted one more crop of corn, putting in $350 an acre but getting back only $150. "We can't continue," he told Blanche. On July 31, the Perrys filed for bankruptcy, listing total assets of $1,143,600 and total claims (from twenty-five creditors) of $1,244,850. Like 13,000 other farmers in North Carolina between 1982 and 1987 (roughly one in five), Perry essentially produced himself out of business. Unlike most others, however, Perry's loss made headlines, from the *Williamston Enterprise* to the *New York Times*. Admitting failure was not easy for someone who had prided himself on being in control. Publicly, Perry could only say, "It's just a farming situation that couldn't be helped." Privately, he deeply regretted having to abandon the farm and not being able to eventually give it to his son, Jack. "I'd just be passing on a liability," he lamented.[43]

Here, Perry spoke as a farmer, not a ballplayer. For more than two decades, sportswriters had sought him out for interviews, both after games and for longer feature stories, knowing that he almost always had candid, animated, and entertaining insights to offer. But like most contemporaries whose farms went under during the crisis of the 1980s, Perry barely knew how to respond to his bankruptcy. While farmers struggled to succeed in the face of more and more factors beyond their control, they believed in their hearts, often until the bitter end and at times even after, that hard work and right values would stave off foreclosure and pull them through the bad times eventually. Because the changes in the agricultural economy that drove people off the land were so complex and difficult to comprehend (even for economists), farmers' feelings of helplessness when trying to come to terms with failure only increased as the crisis deepened. As one farmer from South Carolina put it, "I hated to even admit, it was very hard to tell anybody that I'm quitting. But since that time, farmers that I know are good farmers, I mean they farmed right, they had to quit [also]." Many members of this generation of

Not even Perry's celebrity could sell enough peanuts to prevent his farm from failing during the agricultural crisis of the 1980s.

Photograph by Laura Root; peanut bag in author's possession.

farmers, Perry among them, still search for a satisfactory explanation for what happened to them.[44]

For Perry, the bankruptcy began a string of personal tragedies. In 1987, Blanche, his wife of twenty-eight years, died in a car crash; fourteen months later, his father, Evan, having just recovered from a hip transplant and quadruple bypass surgery, drowned in a boating accident; and in 2005, his son, Jack, died at the young age of thirty-seven, ending a three-year battle with leukemia, just one month before the Giants retired Perry's jersey number 36 in a ceremony at what is now AT&T Park in San Francisco. Perry responded in perfect character. "You got to pick up and start over agin'," he stated. "Too many people still countin' on you, to just lay down. You remember all the good times, and you keep goin'." A lifelong friend, Jim Ward, called Perry "a mountain of strength" and marveled at his "mental toughness and determination" in the face of such anguish—a phrase he also used repeatedly to characterize Perry's pitching and farming.[45]

Throughout his life, baseball and farming reinforced each other in Perry's mind. Both had always carried the expectation that hard work and dedication would pay off in the long run—not with every crop or every pitch, but certainly in the long run. Perry has a lot of Farm Life in him, even today. He still drives home ideas forcefully with his colorful language and country wit; still shouts into the phone as though talking on the old party line; and still wakes up with the sun ready to put in a full day's work.[46] But Perry left the farm almost twenty-five years ago now. For awhile, he coached baseball at Limestone College in Gaffney, South Carolina, where he taught his pitching staff the "hard slider." He retired in 1991, the same year of his induction into the Hall of Fame, and has since lived comfortably on his major league pension and personal memorabilia business (which sells, for the more discerning collector, autographed jars of petroleum jelly).[47] The rural culture that gave him his work ethic, ingenuity, and competitive edge on the pitcher's mound, making him an icon of popular culture, ultimately seduced and humiliated him on the farm. That rural culture now exists primarily in the past and in the memories and idiosyncrasies of its last generation.

EPILOGUE

Vintage Ball

On a brisk, sunny fall Saturday afternoon, the Farmers Branch Mustangs, Fort Concho Enterprise, Richmond Giants, Buffalo Gap Chips, and Tusculum Freethinkers, on the invitation of the host team, the Boerne White Sox, gathered from around the state for the Fourth Annual Veterans Cup. The ball field at the village lake had no diamond or dirt infield, no chalked foul lines, and no outfield fence. It sloped noticeably downward from home plate (a white dish) toward right field and the shimmering lake below and contained numerous bumps and dips in the spacious outfield. Burlap sacks stuffed with sawdust served as bases, and flags positioned behind first and third marked the out-of-bounds territory. A backstop made of chicken wire held a chalkboard for keeping score and a cowbell for ringing in tallies. Perhaps 150 spectators crowded the area behind the dish and around the field, some sitting in chairs but most standing. In addition to the game, they enjoyed the polkas and waltzes played by the village brass band, assembled behind third base, and homemade pie for two bits a slice. Kristy "Horseshoe" Watson, the host team's manager, started the festivities with a warm welcome to one and all, an explanation of the rules, and an announcement that just enough visiting ballists (players) had arrived to field an opposing team, with others still in route. The Blind Tom (umpire) asked the two team captains to grab a bat at the bottom and proceed fist over fist toward the top with the last hand over the knob determining which team would bat first. "Striker to the line," yelled the Blind Tom to the first batter. "Huzzah!" roared the crowd in response. And the match began.[1]

This scene, in many of its details, might easily have taken place at Uncle Seth Doubleday's farm on Otsego Lake in the 1820s, the Phinney farm just outside of Cooperstown in 1840 (perhaps with Abner Doubleday and Abner Graves present), the Y in Davisville in 1887, a pasture field on La Bahia Prairie in south-central Texas at the turn of the twentieth century, Oak View Park on the Feller farm in the early 1930s, the old field next to the elevator bins in Milroy in the late 1940s, or the Farm Life field where the Perry brothers came of age in the 1950s. Instead, it played out in City Lake Park in Boerne, Texas, thirty miles northwest of San Antonio in the year 2010 (November 6, to be precise) and in a game sponsored by the Texas Vintage Base Ball Association (TVBBA), organized in October 2007 to pay homage to the game as it was played in the 1850s and 1860s. The TVBBA is loosely associated with the Vintage Base Ball Association (VBBA), created in 1996 and containing, by this time, more than 250 amateur clubs scattered throughout the country. *Loosely* is the operative word in that vintage ball, like much of baseball over the past two hundred years in rural and small-town America, remains determinedly locally oriented and played, both literally and figuratively, at the grassroots level. Teams adopt old-style rules and customs, determine proper behavior, design (and often make) their own uniforms, schedule their own games, and raise their own funds.[2]

Loose does not mean frivolous, however—far from it. While the players and spectators enjoy themselves at the games, all see vintage ball as a serious affair. Most of the teams in the TVBBA are affiliated with educational institutions of historical parks and organizations. The city's agricultural heritage center and museum, for example, sponsor the Boerne White Sox. Ballists conceive of the games as part living history demonstration (like quiltmaking or blacksmithing) and part historical theater (along the lines of Civil War reenactments). Teams have conducted considerable research over the years in an effort to capture the essence of the mid-nineteenth-century small-town game. They dress in uniforms appropriate to the time period, ranging from jeans and suspenders to more dapper Knickerbocker-style re-creations, play by 1860 rules (as they interpret them), and adopt the vernacular of the old ball game, as epitomized by their insistence on *base ball* (two words). In some instances, they may stray beyond what sticklers might deem historically accurate. The Boerne White Sox, for example, derive their name and uniform from the early-twentieth-century (1914) local team, and the rules they and the other Texas teams use amount to a rough amalgam of townball and baseball. Their unquestioned devotion produces players captivated by the egalitarian and "gentlemanly" nature of the mid-nineteenth-century game. They routinely congratulate opposing players on good plays, assist the lone Blind Tom behind the dish with making calls at the other bases, and impose fines of two to four bits (small in amount but large in symbolism) for spitting, swearing, or other unsportsmanlike behavior. Many participants readily admit that their love for the old game stems at least in part from their disillusionment with the modern, money-driven professional one. "We're in it for the joy of the game," summarized Bob "Bonecrusher" Wettemann, a pioneer organizer of vintage ball in Texas. "It's about having fun and exercising a love of history."[3]

While historical in nature, the games are not staged reenactments but fast-paced, unscripted athletic contests characterized by both tradition and spontaneity. The game in Boerne serves as a case in point. Most striking to the casual observer, at first, is the equipment, or lack thereof: no gloves, no face masks or chest protectors for the catcher (who, quite appropriately, stood a few feet behind the batter), and no batting helmets. Even with a somewhat larger and softer hand-sewn ball, the lack of protective gear makes for plenty of swollen hands and dislocated fingers, which veterans like Debra "Little Egypt" Reid delight in showing off. While most of the ballists were in their thirties and forties, they welcomed with open arms Clancy "Spitball" Haas, age ten, and octogenarian Elmer "Flyboy" Bergmann, who pitched two innings. Women, dressed like the men, are encouraged to play, though on this day only two or three took the field. Toward the middle of the afternoon, spectators were invited to join the game and play for an inning or two, which several did with immense glee. Ballists congratulate each other by shaking hands; they do not, under any circumstances, exchange high fives. Such an act, it became clear early on, would be a boodler (an ungentlemanly maneuver) and as such would simply not have occurred to them.[4]

More of the rules, customs, and idiosyncrasies became evident as the game moved along. Scouts (outfielders) made outs by catching the apple (ball) on the fly or on one bounce. The savvy ones knew when to let a high fly drop intentionally for an easier catch. On one sparkling play, the rover (shortstop) snagged a low line drive (barehanded, of course) on the first bounce and tagged the runner heading into second for an unassisted double play. The next inning, the midfielder (center fielder) caught a lazy fly ball on one bounce for an out and, in one motion, threw a bullet across the field where the basetender (third baseman) caught the ball on one bounce, pivoted, and tagged out the runner trying to advance for another nifty double play. The two right field scouts in this game had the job not only of playing their position but, more importantly, of keeping the apple from rolling all the way down into the lake. With only the one homemade ball, the game would have ended right then and there, had they failed. Feeders (pitchers) threw underhand from forty-five feet away, and the Blind Tom called no balls or strikes; strikers remained up until reaching base safely or making an out (though the Blind Tom has the authority to admonish the feeder for throwing too many unhittable pitches or the hitter for taking too many good ones). Runners were not allowed to slide into bases or overrun first base. Upon scoring (crossing the dish), the jubilant runner continued on to the backstop, asked the scorekeeper for "permission to tally an ace," and, to more cries of "Huzzah!" from the crowd, rang the bell triumphantly. The game came to an end after about an hour and a half—not for any official reason (or because the apple rolled into the lake) but because everyone just got tired. The final score seemed irrelevant. "Vintage ball is for everyone," emphasized one ballist. "It's low-key, high-fun, down-home entertainment."[5]

The Boerne game offered an idealized version of history, to be sure. Vintage base ball allows modern-day players and spectators to express a loose, if deeply felt, bundle of ideas and assumptions about the nature of mid-nineteenth-century rural America. The most noticeable flaw to the authenticity of their approach is that today's teams are not segregated by gender or race, as they most certainly would have been historically. In addition, the emphasis on gentlemanly behavior masks the contemporary realities of gambling, hard-fought competition, and the reactions of winners and losers. And while the colorful nicknames and terminology are all in good fun, they invoke a sense of nostalgia and sentimentality about "the old ball game" in the "good old days" that trivializes the broader cultural significance of the game that vintage ballists are trying to re-create.[6]

Nonetheless, the phenomenon of vintage ball is by no means trivial. It serves as a reminder that there is more to baseball—much more—than major league baseball and that the game has, over the years, been a local pastime every bit as much as a national pastime. Vintage ball also reinforces the fact that baseball has long flourished as a distinguishing characteristic of rural America, not just of urban America, the standard narrative of the game's history notwithstanding. The Boerne White Sox intentionally choose to play in a setting unmistakably rural rather than, for example, the complex of finely manicured baseball and softball diamonds a few miles away next to the freeway near the center of town. They intend to teach what amounts to a history lesson of the game played by farmers, storekeepers, and laborers 150 years ago. "You can tell a person what small-town life in Texas was like in the nineteenth century, or you can show him," boasted one particularly proud ballist.[7]

This book, in essence, serves to expand on that much-needed history lesson and, in that spirit, concludes with three of its own—the first one harking back to the "idol of origins" phenomenon. "In any study seeking the origins of a human activity," warned Marc Bloch, "there lurks the danger of confusing ancestry with explanation." Nowhere has this been more true than with baseball history. "Originologists" of the game, to borrow psychologist Erik Erikson's apt phrase, have pursued, with considerable irony, a curiously ahistorical approach, making "finds" of early ballgames in obscure sources an end in itself. The discovery of the 1816 anti-ball measure in Cooperstown provides a case in point. The irony of banning public ballplaying in the place known for the birth of baseball has not escaped scholars—indeed, it has often delighted them. But few (if any) have studied the ordinance in its immediate or long-term historical context—its significance to Cooperstown itself or, even less so, to the formative years of the American republic. Similarly, scores of enthusiasts have pored over the famous correspondence between Abner Graves and Albert Spalding without investigating the rich detail and historical context of Graves's reminiscences. While the letters have little or no relevance to the ongoing search for the roots of the game, they offer insights galore into the actual history of baseball in Cooperstown. We would do well to adhere to Bloch's insistence that "a historical phenomenon can never be understood apart from its moment in time" or, to paraphrase Jules Tygiel's sage advice once again, to take our eyes *off* the ball when doing baseball history. Perhaps the greatest irony here is that the less-scholarly vintage ballists may have more to teach us along these lines than do the originoligists themselves.[8]

That is certainly the case with regard to rural baseball, which, for too long, has been associated primarily with nostalgia, romantic imagery, and pastoral flights of fancy. Not that such mystical qualities are without meaning or significance. Baseball, lesson two teaches us, does in fact capture the *essence* of the American rural experience. There is something important about the notion (true or not) that Americans think of baseball in rural terms, from Abner Doubleday and Cooperstown to Kevin Costner and *Field of Dreams*. Baseball and agrarianism, in that sense, are very much intertwined. Even in today's predominantly nonrural culture, rural culture continues to be expressed through baseball. Where else other than a major league ballpark does someone sitting in the middle of a row of thirty seats pass a $20 bill down through the many different hands—black, white, brown, male, female, gay, straight—to the hot dog man with the complete and total expectation that they will get back not only the hot dog but every last penny of change? That innate trust and sense of cooperation roots in our agrarian heritage, dating back to the days before the market complicated farmers' lives. It epitomizes what Thomas Jefferson thought a nation of farmers would become. Certainly Will Feller understood this enduring image of farmers. As a modern, commercially successful, technologically sophisticated farmer, Will effectively *manipulated* traditional images of rural people in order to fashion an attractive—and financially lucrative—persona for his son, Bob. So, too, did Gaylord Perry understand how to reap the benefits of his rural background with his "I reckons," "yonders," "y'alls," "fixin' tos," and country-boy, aw-shucks demeanor.

Yet neither the Fellers, Perry, Bob Zwach, Spike Dolan, Grover Williams, Dick Hoover, the Davisville Oletas, Seth Doubleday, nor any of the other historical actors in this book embraced baseball for its abstract qualities—agrarian, nostalgic, pastoral, romantic, or otherwise. For them, baseball's appeal rested on real, tangible attributes. Why then, our final lesson asks, did the game become so popular among rural people in the early nineteenth century and remain so well into the twentieth? On one level, farmers and townspeople simply enjoyed the excitement and camaraderie of the game. Baseball offered recreation, a distraction from their arduous daily routines, and an opportunity for hardworking farm families to gather for a pleasant Sunday afternoon. Yet the widespread, sustained passion for baseball among farm people over the decades indicates that the game had a deeper, more complex cultural meaning than such an explanation suggests. Far from just a simple pastime, baseball became an expression, indeed a symbol, of the way farmers perceived day-to-day reality. With the emergence of market-oriented agriculture in the early nineteenth century, that reality became increasingly defined by skill, competitiveness, and chance: skill, with regard to their ability to produce high-quality crops in prodigious amounts; competitiveness, in terms of their insatiable appetite for achievement in a world of change and unpredictability; and chance, in that for all their skill and competitiveness, a spell of bad weather or a run of bad luck in the marketplace could bring failure, misery, and frustration. Given that perspective on life, farmers and townspeople preferred games that demanded skill, competitiveness, and chance—and baseball, with its intricate set of rules and rituals, action and suspense, and winner-take-all mentality offered them everything they wanted and needed, and more.

Rural baseball now exists primarily in memories and on vintage fields—not because the game has lost popularity but because there are just barely enough farmers left to field a team. For much of American history, however, baseball served as the farmers' game.

NOTES

INTRODUCTION: ABNER DOUBLEDAY AND BASEBALL'S IDOL OF ORIGINS

1. Terry L. Beckenbaugh, "Abner Doubleday," in *Encyclopedia of the American Civil War: A Political, Social, and Military History*, ed. David Stephen Heidler, Jeanne T. Heidler, and David J. Coles (New York: W. W. Norton, 2000), 611–612; Larry Tagg, *The Generals of Gettysburg: Appraisal of the Leaders of America's Greatest Battle* (El Dorado Hills, CA: Savas Publishing, 1998), 25–27; Brooks C. Simpson and Matthew E. Van Atta, "Doubleday, Abner," in *American National Biography*, ed. John A. Garraty and Mark C. Carnes (Oxford: Oxford University Press, 1999), 6:779–780; *Cooperstown Crier*, Sept. 30, 1999 (part of a series entitled "In Our Past," by Tom Heitz); Mark McGuire, "The Ongoing Fable of Baseball," *New York Archives* 2 (Spring 2003): 9.

2. Albert G. Spalding, "The Origin of Baseball," *Spalding's Official Base Ball Guide*, 1906 (Chicago: A. G. Spalding & Bros., 1906), 6 (quote); *Cooperstown Crier*, Sept. 2, 9, 16, and 23, 1999; Harold Seymour, "How Baseball Began," *New York Historical Society Quarterly* 40 (October 1956): 369–371; Robert W. Henderson, *Ball, Bat, and Bishop: The Origin of Ball Games* (1947; reprint, Urbana: University of Illinois Press, 2001), 170–181; David Block, *Baseball before We Knew It: A Search for the Roots of the Game* (Lincoln: University of Nebraska Press, 2005), 1–14.

3. Many of the pertinent documents, including excerpts from *Spalding's Official Base Ball Guide* and the commission's final report, are reprinted in Dean A. Sullivan, ed., *Early Innings: A Documentary History of Baseball, 1825–1908* (Lincoln: University of Nebraska Press, 1995), 279–295 (quotes 284, 287). Numerous others, including the Graves-Spalding exchange and the responses to Sullivan's queries, are in the John Doyle Papers, A. Bartlett Giamatti Research Center, National Baseball Hall of Fame and Museum, Cooperstown, NY. See also Block, *Baseball before We Knew It*, 14–16; Harry Paxton, "The Myths of Cooperstown," *Saturday Evening Post*, Jan. 30, 1960, 18–19, 62, 64; and Victor Salvatore, "The Man Who Didn't Invent Baseball," *American Heritage* 34 (June/July 1983): 65–67.

4. A. G. Spalding to the Special Base Ball Commission, July 28, 1907, reprinted in Sullivan, *Early Innings*, 291 (1st quote); Abraham Mills to Col. Edward Fowler, Dec. 20, 1907 (2nd, 3rd, and 4th quotes); Mills to William Rankin, Jan. 6 and 20, 1908;

Rankin to Mills, June 21, 1908 (5th quote), A. G. Mills Papers, Giamatti Research Center; Henderson, *Ball, Bat, and Bishop*, 179–180; John Thorn, "Abner Cartwright," *Nine: A Journal of Baseball History and Culture* 18 (Fall 2009): 125–129.

5. Abraham Mills, "Final Decision of the Special Baseball Commission," Dec. 30, 1907, reprinted in Sullivan, *Early Innings*, 295; Rankin to Mills, June 21, 1908.

6. *New York Evening Post*, Mar. 20, 1908 (1st and 2nd quotes), along with numerous other such clippings, Mills Papers; *Freeman's Journal*, Mar. 26, 1908 (3rd quote), transcript of article, "Origins of Baseball" file, Giamatti Research Center.

7. Albert G. Spalding, *America's National Game* (New York: American Sports, 1911), 17–26; Henderson, *Ball, Bat, and Bishop*, 170; Block, *Baseball before We Knew It*, 17; Ralph Birdsall, *The Story of Cooperstown* (Cooperstown, NY: Arthur H. Christ, 1917), 233 (quote); John Allen Krout, *Annals of American Sport* (New Haven, CT: Yale University Press, 1929), 117.

8. *A Century of Baseball* (Cooperstown, NY: Freeman's Journal, 1940); James A. Vlasich, *A Legend for the Legendary: The Origin of the Baseball Hall of Fame* (Bowling Green, OH: Bowling Green State University Popular Press, 1990); George Grella, "The Hall of Fame and the American Mythology," in *Baseball and American Culture: Across the Diamond*, ed. Edward J. Rielly (New York: Haworth Press, 2003), 151–160; Brian and Becky Nielsen, *Around Cooperstown in Vintage Postcards* (Charleston, SC: Arcadia, 2000), 98; Block, *Baseball before We Knew It*, 17–18; Steven A. Riess, "The Lead-off Batter Who Slugged Home Runs: Harold Seymour and the Making of the History of Baseball," *Journal of Sport History* 29 (Spring 2002): 136; Richard Peterson, *Extra Innings: Writing on Baseball* (Urbana: University of Illinois Press, 2001), 125–126; Wes D. Gehring, *Mr. Deeds Goes to Yankee Stadium: Baseball Films in the Capra Tradition* (Jefferson, NC: McFarland, 2004); *Cooperstown Crier*, Sept. 30, 1999; "Sport: Immortals," *Time*, Jan. 31, 1938, 56 (quote).

9. Will Irwin, "Baseball: Before the Professionals Came," *Collier's*, May 8, 1909, 12–13; Alfred H. Spink, *The National Game*, 2nd ed. (St. Louis: The National Game, 1911), 54 (Rankin quote); Block, *Baseball before We Knew It*, 16–17.

10. Robert W. Henderson, "How Baseball Began," *Bulletin of the New York Public Library* 41 (April 1937): 287–291; Henderson, "Baseball and Rounders," *Bulletin of the New York Public Library* 43 (April 1939): 303–314; Henderson, *Bat, Ball, and Bishop*.

11. Henderson, *Bat, Ball, and Bishop*, 170–194 (all quotes).

12. Ibid., 132–169; Block, *Baseball before We Knew It*, 18–19.

13. Leonard Koppett, "Foreword to the Illinois Paperback," in Henderson, *Bat, Ball, and Bishop*, xiii–xv; Block, *Baseball before We Knew It*, 55–56; Salvatore, "Man Who Didn't Invent Baseball," 65 (quote).

14. Harold Peterson, "Baseball's Johnny Appleseed," *Sports Illustrated*, Apr. 14, 1969, 56–76, and *The Man Who Invented Baseball* (New York: Scribner's, 1973); Henderson, *Bat, Ball, and Bishop*, 195–196 (quotes); William J. Ryczek, *Baseball's First Inning: A History of the National Pastime through the Civil War* (Jefferson, NC: McFarland, 2009), 28–36.

15. Harold Seymour, *Baseball: The Early Years* (Oxford: Oxford University Press, 1960); David Q. Voigt, *American Baseball: From the Gentleman's Sport to the Commis-*

sioner System (Norman: University of Oklahoma Press, 1966); Benjamin G. Rader, *Baseball: A History of America's Game* (Urbana: University of Illinois Press, 1992); Gunther Barth, *City People: The Rise of Modern City Culture in Nineteenth-Century America* (Oxford: Oxford University Press, 1980), 148–191; John Thorn, *Baseball in the Garden of Eden: The Secret History of the Early Game* (New York: Simon & Schuster, 2011).

16. John Thorn, "The Father of Baseball? You Probably Never Heard of Him," *Elysian Fields Quarterly: The Baseball Review* 11 (Winter 1992): 85–91, and "Abner Cartwright," 128; Nathan Adams Downey, "On Baseball When the Game Was Very New," *New York Times*, Apr. 13, 1980; Randall Brown, "How Baseball Began," *The National Pastime: A Review of Baseball History* 24 (2004): 51–54; "Dr. Daniel Adams and the Knickerbockers of New York," in Sullivan, *Early Innings*, 13–18; Henderson, "Baseball and Rounders," 313; Block, *Baseball before We Knew It*, 20; Ryczek, *Baseball's First Inning*, 28–36.

17. "The Constitution of the Olympic Ball Club of Philadelphia" and "The New York Base Ball Clubs," both in Sullivan, *Early Innings*, 5–8, 19–20; George A. Thompson Jr., "New York Baseball, 1823," *National Pastime* 21 (2001): 6–8; John Thorn, "The Magnolia, the Knickerbocker, and the Age of Flash," *Base Ball: A Journal of the Early Game* 2 (Fall 2008): 100–115; Thorn, "Abner Cartwright," 128; John Thorn, "Important Early Baseball Find," *Thorn Pricks*, Nov. 11, 2007, http://thornpricks.blogspot.com/2007/11/important-early-baseball-find.html (accessed Mar. 12, 2010); Peter Morris, *But Didn't We Have Fun: An Informal History of Baseball's Pioneer Era, 1843–1870* (Chicago: Ivan R. Dee, 2008), 11–25.

18. "The Earliest Known Newspaper Report of a 'Bass-Ball' Challenge," in Sullivan, *Early Innings*, 1–2 (quote 2); *New York Times*, June 3, 1991; *Cooperstown Crier*, Oct. 28, 1999.

19. *Albany Times Union*, May 12, 2004; *New York Times*, May 12, 2004; John Thorn, "1791 and All That: Baseball and the Berkshires," *Base Ball* 1 (Spring 2007): 119–126; Thomas L. Altherr, "'A Place Leavel Enough to Play Ball': Baseball and Baseball-type Games in the Colonial Era, Revolutionary War, and Early American Republic," *Nine* 8 (Spring 2000): 15–49; Henderson, "Baseball and Rounders," 313.

20. *Cooperstown Crier*, Oct. 21, 1999; David Block, "The Story of William Bray's Diary," *Base Ball* 1 (Fall 2007): 5–11; Block, *Baseball before We Knew It*, 21, 94–104 (quote 94), 303; Seymour, "How Baseball Began," 376; Henderson, *Bat, Ball, and Bishop*, 3–31, 70–78, 132–137.

21. See, for example, Thomas R. Heitz and John Thorn, "Early Bat and Ball Games," along with the many bibliographies, biographies, and listservs available on the Society for American Baseball Research Web site, www.sabr.org (accessed Mar. 12, 2010). Similar resources are available at *Project Protoball*, www.retrosheet.org/Protoball, and *Thorn Pricks*, http://thornpricks.blogspot.com (both accessed Mar. 12, 2010). See also David Block's extensive annotated bibliography of early baseball history in *Baseball before We Knew It*, 163–222, 275–286, and Thomas L. Altherr, "Chucking the Old Apple: Recent Discoveries of Pre-1840 North American Ball Games," *Base Ball* 2 (Spring 2008): 29–43.

22. Marc Bloch, *The Historian's Craft* (New York: Alfred A. Knopf, 1953), 29–35 (quote 29); Peter A. Coclanis, "Framing Southeast Asia's Economic History: Cycles of Globalization over *la Longue Durée*," *Journal of the Historical Society* 8 (Mar. 2008): 5; Stephen Jay Gould, "The Creation Myths of Cooperstown," *Natural History* 98 (Nov. 1989): 14–22.

23. Larry R. Gerlach, "Not Quite Ready for Prime Time: Baseball History, 1983–1993," *Journal of Sport History* 21 (Summer 1994): 103–137 (quote 129). The major exception to the emphasis on major league baseball is Harold Seymour, *Baseball: The People's Game* (Oxford: Oxford University Press, 1990).

24. See the studies cited in n. 15, esp. Thorn, *Baseball in the Garden of Eden*. On the dearth of rural sport studies, see Steven A. Riess, "The Historiography of American Sport," *OAH Magazine of History* 7 (Summer 1992): 10–14.

25. Peterson, *Man Who Invented Baseball*; Barth, *City People*, 148–191; Block, *Baseball before We Knew It*, 80–93; Steven Gelber, "Working at Playing: The Culture of the Workplace and the Rise of Baseball," *Journal of Social History* 16 (Summer 1983): 3–22 (quote 6); Frederick Ivor-Campbell, "Knickerbocker Base Ball: The Birth and Infancy of the Modern Game," *Base Ball* 1 (Fall 2007): 55–66.

26. What little we do know about rural baseball comes largely from biographies and autobiographies—usually brief first chapters—of famous professional players who were born and raised on farms. See, for example, Ty Cobb with Al Stump, *My Life in Baseball: The True Record* (New York: Doubleday, 1961); Reed Browning, *Cy Young: A Baseball Life* (Amherst: University of Massachusetts Press, 2000); Henry W. Thomas, *Walter Johnson: Baseball's Big Train* (Lincoln: University of Nebraska Press, 1998); Doug Feldmann, *Dizzy and the Gas House Gang: The 1934 St. Louis Cardinals and Depression-Era Baseball* (Jefferson, NC: McFarland, 2000); Timothy M. Gay, *Tris Speaker: The Rough-and-Tumble Life of a Baseball Legend* (Lincoln: University of Nebraska Press, 2005); Jim "Catfish" Hunter and Armen Keteyian, *Catfish: My Life in Baseball* (New York: McGraw-Hill, 1988); Enos Slaughter with Kevin Reid, *Country Hardball: The Autobiography of Enos "Country" Slaughter* (Greensboro, NC: Tudor Publishers, 1991); and Fred Stein, *Mel Ott: The Little Giant of Baseball* (Jefferson, NC: McFarland, 1999). Other notable, if scattered, contributions include William E. Akin, *West Virginia Baseball: A History, 1865–2000* (Jefferson, NC: McFarland, 2006); Thomas L. Altherr, "Basepaths and Baselines: The Agricultural and Surveying Contexts of the Emergence of Baseball," *Base Ball* 5 (Fall 2011): 63–76; Carl M. Becker, "Crossing Bats: Baseball in the Villages of the Upper Miami Valley, 1865–1900," *Nine* 10 (Spring 2002): 46–70; Paul Edwards, "Farmers and Fastballs: The Culture of Baseball in Depression Era Northeast Arkansas," *Arkansas Review: A Journal of Delta Studies* 41 (August 2010): 109–122; William H. Mullins, "The Impact of Rural Culture on a Baseball Career: Carl Hubbell of Meeker, Oklahoma," *Nine* 12 (September 2003): 102–114; Peter Morris, *Baseball Fever: Early Baseball in Michigan* (Ann Arbor: University of Michigan Press, 2003), esp. chap. 10; Seymour, *Baseball: The People's Game*, parts of chap. 13 and 14; and L. M. Sutter, *Ball, Bat and Bitumen: A History of Coalfield Baseball in the Appalachian South* (Jefferson, NC: McFarland, 2009). For an explanation of why rural historians themselves have not exposed the

standard narrative's urban bias, see my article, "Abner Doubleday, Marc Bloch, and the Cultural Significance of Baseball in Rural America," *Agricultural History* 85 (Winter 2011): 1–20.

27. A. Bartlett Giamatti, "The Green Fields of the Mind," in Kenneth S. Robson, ed., *A Great and Glorious Game: Baseball Writings of A Bartlett Giamatti* (Chapel Hill, NC: Algonquin, 1998), 7 (quote); Jon Miller with Mark Hyman, *Confessions of a Baseball Purist* (Baltimore: Johns Hopkins University Press, 1998), 255 (quote); Roger Angell, "The Sporting Scene: Up at the Hall," *New Yorker*, August 31, 1987, 35–66 (quote 37); Bruce Catton, "The Great American Game," *American Heritage* 10 (April 1959); 17–25, 86; Thomas Boswell, *Why Time Begins on Opening Day* (Garden City, NY: Doubleday, 1984) and *The Heart of the Order* (New York: Penguin Books, 1990), 329 (quote); Jules Tygiel, *Past Time: Baseball as History* (Oxford: Oxford University Press, 2000), 3–14.

28. Clifford Geertz, *The Interpretation of Cultures* (New York: Basic Books, 1973), 3–30, 89, 412–453. See also T. H. Breen, "Horses and Gentlemen: The Cultural Significance of Gambling among the Gentry of Virginia," *William and Mary Quarterly* 34 (April 1977): 239–257; Johan Huizinga, *Homo Ludens: A Study of the Play Element in Culture* (Boston: Beacon, 1955); C. L. R. James, *Beyond a Boundary* (1962; reprint, Durham, NC: Duke University Press, 1993); and Steven A. Riess, *Touching Base: Professional Baseball and American Culture in the Progressive Era* (1983; rev. ed., Urbana: University of Illinois Press, 1999), 3–4.

29. Jules Tygiel, *Extra Bases: Reflections on Jackie Robinson, Race, and Baseball History* (Lincoln: University of Nebraska Press, 2002), x–xi (quote).

30. Jacques Barzun, *God's Country and Mine: A Declaration of Love Spiced with a Few Harsh Words* (Boston: Little, Brown, 1954), 159 (quote).

CHAPTER 1: PLAYING BALL IN COOPERSTOWN IN THE FORMATIVE YEARS OF THE AMERICAN REPUBLIC

1. *Freeman's Journal* (Cooperstown, NY), Feb. 14, 1885; *Otsego Herald*, Mar. 3, 1810; Samuel M. Shaw, *A Centennial Offering: Being a Brief History of Cooperstown with a Biographical Sketch of James Fenimore Cooper* (Cooperstown, NY: Freeman's Journal Office, 1886), 214, 220–221, copy in the New York State Historical Association Research Library, Cooperstown, New York (NYSHA); Margaret B. Curfman and Stephen W. D. Rockstroh, *Doubleday Families of America* (Port Charlotte, FL: Stephen W. D. Rockstroh, 1993), 93–96, NYSHA; James Arthur Frost, *Life on the Upper Susquehanna, 1783–1860* (New York: King's Crown Press, 1951), 7–30; Paul W. Gates, *The Farmer's Age: Agriculture, 1815–1860*, Economic History of the United States, vol. 3 (New York: Holt, Rinehart, and Winston, 1960), 156–157.

2. *Freeman's Journal*, Feb. 14, 1885 (quotes); *Biographical Sketches of the Leading Citizens of Otsego County, New York* (Boston: Biographical Review Publishing, 1893), 414–416; Curfman and Rockstroh, *Doubleday Families of America*, 79–85, 177–178; John R. Betts, "Organized Sport in Industrial America" (PhD diss., Columbia University, 1952), 30–39.

3. *Freeman's Journal*, Feb. 14, 1885 (quote); Curfman and Rockstroh, *Doubleday Families*, 79–85; *Biographical Sketches*, 414–416; Alan Taylor, "The Great Change Begins: Settling the Forest of Central New York," *New York History* 76 (July 1995): 265–290; Marvin Meyers, *The Jacksonian Persuasion: Politics and Belief* (Stanford, CA: Stanford University Press, 1957), 235–236.

4. James Fenimore Cooper, *The Chronicles of Cooperstown* (1838), in *A History of Cooperstown*, ed. Louis C. Jones (Cooperstown, NY: New York State Historical Association, 1976), 6–8, 35; Lyman H. Butterfield, "Judge William Cooper (1754–1809): A Sketch of his Character and Accomplishment," *New York History* 30 (Oct. 1949): 390–395; Alan Taylor, *William Cooper's Town: Power and Persuasion on the Frontier of the Early American Republic* (New York: Vintage, 1995), 57, 87–88; 99–101 (quote 100); Frost, *Life on the Upper Susquehanna*, 17–18.

5. Taylor, "Great Change Begins," 275–276, 278–282; Levi Beardsley, *Reminiscences; Personal and Other Incidents: Early Settlement of Otsego County . . .* (New York: Charles Vinten, 1852), 75–77 (quote 76), NYSHA; Taylor, *William Cooper's Town*, 90–91, 119–126; Frost, *Life on the Upper Susquehanna*, 24–25; Ulysses Prentiss Hedrick, *A History of Agriculture in the State of New York* (1933; reprint, New York: Hill & Wang, 1966), 331–335; Thomas Summerhill, *Harvest of Dissent: Agrarianism in Nineteenth-Century New York* (Urbana: University of Illinois Press, 2005), 20.

6. "Census of Cooperstown for the Year 1802," Mar. 1, 1803, NYSHA; Duane Hamilton Hurd, *History of Otsego County, New York* (Philadelphia: Everts & Fariss, 1878), 247–251, NYSHA; James Taylor Dunn, "Pioneer Cabinet Makers of Cooperstown," *Otsego Farmer*, Apr. 1, 1955, reprint, NYSHA; Taylor, *William Cooper's Town*, 103–104; Frost, *Life on the Upper Susquehanna*, 27–30; Jared Van Wagenen Jr., *The Golden Age of Homespun* (Ithaca, NY: Cornell University Press, 1953), 1–14; Lyman H. Butterfield, "Cooper's Inheritance: The Otsego Country and Its Founders," *New York History* 35 (Oct. 1954): 387; Taylor, "Great Change Begins," 286. The population of Otsego Township, the largest of twenty-one townships in Otsego County and containing Cooperstown, the county seat, grew from 1,362 in 1800 to 3,810 in 1810.

7. This is the central theme of Taylor, *William Cooper's Town*. See also Gordon S. Wood, *The Radicalism of the American Revolution* (New York: Alfred A. Knopf, 1991); Martin Bruegel, *Farm, Shop, Landing: The Rise of a Market Society in the Hudson Valley, 1780–1860* (Durham, NC: Duke University Press, 2002); Richard Lyman Bushman, *The Refinement of America: Persons, Houses, Cities* (New York: Alfred A. Knopf, 1992), esp. chap. 11; Joyce Appleby, *Inheriting the Revolution: The First Generation of Americans* (Cambridge, MA: Belknap Press of Harvard University Press, 2000); Eric J. Sundquist: *Home as Found: Authority and Genealogy in Nineteenth-Century American Literature* (Baltimore: Johns Hopkins University Press, 1979); and Meyers, *Jacksonian Persuasion*.

8. William Cooper, *A Guide in the Wilderness; or the History of the First Settlements in the Western Counties of New York, with Useful Instructions to Future Settlers . . .* (Dublin: Gilbert & Hodges, 1810), passim, NYSHA; Taylor, *William Cooper's Town*, 3–4, 141–146; 319–321, 348–351; 377–381.

9. Cooper, *Guide in the Wilderness*, 8–9; Richard P. Casey, "North Country Nemesis: The Potash Rebellion and the Embargo of 1807–9," *New York Historical Society Quarterly* 64 (Jan. 1980): 34–45; Butterfield, "Judge William Cooper," 386; David M. Ludlum, *Early American Winters, 1604–1820* (Boston: American Meteorological Society, 1966), 190–194 (quote 192); Taylor, *William Cooper's Town*, 321–325, 372–375, 386–389.

10. "Census of Cooperstown 1802"; "Population of Cooperstown, Taken on the First Day of January 1816," NYSHA; Cooper, *Chronicles of Cooperstown*, 26–37; Hurd, *History of Otsego County*, 250, 267; Hiram Doolittle, "Description of Cooperstown," *Freeman's Journal*, Sept. 21, 1829; Martha Reamy, *Early Families of Otsego County, New York* (Westminster, MA: Heritage Books, 2007), 33–37; Edward P. Alexander, "Cooperstown Society in 1820," *Freeman's Journal*, Sept. 24, 1941; James Taylor Dunn, "Social Cooperstown, 1814–1815," *Freeman's Journal*, Mar. 14, 1956, reprint, NYSHA; Ralph Birdsall, *The Story of Cooperstown* (Cooperstown, NY: Arthur H. Christ, 1917), 136–147; Frost, *Life on the Upper Susquehanna*, 39–41; Taylor, *William Cooper's Town*, 375–381.

11. Cooper, *Chronicles of Cooperstown*, 28–29; Hurd, *History of Otsego County*, 260, 267; Taylor, *William Cooper's Town*, 351–355, 383; Bushman, *Refinement of America*, 353–354, 370–390.

12. *Otsego Herald*, Jan. 16, 1813 (1st two quotes); May 29, 1913 (5th quote); Oct. 30, 1813 (3rd quote); Nov. 20, 1813; June 6, 1816 (4th quote); Cooper, *Chronicles of Cooperstown*, 28–29; Taylor, *William Cooper's Town*, 383.

13. Samuel Truesdale Livermore, *A Condensed History of Cooperstown with a Biographical Sketch of J. Fenimore Cooper* (Albany, NY: J. Munsell, 1862), 118, NYSHA; *Otsego Herald*, Jan. 9, 1817; Feb. 20, 1817; Oct. 9, 1817; June 1, 1818; Oct. 9, 1920; *Freeman's Journal*, Feb. 21, 1820; Hurd, *History of Otsego County*, 43; Clifford Lord, "Elkanah Watson and New York's First County Fair," *New York History* 23 (Oct. 1942): 437–445; Donald B. Marti, "Early Agricultural Societies in New York: The Foundations of Improvement," *New York History* 48 (Oct. 1967): 313–333; Geoffrey N. Stein, "*The Otsego County Fair in the Nineteenth Century, 1818–1915*" (MA thesis, State University of New York College at Oneonta, Cooperstown Graduate Program, 1968), chap. 1, NYSHA; Betts, "Organized Sport in Industrial America," 30–39; Frost, *Life on the Upper Susquehanna*, 66–68; Bushman, *Refinement of America*, 378–382; Summerhill, *Harvest of Dissent*, 34; Cooper, *Guide in the Wilderness*, 69–70 (last quote); Taylor, *William Cooper's Town*, 382–385 (all other quotes).

14. *Otsego Herald*, June 6, 1816.

15. See, for example, Thomas L. Altherr, "'A Place Leavel Enough to Play Ball': Baseball and Baseball-type Games in the Colonial Era, Revolutionary War, and Early American Republic," *Nine: A Journal of Baseball History and Social Policy Perspectives* 8 (Spring 2000): 33; William J. Ryczek, *Baseball's First Inning: A History of the National Pastime through the Civil War* (Jefferson, NC: McFarland, 2009), 96.

16. Cooper, *Chronicles of Cooperstown*, 33; James Fenimore Cooper (grandson of the novelist), *The Legends and Traditions of a Northern County* (1921; reprint, Memphis, TN: General Books, 2009), 17–23; *Cooperstown Crier*, Oct. 28, 1999; Nov. 4,

1999; Taylor, *William Cooper's Town*, 381. Second and West, or "The Four Corners," is now Main and Pioneer.

17. Will Irwin, "Baseball: Before the Professionals Came," *Collier's*, May 8, 1909, 12; John Allen Krout, *Annals of American Sport* (New Haven, CT: Yale University Press, 1929), 115–116; Robert W. Henderson, *Ball, Bat, and Bishop: The Origin of Ball Games* (1947; reprint, Urbana: University of Illinois Press, 2001), 151; Harold Seymour, "How Baseball Began," *New York Historical Society Quarterly* 40 (Oct. 1956): 381–383; Jules Tygiel, *Past Time: Baseball as History* (Oxford: Oxford University Press, 2007), 5; Peter Morris, *But Didn't We Have Fun? An Informal History of Baseball's Pioneer Era, 1843–1970* (Chicago: Ivan R. Dee, 2008), 11–25.

18. *Otsego Herald*, June 1, 1818; Oct. 9, 1920; Summerhill, *Harvest of Dissent*, 34; Gates, *Farmer's Age*, 159–160; Carol Sheriff, *The Artificial River: The Erie Canal and the Paradox of Progress, 1817–1862* (New York: Hill & Wang, 1996), chap. 1.

19. Sheriff, *Artificial River*, chap. 3; Gates, *Farmer's Age*, 159–160; Frost, *Life on the Upper Susquehanna*, 75–76; Whitney R. Cross, *The Burned-Over District: The Social and Intellectual History of Enthusiastic Religion in Western New York, 1800–1850* (1950; reprint, New York: Harper Torchbooks, 1965), chap. 4; Tyler O. Hendricks, "Charles Finney and the Utica Revival of 1826: The Social Effect of a New Religious Paradigm" (PhD diss., Vanderbilt University, 1983), 129; Charles Sellars, *The Market Revolution: Jacksonian America, 1815–1846* (New York: Oxford University Press, 1991); George Rogers Taylor, *The Transportation Revolution, 1815–1860*, Economic History of the United States, vol. 4 (New York: Rinehart, 1951).

20. Percy Wells Bidwell and John I. Falconer, *History of Agriculture in the Northern United States, 1620–1860* (Washington, DC: Carnegie Institute of Washington, 1925), 182; Hurd, *History of Otsego County*, 275; Summerhill, *Harvest of Dissent*, 28–29; Frost, *Life on the Upper Susquehanna*, 68–71, 75–82; Gates, *Farmer's Age*, 159–160; Dominick J. Reisen, *Middlefield and the Settling of the New York Frontier* (Voorheesville, NY: Square Circle Press, 2009), 104–106; W. Ross Fullam, "The Farm Account Book as an Economic Instrument in Otsego, County, 1790–1840" (MA thesis, State University of New York College at Oneonta, Cooperstown Graduate Program, 1972), chap. 3, NYSHA.

21. New York (State) Secretary's Office, *Census of the State of New York for 1855*, microfilm (1857; Salt Lake City: Genealogical Society, 1971), NYSHA; Frost, *Life on the Upper Susquehanna*, 82–83; Paul Johnson, *A Shopkeeper's Millennium: Society and Revivals in Rochester, New York, 1815–1837* (New York: Hill & Wang, 1978), chap. 1; Mary P. Ryan, *Cradle of the Middle Class: The Family in Oneida County, New York, 1790–1865* (Cambridge: Cambridge University Press, 1981); 43–58; Hendricks, "Charles Finney," 125–148.

22. U.S. Census, Population Schedules for Otsego Township, Otsego Co., NY, 1850, Ancestry Library, http://ancestrylibrary.com (accessed June 2, 2010), lists numerous journeymen and apprentices (men with different surnames than the head of household) living in craftsmen's homes. For examples of newspaper advertisements for journeymen and apprentices, see *Otsego Republican*, Feb. 16, 1835, and *Freeman's Journal*, Aug. 17, 1838; May 11, 1840; Feb. 22, 1842; Feb. 14, 1852. For a detailed listing

of Cooperstown's businesses and public buildings, see *Freeman's Journal*, Dec. 31, 1852. Wagonmaker John Brewer purchased alcohol for his journeymen and apprentices through the 1840s; see John Brewer, Account Books, 1833–1849, NYSHA. On life as an apprentice hatmaker in Otsego County, see Henry Clarke Wright, *Human Life: Illustrated in My Individual Experience as a Child, a Youth, and a Man* (Boston: Bela Marsh, 1849), 121–138, NYSHA. See also Johnson, *Shopkeeper's Millennium*, chap. 2; Frost, *Life on the Upper Susquehanna*, 83; Fullam, "Farm Account Book," 1–24; and Allan Raymond, "Early Cabinetmakers of Cooperstown, 1794–1840," typescript, 1981, 1–31, NYSHA.

23. Hurd, *History of Otsego County*, 251; Frost, *Life on the Upper Susquehanna*, 90–100; Waldo Ellsworth, "Cooperstown's First Bank," *New York History* 22 (Oct. 1941): 402; Curtis D. Johnson, "Supply-side and Demand-side Revivalism? Evaluating Social Influences on New York State Evangelism in the 1830s," *Social Science History* 19 (Spring 1995): 17; *Portrait and Biographical Record of Kalamazoo, Allegan, and Van Buren Counties, Michigan* (Chicago: Chapman Brothers, 1892), 858–859; *Biographical Sketches*, 414; Curfman and Rockstroh, *Doubleday Families of America*, 79–81, 147–150.

24. Cooper, *Chronicles of Cooperstown*, 42; *Biographical Sketches*, 62; Livermore, *Condensed History of Cooperstown*, 161–163; Hurd, *History of Otsego County*, 260; Birdsall, *Story of Cooperstown*, 129–131; Frost, *Life on the Upper Susquehanna*, 83–84; Stephen R. Wiist, "A History of Printing in Cooperstown, New York, 1795–1850" (MA thesis, State University of New York College at Oneonta, Cooperstown Graduate Program, 1973), chap. 1 and 2, NYSHA; Kathryn Klim Sturrock, "The Phinneys of Cooperstown, 1795–1850" (MA thesis, State University of New York College at Oneonta, Cooperstown Graduate Program, 1972), 53–91, NYSHA.

25. *Cooperstown Watch-Tower*, Nov. 3, 1828; Mar. 30, 1829; *Freeman's Journal*, May 13, 1839; May 27, 1839; June 24, 1839; Sept. 23, 1839; May 4, 1840; Brewer, Account Books (illustrating Doubleday's generous credit); Cooper, *Legends and Traditions of a Northern County*, 17–23; Hurd, *History of Otsego County*, 250–251, 267–268, 274; Meyers, *Jacksonian Persuasion*, 237–253.

26. Charles Giles, *Pioneer: A Narrative of the Nativity, Experience, Travels, and Ministerial Labours of Rev. Charles Giles, with Incidents, Observations, and Reflections* (New York: G. Lane & P. P. Sandford, 1844), 262 (2nd quote), 264 (3rd quote, original emphasis), 306; Sylvester Nash, comp., *The Nash Family; or, Records of the Descendants of Thomas Nash of New Haven, Connecticut, 1640* (Hartford, CT: Case, Tiffany, 1853), 96–103, NYSHA; *Otsego Herald*, Feb. 6, 1817; Cooper, *Chronicles of Cooperstown*, 24; Hurd, *History of Otsego County*, 189, 211–212, 274; Cross, *Burned-Over District*, ix (1st quote); Donald M. Scott, *From Office to Profession: The New England Ministry, 1750–1850* (Philadelphia: University of Pennsylvania Press, 1978), chap. 3; Roger W. Hecht, *The Erie Canal Reader, 1790–1950* (Syracuse, NY: Syracuse University Press, 2003), 30–33; Birdsall, *Story of Cooperstown*, 148–157; Frost, *Life on the Upper Susquehanna*, 32–35; Alison Swift, "*Three Mercantile Ghost Villages of Otsego County: Monticello, Brighton, and Federal Corners*" (MA thesis, State University of New York College at Oneonta, Cooperstown Graduate Program, 1971), 36–49, NYSHA; Marianne

Perciaccante, *Calling Down Fire: Charles Grandison Finney and Revivalism in Jefferson County, New York, 1800–1840* (Albany: State University of New York Press, 2003), 46–47; John H. Wigger, *Taking Heaven by Storm: Methodism and the Rise of Popular Christianity in America* (Urbana: University of Illinois Press, 1998), 18–19.

27. Frank C. Carpenter, *The Baptists of Cooperstown, 1834–1859* (Cooperstown, NY: First Baptist Church, 1959), 1–6, NYSHA; Ashbel Hosmer and John Lawton, *A View of the Rise and Increase of the Churches, Comprising the Otsego Baptist Association* (Morris, NY: L. P. Carpenter, 1871), 3–29, NYSHA; Albert Clarke, *Early Cooperstown and the Methodist Episcopal Church* (Cooperstown, NY: Albert Clarke, 1913), 5–61, NYSHA; Wright, *Human Life*, 141–151; Helen A. Ross, "History of the First Presbyterian Church of Cooperstown, New York," typescript, 1950, NYSHA; Edwin P. Smith, "Father Nash's Record of Baptisms, Central New York, 1797–1827," *New England Historical and Genealogical Register* 115 (Jan.–Apr. 1961): 14–27, 107–188; Cooper, *Chronicles of Cooperstown*, 25, 38; Hurd, *History of Otsego County*, 272–275; Johnson, "Supply-side and Demand-side Revivalism," 17; Hendricks, "Charles Finney," 148–154; Ryan, *Cradle of the Middle Class*, 78–79.

28. Hendricks, "Charles Finney," 154–176; Ryan, *Cradle of the Middle Class*, chap. 2; Scott, *From Office to Profession*, chap. 3.

29. Taylor, *William Cooper's Town*, 406–427; Meyers, *Jacksonian Persuasion*, 57–100 (quote 60); James Grossman, *James Fenimore Cooper* (London: Methuen, 1950), chaps. 2 and 3.

30. James Fenimore Cooper (grandson of the novelist), *Correspondence of James Fenimore Cooper, Volume 1* (New Haven, CT: Yale University Press, 1922), 343–344; Charles R. Tichy, "Otsego Hall and Its Setting, 1786–1940" (MA thesis, State University of New York College at Oneonta, Cooperstown Graduate Program, 1973), 26–27 (village maps showing location of Otsego Hall), chap. 2, NYSHA; Louis C. Jones, ed., *Growing Up in the Cooper Country: Boyhood Recollections of the New York Frontier* (Syracuse, NY: Syracuse University Press, 1965), 7; Ralph Birdsall, "Fenimore Cooper in Cooperstown," *Proceedings of the New York State Historical Association* 16 (1916): 137–143 (2nd quote 143); Hugh Cooke MacDougall, *Cooper's Otsego County: A Bicentennial Guide to Sites in Otsego County Associated with the Life and Fiction of James Fenimore Cooper, 1789–1851* (Cooperstown, NY: New York State Historical Association, 1989), 24–41. At present, Cooper Grounds, still an open space preventing Fair Street from running through the block, is a public park, directly adjacent to the National Baseball Hall of Fame. At the center of the park, where Otsego Hall once stood, sits a large bronze statue of James Fenimore Cooper.

31. Cooper, *Correspondence of James Fenimore Cooper*, 344; MacDougall, *Cooper's Otsego County*, 82–85 (1st quote 82); Birdsall, "Fenimore Cooper in Cooperstown," 142–148 (2nd quote 145; 3rd quote 143); Taylor, *William Cooper's Town*, 425–426.

32. James Fenimore Cooper, *Home as Found* (1838; New York: G. P. Putnam's Sons, 1896), 162–166 (both quotes 164); *Cooperstown Crier*, Nov. 4, 1999; MacDougall, *Cooper's Otsego County*, 14–15, 83–85; Birdsall, *Story of Cooperstown*, 253–260; Meyers, *Jacksonian Persuasion*, 57–100; Taylor, *William Cooper's Town*, 414–415, 424–427.

33. Cooper, *Home as Found*, 156–159; *Cooperstown Crier*, Nov. 4, 1999; Trey Strecker, ed., *Dead Balls and Double Curves: An Anthology of Early Baseball Fiction* (Carbondale: Southern Illinois University Press, 2004), 1–4.

34. Meyers, *Jacksonian Persuasion*, 84–93.

35. Clarence W. Davidson, *Cooperstown and Otsego Lake: Descriptive Sketch of the Village Made Famous by J. Fenimore Cooper . . .* (Cooperstown, NY: Otsego Republican, 1901), NYSHA; *Freeman's Journal*, Dec. 31, 1852; *To Commemorate the Foundation of the Village of Cooperstown and Its Corporate Existence of One Hundred Years . . .* (1907; reprint, Memphis, TN: General Books, 2010), 47 (quote); Hurd, *History of Otsego County*, 263; Tichy, "Otsego Hall and Its Setting," chap. 3; MacDougall, *Cooper's Otsego County*, passim; Charles Fruehling Springwood, *Cooperstown to Dyersville: A Geography of Baseball Nostalgia* (Boulder, CO: Westview, 1996), 29–30.

36. Seymour, "How Baseball Began," 376 (quote).

37. *Akron Beacon Journal*, Apr. 1, 1905 (2nd quote); Apr. 4, 1905; Abner Graves to Editor, *Akron Beacon Journal*, Apr. 3, 1905; Graves to Albert G. Spalding, Nov. 17, 1905, John Doyle Papers, A. Bartlett Giamatti Research Center, National Baseball Hall of Fame and Museum, Cooperstown, NY; Donald Honig, *Baseball America* (New York: Fireside, 1985), 4 (1st quote); Stephen Jay Gould, "The Creation Myths of Cooperstown," *Natural History* 98 (Nov. 1989): 20 (quoting Honig); David Block, *Baseball before We Knew It: A Search for the Roots of the Game* (Lincoln: University of Nebraska Press, 2005), 50–61; Harry Paxton, "The Myths of Cooperstown," *Saturday Evening Post*, Jan. 30, 1960, 64.

38. Birdsall, *Story of Cooperstown*, 249; Cooper, *Correspondence of James Fenimore Cooper*, 343; Hurd, *History of Otsego County*, 260; Sturrock, "Phinneys of Cooperstown." Each boy's age is based on his estimated year of birth in the 1850 census schedules and thus may be off by a year, depending on what month a boy was born.

39. Carlton Lee Starkweather, *A Brief Genealogical History of Robert Starkweather of Roxbury and Ipswich, Massachusetts . . .* (Auburn, NY: Knapp, Peck, & Thompson, 1904), 134–135, NYSHA; *Freeman's Journal*, July 6, 1818; Oct. 13, 1823; Hurd, *History of Otsego County*, 29, 31, 261.

40. U.S. Census, Population Schedules for Otsego Township 1850; Curfman and Rockstroh, *Doubleday Families of America*, 173–174. The 1850 census was the first to identify all members in a given household by name.

41. Brewer, Account Books, 1833–1849; U.S. Census, Population Schedules for Otsego Township, 1850; U.S. Census, Population Schedules for Otsego Township, Otsego Co., NY, 1840, Ancestry Library, http://ancestrylibrary.com (accessed June 15, 2010); Hurd, *History of Otsego County*, 261.

42. U.S. Census, Population Schedules for Otsego Township, 1850; Hurd, *History of Otsego County*, 268.

43. U.S. Census, Population Schedules for Otsego Township, 1840 and 1850; New York (State) Secretary's Office, *Census of the State of New York for 1825: Town of Otsego, Otsego County*, microfilm (Salt Lake City: Genealogical Society, 1968), NYSHA; *Cooperstown Watch-Tower*, Feb. 18, 1828; Mar. 23, 1829; Hurd, *History of Otsego County*, 261, 279–280.

44. U.S. Census, Population Schedules for Otsego Township, 1840. From the 1840 census, we know only that Joseph's age was between ten and fifteen.

45. Graves to Editor, Apr. 3, 1905; Graves to Spalding, Nov. 17, 1905 (both quotes).

46. Graves to Editor, Apr. 3, 1905 (1st two quotes); Graves to Spalding, Nov. 17, 1905 (4th quote); Birdsall, *Story of Cooperstown*, 230–231 (5th quote 231), 396–397; James Fenimore Cooper, *Reminiscences of Mid-Victorian Cooperstown and a Sketch of William Cooper* (1935–1936; reprint, Cooperstown, NY: Smithy-Pioneer Gallery, 1986), 22; Walter R. Littell, *The History of Cooperstown, 1886–1928* (1929), reprinted in Lewis C. Jones, ed., *A History of Cooperstown* (Cooperstown, NY: New York State Historical Association, 1976), 191; *Cooperstown Crier*, Nov. 19, 1998; Robert Kossuth, "Boondoggling, Baseball, and the WPA: Cooperstown's Doubleday Field," *Nine* 9 (Fall 2000): 63–64 (3rd quote 64).

47. Graves to Editor, Apr. 3, 1905 (1st quote); Graves to Spalding, Nov. 17, 1905; Order No. 30, June 18, 1840, Post Orders, Records of the Deputy Chief of Staff, Personnel, and Administration, Records of the U.S. Military Academy, RG 404, National Archives—Affiliated Archives, record on deposit at U.S. Military Academy Archives, West Point, NY (2nd quote). My thanks to Alicia Mauldin-Ware, archives curator, for tracking this down for me.

48. Hurd, *History of Otsego County*, 261; "Doubleday, Ulysses Freeman," *Appletons' Cyclopaedia of American Biography*, ed. James Grant Wilson and John Fiske (New York: Appleton, 1888), 2:210; "Doubleday, Ulysses Freeman," *Biographical Directory of the American Congress, 1774–1961*, ed. U.S. Congress, Joint Committee on Printing (Washington, DC: Government Printing Office, 1961), 824; Brooks C. Simpson and Matthew E. Van Atta, "Doubleday, Abner," *American National Biography*, ed. John A. Garraty and Mark C. Carnes (Oxford: Oxford University Press, 1999), 6:779; Curfman and Rockstroh, *Doubleday Families of America*, 151; Stephen D. Rockstroh (Abner's grand-nephew), "A Few Words on Behalf of Uncle Abner," *American Heritage* 35 (June–July 1984): 9.

49. Graves to Spalding, Nov. 17, 1905; Rockstroh, "Few Words," 9; Block, *Baseball before We Knew It*, 58; Victor Salvatore, "The Man Who Didn't Invent Baseball," *American Heritage* 34 (June–July 1983): 66–67; Peter Morris, *Baseball Fever: Early Baseball in Michigan* (Ann Arbor: University of Michigan Press, 2003), 363–364.

50. *Freeman's Journal*, Aug. 16, 1877 (all quotes); Aug. 23, 1877; *Cooperstown Republican and Democrat*, Aug. 15, 1877 (lists names of all participants); Aug. 22, 1877; U.S. Census, Population Schedules for Otsego Township, Otsego Co., NY, 1870 and 1880, Ancestry Library, http://ancestrylibrary.com (accessed June 29, 2010); Hurd, *History of Otsego County*, 247–286 (firemen listed on 270; name index available at NYSHA); *Cooperstown Crier*, Nov. 11, 1999; Dec. 2, 1999; Douglas M. Preston, "*The Clang of the Bell, the Wail of the Whistle: A History of the Cooperstown Fire Department*" (MA thesis, State University of New York College at Oneonta, Cooperstown Graduate Program, 1975), 240–348, NYSHA. Another "old-fashioned game" was played in early August 1890, as reported in the *Freeman's Journal*, Aug. 1, 1890. See also Priscilla Astifan and Larry McCray, "'Old Fashioned Base Ball' in Western New York, 1825–1860," *Base Ball: A Journal of the Early Game* 2 (Fall 2008): 26–34, and Thomas

L. Altherr, "Chucking the Old Apple: Recent Discoveries of Pre-1840 North American Ball Games," *Base Ball* 2 (Spring 2008): 29–43.

CHAPTER 2: BASEBALL AND THE TRANSFORMATION OF RURAL CALIFORNIA

1. *Dixon Tribune*, June 4, 1887 (1st five quotes); June 11, 1887; Sept. 17, 1887 (6th quote); May 19, 1888.

2. *Dixon Tribune*, Oct. 17, 1885 (1st quote); Oct. 24, 1885 (2nd and 3rd quotes); Nov. 14, 1885 (4th and 5th quotes). While this essay focuses primarily on Davisville and Dixon, baseball flourished in rural communities throughout northern California, as documented in many local newspapers; see, for example, Frank Herzog, "Early Baseball in Siskiyou County," *Siskiyou Pioneer* 2 (Spring 1954): 11–13, and the several accompanying articles in the same issue. See also Harold Seymour, *Baseball: The People's Game* (Oxford: Oxford University Press, 1990), 192.

3. On the new rural history, see David B. Danbom, *Born in the Country: A History of Rural America* (Baltimore: Johns Hopkins University Press, 1995); Hal S. Barron, "Old Wine in New Bottles? The Perspective of Rural History," in *Outstanding in His Field: Perspectives on American Agriculture in Honor of Wayne D. Rasmussen*, ed. Frederick V. Carstensen, Morton Rothstein, and Joseph A. Swanson (Ames: Iowa State University Press, 1993), 48–60; and David Vaught, "State of the Art—Rural History, or Why Is There No Rural History of California?" *Agricultural History* 74 (Fall 2000): 759–774. On the new baseball and, more broadly, sport history, see Steven A. Riess, "The Historiography of American Sport," *OAH Magazine of History* 7 (Summer 1992): 10–14; Larry R. Gerlach, "Not Quite Ready for Prime Time: Baseball History, 1983–1993," *Journal of Sport History* 21 (Summer 1994): 103–137; and S. W. Pope, ed., *The New American Sport History: Recent Approaches and Perspectives* (Urbana: University of Illinois Press, 1997). In the interest of full disclosure, my own full-length contributions to the new rural history, *Cultivating California: Growers, Specialty Crops, and Labor, 1875–1920* (Baltimore: Johns Hopkins University Press, 1999) and *After the Gold Rush: Tarnished Dreams in the Sacramento Valley* (Baltimore: Johns Hopkins University Press, 2007), are two cases in point. The second devotes all of one paragraph to baseball while the first makes no mention whatsoever of the game.

4. *Dixon Tribune*, June 6, 1885 (quote).

5. Seymour, *Baseball: The People's Game*, chap. 13 and 14; Carl M. Becker, "Crossing Bats: Baseball in the Villages of the Upper Miami Valley, 1865–1900," *Nine: A Journal of Baseball History and Culture* 10 (Spring 2002): 47–50; Peter Morris, *Baseball Fever: Early Baseball in Michigan* (Ann Arbor: University of Michigan Press, 2003), chap. 6 and 7.

6. *Dixon Tribune*, Feb. 6, 1875; Mar. 21, 1885; Aug. 29, 1885; Sept. 5, 1885; Sept. 12, 1885; Oct. 31, 1885; July 6, 1889; Mar. 15, 1890; May 31, 1890; Mar. 8, 1895; Mar. 15, 1895; June 21, 1895; June 28, 1895; *Weekly Solano Republican*, May 1, 1878; U.S. Census, Population Schedules for Putah Township, Yolo Co., Tremont Township, Solano Co., and Silveyville Township, Solano Co., California, 1880 and 1900, microfilm (Washington, D.C.: National Archives, 1967); Joann Leach Larkey, *Davisville '68: The His-*

tory and Heritage of the City of Davis, Yolo County, California (Davis: Davis Historical and Landmarks Commission, 1969), 143–229; Obituary file, Yolo County Archives, Woodland, California (YCA).

7. J. M. Guinn, *History of the State of California and Biographical Record of the Sacramento Valley, California* (Chicago: Chapman, 1906), 425; Larkey, *Davisville '68*, 146; *James T. Lillard v. E. W. Brown* (1885), Yolo Co., Superior Court Case Files, no. 441, YCA; *E. W. Brown v. Sinclair Manufacturing Company* (1894), Yolo Co., Superior Court Case Files, no. 1780, YCA.

8. On migration from the Midwest to the gold fields of the Sierra foothills to Putah Creek, see Vaught, *After the Gold Rush*, chap. 1.

9. Farmers' successes and struggles in the 1850s are richly documented in numerous contemporary lawsuits. See, especially, *Charles E. Greene v. His Creditors* (1861), Yolo Co., County Court Case Files, Civil Case no. 107, YCA; *Benjamin Cahoon v. Jerome C. Davis and Isaac Davis* (1867), Sacramento Co., District Court Case Files, no. 11590, Sacramento Archives and Museum Collection Center, Sacramento (SAMCC); *George W. Pierce v. Henry E. Robinson* (1859), California Supreme Court, no. 2329, "Transcript on Appeal," California State Archives, Sacramento; *H. O. Beatty v. R. C. Clark* (1861), California Supreme Court, no. 3223, "Transcript on Appeal," California State Archives; *W. W. Brown v. C. E. Greene* (1884), California State Supreme Court, no. 9443, "Transcript on Appeal," California State Archives. See also *Sacramento Daily Union*, Oct. 8, 1852 (quote); Jim Gerber, "The Origin of California's Export Surplus in Cereals," *Agricultural History* 67 (Fall 1992): 40–57; and David Vaught, "After the Gold Rush: Replicating the Rural Midwest in the Sacramento Valley," *Western Historical Quarterly* 34 (Winter 2003): 447–467.

10. United States Land Case no. 232, Northern District, Rio de los Putos Grant; United States Land Case no. 74, Northern District, Los Putos Grant; and United States Land Case no. 411, Northern District, Laguna de Santos Callé Grant, all in the Bancroft Library, University of California, Berkeley; David Vaught, "A Tale of Three Land Grants on the Northern California Border Lands," *Agricultural History* 78 (Spring 2004): 140–154.

11. Lacking a town center before the founding of Davisville in 1868, Putah Creek was, in essence, what rural sociologists call an "open-country settlement." See John Mack Faragher, "Open-Country Community: Sugar Creek, Illinois, 1820–1850," in *The Countryside in the Age of Capitalist Transformation: Essays in the Social History of Rural America*, ed. Steven Hahn and Jonathan Prude (Chapel Hill: University of North Carolina Press, 1985), 233–258, for an extended discussion. On the social and cultural development of the community in the 1850s, see Vaught, *After the Gold Rush*, chap. 4.

12. *Sacramento Daily Union*, Oct. 5, 1857; Apr. 26, 1860; Sept. 29, 1862; Mar. 13, 1863; Apr. 13, 1863 (quote); *Knights Landing News*, Mar. 24, 1860; *Porter's Spirit of the Times: A Chronicle of the Turf, Field Sports, Literature, and the Stage*, Mar. 12, 1859; "Rattler Mare Account, 1861," Jerome C. Davis Collection, MS box 205, California Room, California State Library, Sacramento; *Transactions of the California State Agricultural Society during the Year 1858* (Sacramento: State Printer, 1859), 84–85, 115,

160, 236–237; *Transactions of the California State Agricultural Society during the Year 1861* (Sacramento: State Printer, 1862), 82–83, 122; "Fine Horses" folder, box 12, James L. Warren Papers, Bancroft Library; Joel Franks, "California and the Rise of Spectator Sports, 1850–1900," *Southern California Quarterly* 71 (Winter 1989): 290–291; T. H. Breen, "Horses and Gentlemen: The Cultural Significance of Gambling among the Gentry of Virginia," *William and Mary Quarterly* 34 (Apr. 1977): 239–257; Bertram Wyatt-Brown, *Southern Honor: Ethics and Behavior in the Old South* (Oxford: Oxford University Press, 1982), 339–350; Kenneth S. Greenberg, *Honor and Slavery* (Princeton: Princeton University Press, 1996), 135–140; Melvin L. Adelman, *A Sporting Time: New York City and the Rise of Modern Athletics, 1820–70* (Urbana: University of Illinois Press, 1986), 27–89; Paul W. Gates, *The Farmer's Age: Agriculture, 1815–1860* (New York: Harper & Row, 1960), 228–230.

13. *Daily Alta California*, Jan. 14, 1852; *Dixon Tribune*, June 6, 1885; June 28, 1895 (quote); *Weekly Solano Press*, May 5, 1869; Kevin Nelson, *The Golden Game: The Story of California Baseball* (San Francisco: California Historical Society Press, 2004), 2–7; John E. Spalding, *Always on Sunday: The California Baseball League, 1886–1915* (Manhattan, KS: Ag Press, 1992), 9; David Block, *Baseball before We Knew It: A Search for the Roots of the Game* (Lincoln: University of Nebraska Press, 2005), chap. 6; Harold Peterson, *The Man Who Invented Baseball* (New York: Scribner's, 1973); Harold Seymour, *Baseball: The Early Years* (Oxford: Oxford University Press, 1960), 15–34; Seymour, *Baseball: The People's Game*, 192–194; Anne Cartwright, "Cartwright's Trip West," *The National Pastime: A Review of Baseball History*, vol. 18 (Cleveland: Society for American Baseball Research, 1998), 14–16; Brian McGinty, "The Old Ball Game," *Pacific Historian* 25 (Spring 1981): 13–17; Natalie Vermilyea, "Kranks' Delight: California Baseball, 1858–1888," *Californians* 8 (Mar./Apr. 1991): 32–35.

14. On baseball in San Francisco in the 1860s, see Joel Franks, "Organizing California Baseball, 1859–1893," *Baseball History* 4 (1991): 1–5; McGinty, "Old Ball Game," 17; and Nelson, *Golden Game*, 10–14.

15. *Knights Landing News*, Jan. 25, 1862 (quote). The *Sacramento Daily Union* covered the flood extensively. For a concise overview, see its one-year "anniversary" stories, Dec. 9, 1862, and Jan. 10, 1863. On the drought, see especially W. H. Fraser, "Rainfall and Wheat in California," *Overland Monthly* 33 (Jan. 1899): 521–523; Frank T. Gilbert, *The Illustrated Atlas and History of Yolo County* (San Francisco: De Pue, 1879), 40–41; and Hazel Adele Pulling, "A History of California's Range-Cattle Industry, 1770–1912" (PhD diss., University of Southern California, 1944), 111–117.

16. Rodman W. Paul, "The Beginnings of Agriculture in California: Innovation vs. Continuity," *California Historical Quarterly* 52 (Spring 1973): 22 (quote); Rodman W. Paul, "The Wheat Trade Between California and the United Kingdom," *Mississippi Valley Historical Review* 45 (Dec. 1958): 396; Morton Rothstein, *The California Wheat Kings* (Davis: University of California, Davis, 1987), 3–5; Vaught, "After the Gold Rush," 465–466.

17. *Sacramento Daily Union*, Aug. 13, 1860; Apr. 13, 1863; Sept. 8, 1870; *Yolo Weekly Mail*, Mar. 9, 1871; *Davis Enterprise*, Oct. 8, 1970; Joann L. Larkey and Shipley Walters, *Yolo County: Land of Changing Patterns* (Northridge, CA: Windsor Publications,

1987), 37–38; Larkey, *Davisville '68*, 23, 192, 194; Joseph A. McGowan, *History of the Sacramento Valley*, 3 vols. (New York: Lewis Historical Publishing, 1961), 1:164–165, 263–264, 279.

18. Stephen D. Guschov, *The Red Stockings of Cincinnati: Base Ball's First All-Professional Team and Its Historic 1869 and 1870 Seasons* (Jefferson, NC: McFarland, 1998); Joseph S. Stern Jr., "The Team That Couldn't Be Beat: The Red Stockings of 1869," *Cincinnati Historical Society Bulletin* 27 (Spring 1969): 25–41; Robert Knight Barney, "Of Rails and Red Stockings: Episodes in the Expansion of the 'National Pastime' in the American West," *Journal of the West* 17 (July 1978): 61–70; Spalding, *Always on Sunday*, 10; McGinty, "Old Ball Game," 17–24; Nelson, *Golden Game*, 16–19; David Q. Voigt, "America's First Red Scare: The Cincinnati Reds of 1869," in *America through Baseball* (Chicago: Nelson-Hall, 1976), 29–41; Warren Goldstein, *Playing for Keeps: A History of Early Baseball* (Ithaca, NY: Cornell University Press, 1989), 101–119.

19. *Daily Alta California*, Sept. 24, 26, 28, 29, 30, 1869; Oct. 1, 2, 3, 4, 5, 6, 1869; *Sacramento Daily Union*, Sept. 28, 1869; Oct. 1, 2, 3, 6, 1869; *Weekly Solano Herald*, Oct. 2, 1869; *Weekly Solano Press*, Oct. 20, 1869; Spalding, *Always on Sunday*, 10; Barney, "Of Rails and Red Stockings," 64 (quote). The *San Francisco Chronicle*, *Examiner*, and *Call* all covered the story of the Red Stockings in California as well.

20. *Sacramento Daily Union*, May 16, 1870; June 13 and 27, 1870; Sept. 10, 15, 1870; Vermilyea, "Kranks' Delight," 38; Franks, "Organizing California Baseball," 3–6; Spalding, *Always on Sunday*, 11–13; Nelson, *Golden Game*, 21.

21. *Weekly Solano Press*, Oct. 20, 1869; *Weekly Solano Herald*, Oct. 16, 1869; *Yolo Weekly Mail*, May 11, 1871; May 8, 1879; Apr. 8, 1880; May 6, 1880; *Dixon Tribune*, Apr. 17, 1875; June 23, 1877; Aug. 25, 1877; Aug. 28, 1879; June 28, 1895 (quote).

22. *Dixon Tribune*, June 6, 1885; Seymour, *Baseball: The Early Years*, 61–65; John P. Rossi, *The National Game: Baseball and American Culture* (Chicago: Ivan R. Dee, 2000), 33; Gunther Barth, *City People: The Rise of Modern City Culture in Nineteenth-Century America* (Oxford: Oxford University Press, 1980), 159–161; Joel Zoss and John Bowman, *Diamonds in the Rough: The Untold History of Baseball* (Lincoln: University of Nebraska Press, 1989), 5–8, 70–76; Benjamin G. Rader, introduction to *Early Innings: A Documentary History of Baseball, 1825–1908*, ed. Dean A Sullivan (Lincoln: University of Nebraska Press, 1995), xviii–xix; Reed Browning, *Cy Young: A Baseball Life* (Amherst: University of Massachusetts Press, 2000), 32–33; Voigt, *America through Baseball*, 8; Vermilyea, "Kranks' Delight," 37.

23. *Dixon Tribune*, Feb. 14, 1885; Oct. 10, 1885 (1st two quotes); Mar. 15, 1895; June 28, 1895 (3rd quote); Seymour, *Baseball: The People's Game*, 193–194; Frank Herzog, "Bats and Balls," *Siskiyou Pioneer* 2 (Spring 1954): 25; Vermilyea, "Kranks' Delight," 37.

24. *Dixon Tribune*, Aug. 9, 1884; Jan. 3, 1885 (2nd quote); Nov. 14, 1891; *Yolo Weekly Mail*, Nov. 12, 1887; *Pacific Rural Press*, Jan. 21, 1885; *Wheat: An Illustrated Description of California's Leading Industry* (San Francisco: Commercial Publication Co., 1887), 35, Bancroft Library; Horace Davis, "Wheat in California: A Retrospect and Prospect," *Overland Monthly* 32 (July 1898): 60–63, and "California Breadstuffs," *Journal of Political Economy* 2 (Sept. 1894): 530–532; Alfred Bannister,

"California and Her Wheat Culture," *Overland Monthly* 12 (July 1888): 67; Rothstein, *California Wheat Kings*, 2 (1st quote); Paul Rhode, "Learning, Capital Accumulation, and the Transformation of California Agriculture," *Journal of Economic History* 55 (Dec. 1995): 773–800.

25. *Dixon Tribune*, Nov. 14, 1891 (1st quote); *Yolo Weekly Mail*, Jan. 1, 1892 (2nd quote).

26. George Robertson, "Statistical Summary of the Production and Resources of California" (1850–1910), in California State Board of Agriculture, *Fifty-eighth Annual Report for 1911* (Sacramento: State Printing Office, 1912), 119–121, 400–401; Rhode, "Learning, Capital Accumulation," 773 (quote). For a full, detailed analysis of the new generation's emergence during the transformation, see Vaught, *After the Gold Rush*, chap. 11.

27. *Dixon Tribune*, Sept. 12, 1885; U.S. Census, Population Schedules for Putah Township, Yolo Co., Tremont Township, Solano Co., and Silveyville Township, Solano Co., California, 1860, 1880, and 1900; Davisville Almond Growers' Association, Constitution and Minute Book, Jan. 23, 1897, Board of Directors file, Predecessor and Concurrent Organizations, box 1, California Almond Growers' Exchange Records, SAMCC.

28. *Dixon Tribune*, July 14, 1877; Aug. 28, 1879; Sept. 5, 1885; Nov. 7, 1885; Aug. 28, 1886; Oct. 23, 1886; Mar. 15, 1895; Ronald Story, "The Country of the Young: The Meaning of Baseball and Early American Culture," *Baseball History from Outside the Lines: A Reader*, ed. John E. Dreifort (Lincoln: University of Nebraska Press, 2001), 19–33; Barth, *City People*, 151; Vaught, *After the Gold Rush*, chap. 11.

29. *Dixon Tribune*, Oct. 26, 1878; May 27, 1880; June 6, 1885; July 4, 1885; Nov. 14, 1885; Dec. 19, 1885; Apr. 10, 1886 (1st quote); Feb. 5, 1887 (quote); Aug. 6, 1887; Feb. 11, 1888; Feb. 18, 1888; Apr. 6, 1889; Mar. 15, 1895 (2nd quote); May 17, 1895; *Yolo Weekly Mail*, Feb. 8, 1877; May 8, 1879; May 6, 1880; "Presbyterian Church of Davisville, California: Minutes of the Session and Register of Communicants, 13 Nov. 1873–14 Apr. 1918," transcribed by Clare L. Childers, 1997, 3–40, YCA; Sullivan, *Early Innings*, 21–22; Goldstein, *Playing for Keeps*, 43–63; Michael S. Kimmel, "Baseball and the Reconstitution of American Masculinity, 1880–1920," in Dreifort, *Baseball History*, 47–61.

30. *Dixon Tribune*, Mar. 21, 1885; Apr. 11, 1885; Sept. 12, 1885; *S. H. Cowell v. Lydia T. Armstrong* (1930), California State Supreme Court, no. 4341 (SAC), "Transcript on Appeal," 292–367, California State Archives; Larkey, *Davisville '68*, 198–199, 219–221; Wood Young, *Vaca-Peña Los Putos Rancho and the Peña Adobe* (Vallejo, CA: Wheeler, 1971), 11–29, appendix N; Nelson, *Golden Game*, 65–66, 73, 106–107, 168–172, 207–214; Samuel O. Regalado, "Sport and Community in California's Japanese American 'Yamato Colony,'" *Journal of Sport History* 19 (Summer 1992): 130–143; Regalado, "'Invisible Baseball': Japanese Americans and Their Game in the 1930s," in *Baseball in America and America in Baseball*, ed. Donald G. Kyle and Robert B. Fairbanks (College Station: Texas A&M University Press, 2008), 32–51.

31. *Dixon Tribune*, Dec. 12, 1874; Feb. 6, 1875; Oct. 27, 1877; Nov. 24, 1877; May 9, 1885; July 4, 1885; Nov. 14, Feb. 12, 1887 (quote); Apr. 2, 1887; Mar. 9, 1889; Apr.

12, 1890; July 26, 1890; *Yolo Daily Democrat*, Mar. 5, 1875; *Woodland Daily Democrat*, Nov. 15, 1892; *Sam N. Chantry v. William W. Montgomery* (1885), Yolo Co., Superior Court Case Files, no. 463, YCA; Barth, *City People*, 156–157; Nelson, *Golden Game*, 18.

32. *Dixon Tribune*, Mar. 21, 1885; Apr. 18, 1885; May 16, 1885; May 23, 1885; June 20, 1885; Apr. 3, 1886; July 6, 1889; Apr. 19, 1895; June 7, 1895; June 28, 1895; Seymour, *Baseball: The People's Game*, 206–207; Seymour, *Baseball: The Early Years*, 51–53; Nelson, *The Golden Game*, 18–19; Larkey, *Davisville '68*, 121–122.

33. *Dixon Tribune*, Sept. 5, 1885; Mar. 12, 1887; July 6, 1889; July 5, 1895 (quote); Sept. 17, 1897; Apr. 1, 1898; Apr. 21, 1899; Jackson Lears, *Something for Nothing: Luck in America* (New York: Viking, 2003), 1–24, 147–186; Larkey, *Davisville '68*, 121–122.

CHAPTER 3: MULTICULTURAL BALL IN THE HEYDAY OF TEXAS COTTON AGRICULTURE

1. *La Grange Journal*, June 1, 1911; July 6, 1911; *First Annual Report of the Agricultural Bureau of the Department of Agriculture, Insurance, Statistics, and History, 1887–1888* (1889; reprint, Austin: Texas State Historical Association, 2001), 71 (2nd quote); Fayette County History Book Committee (FCHBC), *Fayette County, Texas Heritage* (Dallas, TX: Curtis Media, 1996), 1:474–475, Institute of Texan Cultures Reading Room, University of Texas at San Antonio (ITC); "Parallel Pragues: Little Bit of Czechoslovakia in Texas," *Austin American-Statesman*, Feb. 7, 1993, Czechs in Texas vertical file, Briscoe Center for American History, University of Texas at Austin (BCAH); Clinton Machann and James W. Mendl, *Krásná Amerika: A Study of the Texas Czechs, 1851–1939* (Austin, TX: Eakin Press, 1983), 82–83, 97–99; W. Phil Hewitt, *The Czech Texans* (San Antonio: University of Texas, San Antonio, Institute of Texan Cultures, 1972), 6 (1st quote), 18, 20.

2. *La Grange Journal*, Sept. 2, 1909; June 1, 1911; June 29, 1911; July 6, 1911 (all quotes); July 13, 1911; July 27, 1911; Frank Lotto, *Fayette County: Her History and Her People* (1902; reprint, Schulenburg, TX: Schulenburg Printing, 2010), 340–350, 355–358. The *La Grange Journal* is an especially valuable source in that it regularly published articles and box scores concerning community teams from throughout Fayette County.

3. *La Grange Journal*, Aug. 19, 1909 (quote); Deborah Fitzgerald, *Every Farm a Factory: The Industrial Ideal in American Agriculture* (New Haven, CT: Yale University Press, 2003); Gilbert C. Fite, *American Farmers: The New Minority* (Bloomington: Indiana University Press, 1981); William E. Akin, *West Virginia Baseball: A History, 1865–2000* (Jefferson, NC: McFarland, 2006), 2; Thad Sitton and Dan K. Utley, *From Can See to Can't: Texas Cotton Farmers on the Southern Prairies* (Austin: University of Texas Press, 1997), 11 (quote), passim; Pete Daniel, *Breaking the Land: The Transformation of Cotton, Tobacco, and Rice Cultures since 1880* (Urbana: University of Illinois Press, 1986), 3–22, 290–298.

4. John M. Carroll, "The Doubleday Myth and Texas Baseball," *Southwestern Historical Quarterly* 92 (Apr. 1989): 597–612; Paul H. Carlson, "Baseball's Abner Dou-

bleday on the Texas Frontier," *Military History of Texas and the Southwest* 12 (1974): 236–243; George W. Kirsch, *Baseball in Blue and Gray: The National Pastime during the Civil War* (Princeton, NJ: Princeton University Press, 2003); William J. Ryczek, *When Johnny Came Sliding Home: The Post–Civil War Baseball Boom, 1865–1870* (Jefferson, NC: McFarland, 1998); Joel Zoss and John Bowman, *Diamonds in the Rough: The Untold History of Baseball* (Lincoln: University of Nebraska Press, 2004), 77–87; Larry Bowman, "Soldiers at Play: Baseball on the American Frontier," *Nine: A Journal of Baseball History and Culture* 9 (Fall 2000): 35–49.

5. *Schulenburg Argus*, Mar. 30, 1877 (clothes quotes); *Fayette County Record*, Apr. 1, 2001; May 13, 2001; Aug. 4, 2001; Sept. 25, 2001; U.S. Census, Population Schedules for the Town of Schulenburg, Fayette Co., TX, 1880, Ancestry Library, http://ancestry library.com (accessed Aug. 18, 2010); Jane Knapik, *Schulenburg: 100 Years on the Road, 1873–1973* (Yoakum, TX: Nortex Offset, 1973), 16–27, 40 (Little Germany quote).

6. Glen E. Lich, *The German Texans* (San Antonio: University of Texas, San Antonio, Institute of Texan Cultures, 1981), 64–73; Terry G. Jordan, *German Seed in Texas Soil: Immigrant Farmers in Nineteenth-Century Texas* (Austin: University of Texas Press, 1966), chap. 2 and 3; Terry G. Jordan, "Germans," *Handbook of Texas Online*, www.tshaonline.org/handbook/online/articles/GG/png2.html (accessed Oct. 4, 2010); FCHBC, *Fayette County*, 1:24–25; Walter D. Kamphoefner, *The Westfalians: From Germany to Missouri* (Princeton, NJ: Princeton University Press, 1987), 3–11, and "The Handwriting on the Wall: The Klan, Language Issues, and Prohibition in the German Settlements of Eastern Texas," *Southwestern Historical Quarterly* 112 (July 2008): 54; *First Annual Report of the Agricultural Bureau*, 71; C. Allan Jones, *Texas Roots: Agriculture and Rural Life before the Civil War* (College Station: Texas A&M University Press, 2005), 101–107, 125–132; Lonn Taylor, "Some Neighbors," *Texas Observer*, Apr. 11, 1975, 12, Fayette County vertical file, BCAH; Donna Gholson Cook, ed., *Fritz and Annie Lippe Family: German Cotton Farmers in Early 1900s Texas: Washington, Mills, Hamilton, and Tom Green Counties* (Bloomington, IN: Author House, 2009), 6–8.

The Mexican American population in both Fayette and Washington Counties, in contrast, was very small in 1887—less than 100 in both cases—and would not become significantly larger until the 1920s; *First Annual Report of the Agricultural Bureau*, 71, 229; *The 1928 Texas Almanac and State Industrial Guide* (N.p.: n.p., ca. 1928), Texas State Historical Association, Denton, online at *The Portal to Texas History*, University of North Texas Libraries, http://texashistory.unt.edu/ark:/67531/metapth123786 (accessed Nov. 18, 2010), 63, 65.

7. Jordan, *German Seed in Texas Soil*, chap. 4; Jones, *Texas Roots*, 195–201; Thomas Supak, Charles Hensel, and Ricky Dippel, "German Settlers in Fayette County," in *Fayette County: Past and Present*, ed. Marjorie L. Williams (La Grange: La Grange High School, 1976), 22–26; Wilfred O. Dietrich, "German Immigrant Pioneers in Washington County and Their Influence," *German-Texan Heritage Society Journal* 13 (1991): 123–125; FCHBC, *Fayette County*, 1:24–25; Cook, *Fritz and Annie Lippe Family*, 23–24; Sitton and Utley, *From Can See to Can't*, 19–23.

8. Lich, *German Texans*, 123–183; Kermit W. Fox, *A Son of La Bahia Remembers* (Austin, TX: Aus-Tex, 1991), 1–5, 31; Thomas Oliver Whitener, interviewed on three

occasions by Thomas Lee Charlton and Dan K. Utley, Mar. 25–Dec. 3, 1992, in Burton, TX, transcript, p. 8, Baylor University Institute for Oral History, Waco, TX (BUIOH); Robert Lee Dement, interviewed by Dan K. Utley, June 28, 1993, in Burton, TX, transcript, pp. 1–2, BUIOH; Dietrich, "German Immigrant Pioneers in Washington County," 123–125; Supak, Hensel, and Dippel, "German Settlers," 22–26; Lois Krause, "Round Top Rifle Association Hall," in *Fayette County: Past and Present*, 380–386; FCHBC, *Fayette County*, 1:3, 24–25, 70–71; Joseph B. Wilson, "The Texas Germans of Lee and Fayette Counties," *Rice Institute Pamphlet* 47 (Apr. 1960): 83–98, Germans-Fayette County vertical file, ITC; Kamphoefner, "Handwriting on the Wall," 65–66; Walter D. Kamphoefner, "German Texans: In the Mainstream or Backwaters of Lone Star Society?" *Yearbook of German-American Studies* (2003): 132–134; Sitton and Utley, *From Can See to Can't*, 197.

La Bahia Prairie was named for the Old La Bahia Road, one of the first overland routes used by European explorers of Texas dating back to the 1680s. Following the route of present-day Farm to Market Road 390 and State Highway 237, it ran through Washington-on-the-Brazos, Independence, Burton, Round Top, and La Grange. See Wilfred O. Dietrich, *The Blazing Story of Washington County* (1950; revised ed., Wichita Falls, TX: Nortex Offset, 1973), 151–152.

9. Dement interview, 83–84; Annie Maud Knittel Avis, interviewed by Anne Radford Phillips, Nov. 11, 1991 and Dec. 5, 1991, in Burton, TX, transcript, pp. 26–27, BUIOH; Gladys J. Krause, interviewed by Thad Sitton, Dec. 2, 1994, in Round Top, TX, transcript, p. 7, BUIOH; Ora Nell Wehring Moseley, interviewed by Lois E. Myers, Jan. 22, 1992, in Burton, TX, transcript, p. 21, BUIOH; Ilo A. Ullrich, interviewed by Thad Sitton, Nov. 4, 1994, in Carmine, TX, transcript, p. 20, BUIOH; Edward F. Wegner, interviewed on seven occasions by Dan K. Utley, Jan. 22, 1992–Sept. 16, 1994, in Burton, TX, transcript, p. 225, BUIOH; Fox, *Son of La Bahia*, 27; Cook, *Fritz and Annie Lippe Family*, 68. See Jennifer Ring, *Stolen Bases: Why American Girls Don't Play Baseball* (Urbana: University of Illinois Press, 2009), for a historical analysis, albeit largely urban-oriented, of women's exclusion from participation in the game.

10. Dement interview, 83–84; Howard Herbert Matthies and Olefa Koerth Matthies, interviewed on seven occasions by Thomas Lee Charlton, Deborah J. Hoskins, Thad Sitton, and Dan K. Utley, Dec. 20, 1991–Dec. 2, 1994, in Burton, TX, transcript, pp. 130–131 (1st quote 130), BUIOH; Ullrich interview, 20 (2nd quote); W. F. "Boy" Hasskarl Jr., *Remembering Brenham: A Collection of Stories as told to by Dr. "Boy" Hasskarl* (Brenham, TX: Webb Printing, 2005), 92; Timothy M. Gay, *Tris Speaker: The Rough and Tumble Life of a Baseball Legend* (Lincoln: University of Nebraska Press, 2005), 38–39.

11. *Brenham Banner*, Apr. 30, 1874; *Brenham Daily Banner*, Apr. 6, 1879; May 10, 1879 (1st quote); May 8, 1880; May 2, 1884 (2nd quote); *Brenham Daily Banner-Press*, May 26, 1914; William O. Dietrich, *History of the Brenham Maifest* (Brenham, TX: Brenham Maifest Association, 1990), 5–21; Dietrich, "German Immigrant Pioneers in Washington County," 126; Robert A. Hasskarl Jr. *Brenham, Texas, 1844–1958* (Brenham, TX: Banner-Press Publishing, 1958), 70–72; Hasskarl, *Remembering Brenham*,

42; Lich, *German Texans*, 133. "Cochatte" was probably a variant of the Alabama-Coushatta Tribe of Texas.

12. Marguerite Johnston, "Round Top: For 112 Years, a Grand Tradition," *Houston Post*, June 30, 1963, Round Top vertical file, BCAH; "La Grange in 1886," *La Grange Journal*, June 4, 1931, Fayette County Scrapbook, BCAH; *La Grange Journal*, July 10, 1902 (both quotes); July 9, 1903; July 23, 1903; June 30, 1904; Matthies interview, 131; Krause, "Round Top Rifle Association Hall," 380–386; Sitton and Utley, *From Can See to Can't*, 197–198.

13. Matthies interview, 260–261; Dement interview, 83–84; Daniel, *Breaking the Land*, 3–4; J. B. Coltharp, "Reminiscences of Cotton Pickin' Days," *Southwestern Historical Quarterly* 73 (Apr. 1970): 539–542; Fox, *Son of La Bahia*, 54–92; Sitton and Utley, *From Can See to Can't*, chap. 5.

14. Dement interview, 83–84; Matthies interview, 130–131; Ullrich interview, 20–21; Wegner interview, 225; *La Grange Journal*, July 4, 1901; July 18, 1901; Aug. 8, 1901; Aug. 21, 1902; Aug. 13, 1903; Sept. 3, 1903; June 16, 1904; Aug. 25, 1904; June 15, 1905; Aug. 17, 1905; June 6, 1907; July 4, 1907; Aug. 15, 1907; Sept. 19, 1907; July 23, 1908; Aug. 13, 1908; Aug. 20, 1908; Aug 5, 1909; Aug. 4, 1910; Knapik, *Schulenburg*, appendix B; Aileen Loehr, *The Fayette County Record: 80th Anniversary: 1922–2002 Pictorial History* (Dallas, TX: Taylor Publishing, 2002), 110; Annie Maud Knittel Avis, *History of Burton, Including the Area of the Burton Independent School District* (Burton, TX: s.n., 1974), 376; FCHBC, *Fayette County*, 1:416; William T. Chambers, "Life in a Cotton Farming Community," *Journal of Geography* 28 (1930): 141–147; Sitton and Utley, *From Can See to Can't*, 200–203.

15. Robert L. Skrabanek, *We're Czechs* (College Station: Texas A&M University Press, 1998), xii, 3 (quote); Sean N. Gallup, *Journeys into Czech-Moravian Texas* (College Station: Texas A&M University Press, 1998), 9.

16. Le Roy Hodges, "The Bohemian Farmers of Texas," *Texas Magazine* 6 (June 1912): 87–96, Czechosloakian-Agriculture vertical file, ITC; Olga Pazdral, "Czech Folklore in Texas" (MA thesis, University of Texas at Austin, 1942), 166–167, Czechosloakian-Social Life and Customs vertical file, ITC; Machann and Mendl, *Krásná Amerika*, 22–38 (quote 28), 205–234; Clinton Machann and James W. Mendl Jr., eds., *Czech Voices: Stories from Texas in the Amerikán Národní Kalendář* (College Station: Texas A&M University Press, 1991), 128; Hewitt, *Czech Texans*, 1–5, 11; Gallup, *Journeys into Czech-Moravian Texas*, 3–9; William Phillip Hewitt, "The Czechs in Texas: A Study of the Immigration and the Development of Czech Ethnicity, 1850–1920" (PhD diss., University of Texas at Austin, 1978), chap. 2 and 3.

17. Hodges, "Bohemian Farmers of Texas," 87–96; Machann and Mendl, *Krásná Amerika*, 209; Hewitt, "Czechs in Texas," 256–257; Gallup, *Journeys into Czech-Moravian Texas*, 4; Machann and Mendl, *Czech Voices*, xviii; *First Annual Report of the Agricultural Bureau*, 71; FCHBC, *Fayette County*, 1:25–27, 47–48.

18. "Communities in Texas having more than 100 People of Czech Stock (1900)," Czechs in Texas vertical file, BCAH; Kamphoefner, *Westfalians*, chap. 2 (quote chapter title); Machann and Mendl, *Krásná Amerika*, 42–47, 71–72, 208–213, 219; Hewitt, *Czech Texans*, 1; Leonie Rummel Weyland and Houston Wade, *An Early History of*

Fayette County (1936; reprint, La Grange, TX: Fayette County Historical Commission, 2002), 240–243; Robert Janak, *Dubina, Hostyn, and Ammannsville: The Geographic Origin of Three Czech Communities in Fayette County, Texas* (Beaumont, TX: By author, 1978); Henrietta Remmert Arning, "Arning Tells Her Story," *German-Texan Heritage Society Journal* 15 (1992): 179; Robert L. Skrabanek, "The Influence of Cultural Backgrounds on Farming Practices in a Czech-American Rural Community," *Southwestern Social Science Quarterly* 31 (1951): 262; Robert L. Skrabanek and Vernon J. Parenton, "Social Life in a Czech-American Community," *Rural Sociology* 15 (Fall 1949): 221–222.

19. Gallup, *Journeys into Czech-Moravian Texas*, 6–8; Skrabanek, "Influence of Cultural Backgrounds," 261–263; Skrabanek and Parenton, "Social Life in a Czech-American Community," 221–231 (quote 229); Machann and Mendl, *Krásná Amerika*, 72–86; Hewitt, "Czechs in Texas," 147–175; Robert L. Skrabanek, "Forms of Cooperation and Mutual Aid in a Czech-American Rural Community," *Southwestern Social Science Quarterly* 30 (Dec. 1949): 183–187; Henry Wolff Jr., "Dubina's Heyday Remembered," *Victoria Advocate*, Nov. 19, 1989, Dubina vertical file, BCAH; Henry Wolff Jr., "Hardships Bested by Settlers," *Victoria Advocate*, Dec. 17, 1989, Czechs in Texas vertical file, BCAH; Richard Pierce, "Maticka Praha," *Texas Highways*, Dec. 1974, Czechs in Texas vertical file, BCAH; "Hail Freedom! A Bit of Old Europe in a Texas Setting," *Dallas Morning News*, June 16, 1940, Hostyn vertical file, BCAH.

20. Machann and Mendl, *Krásná Amerika*, 78–83; Skrabanek, "Influence of Cultural Backgrounds," 259–266; Skrabanek and Parenton, "Social Life in a Czech-American Community," 223; Skrabanek, "Forms of Cooperation," 184–185; Skrabanek, *We're Czechs*, 8, 63; Gallup, *Journeys into Czech-Moravian Texas*, 8.

21. Skrabanek, *We're Czechs*, 16 (quote), 75–100; Tomáš Grulich, "Prague: Sports as History," *Museum* 43 (1991): 67–70, Czechosloakian-Sports vertical file, ITC; Hodges, "Bohemian Farmers of Texas," 87–96; Kay Kallina, "Czech Customs and Folklore in Texas: Literature of the Southwest," Dec. 11, 1964, unpublished manuscript, Czechosloakian-Social Life and Customs vertical file, ITC; Pazdral, "Czech Folklore in Texas," 111; Gallup, *Journeys into Czech-Moravian Texas*, 9; Machann and Mendl, *Krásná Amerika*, 82; FCHBC, *Fayette County*, 1:474–479.

22. Skrabanek, *We're Czechs*, 62, 77, 80, 105, 114, 160.

23. *La Grange Journal*, June 15, 1905; Aug. 17, 1905; June 14, 1906; June 6, 1907; June 13, 1907; June 20, 1907; July 4, 1907; July 11, 1907; July 18, 1907; July 25, 1907; Aug. 8, 1907; Aug. 15, 1907; Aug. 22, 1907; Sept. 5, 1907; June 18, 1908; June 10, 1909; Aug. 5, 1909; Aug. 12, 1909; Sept. 2, 1909; July 14, 1910; June 1, 1911; June 15, 1911; June 22, 1911; July 6, 1911; July 13, 1911; July 27, 1911; Aug. 9, 1911; Aug. 16, 1911; July 23, 1927; Machann and Mendl, *Krásná Amerika*, 205–234; Gallup, *Journeys into Czech-Moravian Texas*, 6–7.

24. *La Grange Journal*, June 14, 1906 (1st and 2nd quotes); June 18, 1907 (3rd quote); Aug. 22, 1907 (4th quote); June 10, 1909 (6th quote); July 27, 1911 (5th quote).

25. Kamphoefner, "Handwriting on the Wall," 54; Donald G. Nieman, "Black Political Power and Criminal Justice: Washington County, Texas, 1868–1884," *Journal*

of Southern History 55 (Aug. 1989): 393; Thad Sitton and James H. Conrad, *Freedom Colonies: Independent Black Texans in the Time of Jim Crow* (Austin: University of Texas Press, 2005), 1–8, 60; Sitton and Utley, *From Can See to Can't*, 51, 71–80.

26. Sitton and Conrad, *Freedom Colonies*, 3, 15–19, 190–198; Sitton and Utley, *From Can See to Can't*, 28–29; Mance Lipscomb and Glen Alyn, *I Say Me for a Parable: The Oral Autobiography of Mance Lipscomb, Texas Bluesman* (New York: W. W. Norton, 1993), 272–314; Thad Sitton, "Freedmen's Settlements," *Handbook of Texas Online*, www.tshaonline.org/handbook/online/articles/uef20 (accessed Oct. 27, 2010); Nieman, "Black Political Power," 420.

27. Charlie Lincecum, interviewed by Dan K. Utley, Aug. 28, 1992, in Post Oak (Lee Co.), TX, transcript, pp. 2–5, BUIOH; Matthies interview, 268; Wegner interview, 258–259; Grover L. Williams Sr., interviewed on five occasions by Dan K. Utley, Nov. 25, 1991–June 12, 1992, in Burton, TX, transcript, pp. 1, 32, 140, 225, BUIOH; U.S. Census, Population Schedules, Precincts 3 and 4, Washington Co., TX, 1870, Ancestry Library, http://ancestrylibrary.com (accessed Oct. 20, 2010); U.S. Census, Population Schedules, Precinct 4, Washington Co., TX, 1880, 1930, Ancestry Library, http://ancestrylibrary.com (accessed Oct. 20, 2010); Donaly E. Brice and John C. Barron, *An Index to the 1867 Voters' Registration of Texas*, CD-ROM 1354 (Bowie, MD: Heritage Books, 2000); Sitton and Conrad, *Freedom Colonies*, 4, 18–19, 30; Sitton, "Freedmen's Settlements"; *First Annual Report of the Agricultural Bureau*, 229; Lois Wood Burkhalter, *Gideon Lincecum, 1793–1874: A Biography* (Austin: University of Texas Press, 1965), 74–79, 167–169 (quote 168); Hasskarl, *Remembering Brenham*, 51–53; Jerry Bryan Lincecum and Edward Hake Phillips, "Civil War Letters of Dr. Gideon Lincecum: 'I am Out and Out a Secessionist,'" *Texas Studies* 2 (1995): 159, 164; *Adventures of a Frontier Naturalist: The Life and Times of Dr. Gideon Lincecum*, ed. Jerry Bryan Lincecum and Edward Hake Phillips (College Station: Texas A&M University Press, 1994).

28. Williams interview, 38–39, 71, 82–84, 125–132, 161–169, 189; Dement interview, 35–38; Matthies interview, 244; Wegner interview, 148–150; Sitton and Conrad, *Freedom Colonies*, 23–24 (quote 24), 52, 73; Sitton and Utley, *From Can See to Can't*, 52, 236–240; Rebecca Sharpless, *Fertile Ground Narrow Choices: Women on Texas Cotton Farms: 1900–1940* (Chapel Hill: University of North Carolina Press, 1999), 173.

29. Lipscomb and Alyn, *I Say Me for a Parable*, 272–314 (2nd quote 305); Sitton and Conrad, *Freedom Colonies*, 16–18 (1st quote 17); Sitton and Utley, *From Can See to Can't*, 28–29, 44–46, 65–66; Ruth Loessin Giesber, *The Hanging Rope* (La Grange, TX: La Grange Journal, 1969).

30. Williams interview, 32–33, 212 (1st quote); Wegner interview, 110 (4th quote); Matthies interview, 126; Sitton and Conrad, *Freedom Colonies*, 24, 33 (3rd quote); 157, 159–164 (2nd quote 159).

31. Lipscomb and Alyn, *I Say Me for a Parable*, 282, 297 (quotes); Ed and Lilly Latham, interviewed by Glen Alyn, Nov. 28, 1976, CD, box 2.325/R, Lipscomb-Alyn Collection, 1960–1995, BCAH (quotes); Bubba and Eula Lee Bowser, interviewed by Glen Alyn, Aug. 11, 1977, CD, box 2.325/R, Lipscomb-Alyn Collection, 1960–1995, BCAH (quotes); Williams interview, 140; Sitton and Conrad, *Freedom Colonies*, 60–62; Sitton and Utley, *From Can See to Can't*, 29, 52.

32. Williams interview, 34, 56, 60–64, 141–145, 179, 225; Lipscomb and Alyn, *I Say Me for a Parable*, 272 (quote); Sitton and Conrad, *Freedom Colonies*, 93–97, 145–147.

33. Williams interview, 140–141, 222; Dement interview, 83 (both quotes); Wegner interview, 113–114; Sitton and Conrad, *Freedom Colonies*, 83–84, 93–94, 97–98, 147; Dietrich, *Blazing Story of Washington County*, 55; Avis, *History of Burton*, 28; Sitton and Utley, *From Can See to Can't*, 236–240.

34. Williams interview, 211, 222; *La Grange Journal*, July 24, 1902; June 30, 1904; June 27, 1912; Sitton and Conrad, *Freedom Colonies*, 104–107; William H. Wiggins Jr., "'They Closed the Town Up, Man!': Reflections on the Civil and Political Dimensions of Juneteenth," in *Celebration: Studies in Festivity and Ritual*, ed. Victor Witter Turner (Washington, DC: Smithsonian Institution Press, 1982), 284–295 (quote 291), Afro-American Holidays vertical file, ITC; William H. Wiggins Jr., *O Freedom! Afro-American Emancipation Celebrations* (Knoxville: University of Tennessee Press, 1987); Hasskarl, *Brenham, Texas, 1844–1958*, 73; Teresa Palomo Acosta, "Juneteenth," *Handbook of Texas Online*, www.tshaonline.org/handbook/online/articles/lkj01 (accessed Oct. 25, 2010); Elizabeth Hayes Turner, "Juneteenth: Emancipation and Memory," in *Lone Star Pasts: Memory and History in Texas*, ed. Gregg Cantrell and Elizabeth Hayes Turner (College Station: Texas A&M University Press, 2007), 143–175.

35. Williams interview, 222–226 (1st and 2nd quotes); Latham interview; Bowser interview; *La Grange Journal*, July 20, 1922; Aug. 7, 1924; June 9, 1927; *Brenham Daily Banner-Press*, May 11, 1925; June 10, 1925; June 15, 1925; June 23, 1925 (3rd and 4th quotes); June 29, 1925; July 8, 1925; July 18, 1925; Sitton and Conrad, *Freedom Colonies*, 33, 195, 198; Sitton and Utley, *From Can See to Can't*, 200–201.

36. Randolph B. Campbell, *Grassroots Reconstruction in Texas, 1865–1880* (Baton Rouge: Louisiana State University Press, 1997), esp. chap. 2; Walter L. Buenger, *Path to a Modern South: Northeast Texas between Reconstruction and the Great Depression* (Austin: University of Texas Press, 2001); Louis L. Gould, *Progressives and Prohibitionists: Texas Democrats in the Wilson Era* (Austin: University of Texas Press, 1973); Machann and Mendl, *Krásná Amerika*, 214. The ethnic makeup of the various teams has been determined by surveying hundreds of box scores printed in the *La Grange Journal* and the *Brenham Daily Banner-Press* from 1880 to 1929.

37. Matthies interview, 49–53; Wegner interview, 111–112; *Schulenburg Sticker*, May 28, 1915; Knapik, *Schulenburg*, 71, appendix B; Charles F. Schmidt, *History of Washington County* (San Antonio, TX: Naylor, 1949), 33; Dietrich, "German Immigrant Pioneers," 125; Dietrich, *History of the Brenham Maifest*, 169; Fox, *Son of La Bahia*, 363; Hasskarl, *Brenham, Texas, 1844–1958*, 77; Hasskarl, *Remembering Brenham*, 13; Sitton and Utley, *From Can See to Can't*, 53–54; Matthew D. Tippens, *Turning Germans into Texans: World War I and the Assimilation and Survival of German Culture in Texas, 1900–1930* (Austin, TX: Kleingarten Press, 2010), 89–126.

38. *Brenham Daily Banner-Press*, May 19, 1921; July 22, 1924; *Brenham Morning Messenger*, May 19 and 21, 1921; *Austin Statesman*, May 21 and 28, 1921; *La Grange Journal*, July 27, 1921; Wegner interview, 111–112; Fox, *Son of La Bahia*, 13–14; Dietrich, "German Immigrant Pioneers," 125; Hasskarl, *Brenham, Texas, 1844–1958*, 77–78; Has-

skarl, *Remembering Brenham*, 13; Kamphoefner, "Handwriting on the Wall," 55–58; Tippens, *Turning Germans into Texans*, 176–177; Sitton and Utley, *From Can See to Can't*, 54; Walter L. Buenger, "Memory and the 1920s Ku Klux Klan in Texas," in Cantrell and Turner, *Lone Star Pasts*, 119–142.

39. *Brenham Daily Banner-Press*, Aug. 13, 1923; Oct. 27, 1923; Oct. 29, 1923 (2nd and 3rd quotes); Oct. 31, 1923 (4th quote); July 22, 1924 (1st and 5th quotes); Hasskarl, *Brenham, Texas, 1844–1958*, 78, 83–84; Hasskarl, *Remembering Brenham*, 13, 84–86; Kamphoefner, "Handwriting on the Wall," 58; Shannon Lowry, "Bootleggers, Baseball & Barbecue: Brenham in the 20s," *Texas Co-Op Power* 64 (Jan. 2008): 12–15.

40. *Brenham Daily Banner-Press*, Apr. 22, 1925 (all quotes); Hasskarl, *Remembering Brenham*, 46.

41. *Brenham Daily Banner-Press*, Apr. 22; May 4; May 11 (1st quote); May 18; May 19 (2nd quote); May 21 (3rd quote); May 22; May 23; and June 20, 1925.

42. *Brenham Daily Banner-Press*, May 25; June 1; June 8; June 12; June 13; June 15 (1st quote); June 23; June 27; June 29; July 1; July 6 (2nd quote); July 7 (5th quote); July 10 (4th quote); July 11; July 13; July 17 (3rd quote); July 20; July 29; and Aug. 5, 1925 (6th and 7th quotes).

43. Fox, *Son of La Bahia*, 77, 96–97; Ulrich interview, 31; Skrabanek, *We're Czechs*, 37; *Brenham Daily Banner-Press*, Apr. 22; Apr. 27; and July 28, 1925; Sitton and Utley, *From Can See to Can't*, 57–61.

44. *Brenham Daily Banner-Press*, July 27 (1st quote); July 29 (3rd quote); July 31 (2nd quote); Aug. 1; Aug. 4; Aug. 5 (4th quote); Aug. 7 (5th quote); Aug. 8; Aug. 10; Aug. 11 (6th quote); Aug. 12; Aug. 15; Aug. 17 (7th quote); Aug. 19 (8th quote); Aug. 20; and Aug. 21, 1925 (9th and 10th quotes).

45. Tippens, *Turning Germans into Texans*, 187–192; Supak, Hensel, and Dippel, "German Settlers in Fayette County," 25–26; Kamphoefner, "Handwriting on the Wall," 65–66. By the mid 1920s, Mexican Americans increasingly became the focus of discrimination in the region—a significant topic, though beyond the scope of this essay.

CHAPTER 4: THE MAKING OF BOB FELLER AND THE MODERN AMERICAN FARMER

1. *Dallas County News*, Jan. 20, 1937; Kyle Crichton, "High School Hero," *Collier's*, Mar. 6, 1937, 22, 42, 46 (1st three quotes), Bob Feller player file, A. Bartlett Giamatti Research Center, National Baseball Hall of Fame and Museum, Cooperstown, NY (Feller HOF file); Roy J. Stockton, "Bob Feller—Storybook Ball Player," *Saturday Evening Post*, Feb. 20, 1937, 12–13, 66, 70; Ken Smith, "Pa Feller Raised Bob to Be a Baseball Star," *New York Daily Mirror*, Apr. 18, 1937, Feller HOF file; O. K. Armstrong, "Young Feller," *New York Herald Tribune*, Mar. 7, 1937, Feller HOF file (4th quote); "Baseball: New Season," *Time*, Apr. 19, 1937, 31; H. G. Salsinger, "The Umpire," *Cleveland Plain Dealer*, Feb. 21, 1937, Feller HOF file; "Feller Surveys Ornament on Christmas Tree in Farmhouse Parlor, Finds It's High, Outside," *Cleveland Press*, Dec. 24, 1936, Feller HOF file; "Sensational Rookie Grew Up with Baseball in

Hand," *Chicago Herald-Examiner*, Apr. 19, 1937, Feller HOF file; Kyle Samuel Crichton, *Total Recoil* (Garden City, NY: Doubleday, 1960).

2. Crichton, "High School Hero," 22, 42, 46; *Des Moines Tribune*, Oct. 10, 1936; Richard Goldstein, "Bob Feller, Whose Fastball Dazzled, Dies at 92," *New York Times*, Dec. 15, 2010 (1st quote); Franklin Lewis, "Farm Boy Turns Laughs into Gasps," *Cleveland Press*, July 7, 1936, Feller HOF file; Franklin Lewis, "Feller Leaps from Farm Field to Major Stardom," *Cleveland Press*, Aug. 26, 1936, Feller HOF file (2nd quote); "Feller Coached by Dad: Grandfather Also Had Hand in Developing New Mound Ace While on Farm," *New York World Telegram*, Aug. 26, 1936, Feller HOF file; Frank Deford, "Rapid Robert Can Still Bring It," *Sports Illustrated* May 8, 2005, 60–69.

3. The *Des Moines Tribune* was the first to publish "My Own Story," with the series starting on Apr. 5, 1937 (all quotes). The *Chicago Herald-Examiner, Cleveland Press, Toledo News-Bee, St. Louis Star-Times, New York American*, among many other papers, printed the series in full, including photographs, later in the month. Copies available at the Bob Feller Museum, Van Meter, IA, and Feller HOF file.

4. See, for example, Smith, "Pa Feller." While the print media generally referred to Bob's father as Bill, his family, friends, and community knew him over the course of his life as Will; see "Reminiscences of Marie Jamison," in Van Meter Tuesday Club, *Echoes from the Past* (Des Moines: Best Fast Printing, 1976), Roy R. Estle Memorial Library, Dallas Center, IA.

5. *New York Passenger Lists, 1820–1957*, Ancestry Library, http://ancestrylibrary.com (accessed Feb. 1, 2011); John Feller obituary, Mar. 1, 1928, Obituary file, Estle Memorial Library; Jacob Feller obituary, Jan. 9, 1924, Obituary file, Estle Memorial Library; U.S. Census, Population Schedules for Boone Township, Dallas Co., IA, 1860, Ancestry Library, http://ancestrylibrary.com (accessed Feb. 1, 2011); *Dallas County News*, Jan. 20, 1943; Dorothy Schwieder, *Iowa: The Middle Land* (Ames: Iowa State University Press, 1996), 38–44; Thomas J. Morain, *Prairie Grass Roots: An Iowa Small Town in the Early Twentieth Century* (Ames: Iowa State University Press, 1988), 4–6.

6. The previous four paragraphs draw from David Vaught, introduction to *The John Deere Story: A Biography of Plowmakers John and Charles Deere*, by Neil Dahlstrom and Jeremy Dahlstrom (DeKalb: Northern Illinois University Press, 2005), xiii–xix, which in turn draws from Paul W. Gates, *The Farmer's Age: Agriculture, 1815–1860*, Economic History of the United States, vol. 3 (New York: Holt, Rinehart & Winston, 1960), vi, 420; Fred Shannon, *The Farmer's Last Frontier: Agriculture, 1860–1897*, Economic History of the United States, vol. 5 (New York: Rinehart, 1945); Martin Bruegel, *Farm, Shop, Landing: The Rise of a Market Society in the Hudson Valley, 1780–1860* (Durham: Duke University Press, 2002); William Cronon, *Nature's Metropolis: Chicago and the Great West* (New York: W. W. Norton, 1991); James A Henretta et al., *America's History*, 3rd ed. (New York: Worth, 1997), 519–549; R. Douglas Hurt, *American Farm Tools from Hand-Power to Steam-Power* (Manhattan, KS: Sunflower University Press, 1982) and *American Agriculture: A Brief History* (Ames: Iowa State University Press, 1994); Morton Rothstein, "The American West and Foreign Markets,

1850–1900," in *The Frontier in American Development: Essays in Honor of Paul Wallace Gates*, ed. David M. Ellis (Ithaca, NY: Cornell University Press, 1969), 381–406; Morton Rothstein, "The Big Farm: Abundance and Scale in American Agriculture," *Agricultural History* 49 (Oct. 1975): 583–597; Charles Sellars, *The Market Revolution: Jacksonian America, 1815–1846* (New York: Oxford University Press, 1991); and George Rogers Taylor, *The Transportation Revolution, 1815–1860*, Economic History of the United States, vol. 4 (New York: Rinehart, 1951).

7. John Feller obituary; Jacob Feller obituary; U.S. Census, Boone Township, IA, 1860; Dallas Co., Deeds I:159, State Historical Society of Iowa Library and Archives, Des Moines (SHSI-DM); Howard E. Sneeden and Barbara A Sneeden, *Iowa: Dallas County Records* (Des Moines: s.n., 1972), 2:56, SHSI-DM; Schwieder, *Iowa*, 35–37, 134; *Van Meter Centennial History, 1868–1970* (Van Meter, IA: Van Meter Centennial Committee, 1970), 4–8, 19, 115–116, Van Meter Public Library, Van Meter, IA; Union Historical Company, *The History of Dallas County, Iowa: Containing a History of the County, Its Cities, Towns, & c. . . .* (Des Moines, IA: Union Historical Co., 1879), 503–506, Van Meter Public Library; Bob Feller with Will Gilbert, *Now Pitching, Bob Feller: A Baseball Memoir* (New York: Kensington, 1990), 33; Bob Feller with Burton Rocks, *Bob Feller's Little Black Book of Baseball Wisdom* (Chicago: Contemporary Books, 2001), 6.

8. U.S. Census, Population Schedules for Van Meter Township, Dallas Co., IA, 1870, Ancestry Library, http://ancestrylibrary.com (accessed Feb. 4, 2011); Elizabeth Feller obituary, Mar. 1930, Obituary file, Estle Memorial Library; Dallas Co., Deeds J:688, SHSI-DM; "Plat of Van Meter Township, 1901," *Plat Book of Dallas County, Iowa* (Minneapolis: Northwest Publishing, 1901), 8, Estle Memorial Library; *Van Meter Centennial History*, 11–15; Union Historical Company, *History of Dallas County*, 503–506; R. F. Wood, *Past and Present of Dallas County, Iowa* (Chicago: S. J. Clarke, 1907), 217–223, 233–236; Eugene N. Hastie, *Hastie's History of Dallas County, Iowa* (Des Moines, IA: Wallace-Homestead, 1938), 166–168; Earle D. Ross, *Iowa Agriculture: An Historical Survey* (Iowa City: State Historical Society of Iowa, 1951), 71–72; Alan G. Bogue, *From Prairie to Corn Belt: Farming on the Illinois and Iowa Prairies in the Nineteenth Century* (1963; reprint, Ames: Iowa State University Press, 1994), 193–215; John Sickels, *Bob Feller: Ace of the Greatest Generation* (Dulles, VA: Potomac Books, 2004), 2; Morain, *Prairie Grass Roots*, 27; Schwieder, *Iowa*, 47–48, 240–242. In 1869, the portion of Boone Township where the Feller farm was located became part of the newly created Van Meter Township (township 78, north of range 27, west of the 5th principal meridian). The Feller farm covered portions of sections 13 and 24.

9. Vaught, introduction, xvi–xviii.

10. Ibid.; Ross, *Iowa Agriculture*, 92–116; Schwieder, *Iowa*, 136–138; Jeffrey Ostler, *Prairie Populism: The Fate of Agrarian Radicalism in Kansas, Nebraska, and Iowa, 1880–1892* (Lawrence: University Press of Kansas, 1993), 154–174.

11. Dallas Co., Deeds K:310, K:375, 7:357, 36:612, 41:318, 41:457, 43:207, 43:260, 97:562, SHSI-DM; Dallas Co., Probate Case Files, Andrew Feller, no. 1167 (1898), Dallas Co. Archives, Adel, IA; Dallas Co., "Register of Deaths, vol. 1, 1880–1897," SHSI-DM;

Dallas Co., "Death Record, vol. 2, 1897–1910," SHSI-DM; U.S. Census, Population Schedules for Van Meter Township, Dallas Co., IA, 1880, 1900, Ancestry Library, http://ancestrylibrary.com (accessed Feb. 7, 2011); Iowa State Census, Population Schedules for Van Meter Township, Dallas Co., 1885, SHSI-DM; Annie Feller obituary, Jan. 6, 1937, Obituary file, Estle Memorial Library; Jacob Feller obituary; Elizabeth Feller obituary; "Plat of Van Meter Township, 1901"; Sneeden and Sneeden, *Iowa: Dallas County Records*, 2:146, 195; Feller and Rocks, *Bob Feller's Little Black Book*, 9; Ross, *Iowa Agriculture*, 71–91; Bogue, *From Prairie to Corn Belt*, 238–240; Morain, *Prairie Grass Roots*, 28–32, 59; Schwieder, *Iowa*, 134–136.

12. Vaught, introduction, xvi–xviii.

13. Ibid.

14. The ironies embedded in "the vanishing majority" constitute the central theme of Gilbert C. Fite, *American Farmers: The New Minority* (Bloomington: Indiana University Press, 1981). See also Hal S. Barron, *Mixed Harvest: The Second Great Transformation in the Rural North, 1870–1930* (Chapel Hill: University of North Carolina Press, 1997); John L. Shover, *First Majority—Last Minority: The Transformation of Rural Life in America* (DeKalb: Northern Illinois University Press, 1976); Joseph Frazier Wall, "The Iowa Farmer Crisis, 1920–1936," *Annals of Iowa* 47 (Spring 1983): 116–127; Schwieder, *Iowa*, 143–152; Ross, *Iowa Agriculture*, 117–186; and David B. Danbom, *Born in the Country: A History of Rural America* (Baltimore: Johns Hopkins University Press, 1995), 161–205.

15. Elizabeth Feller obituary; "Plat of Van Meter Township, 1901"; Dallas Co., Probate Case Files, Andrew Feller; U.S. Census, Population Schedules for Van Meter Township, Dallas Co., IA, 1900, 1910, Ancestry Library, http://ancestrylibrary.com (accessed Feb. 9, 2011).

16. *Dallas County News*, Jan. 13 and 20, 1943; "Plat of Van Meter Township," *Atlas of Dallas County, Iowa, 1916* (Mason City: IA: Anderson Publishing, 1916), State Historical Society of Iowa Library and Archives, Iowa City (SHSI-IC); Jack Sher, "Will Feller's Boy," *American Legion Magazine* 41 (June 1947): 24–30, Feller HOF file; *Van Meter Centennial History*, 71–72; Danbom, *Born in the Country*, 161–164; Fite, *American Farmers*, 16–19; Ross, *Iowa Agriculture*, 117–122; Morain, *Prairie Grass Roots*, 212–232.

17. Sher, "Will Feller's Boy," 24–30; *Dallas County News*, Jan. 20, 1943; Danbom, *Born in the Country*, 164–167; Barron, *Mixed Harvest*, 194–200; Morain, *Prairie Grass Roots*, 114–117; Ronald R. Kline, *Consumers in the Country: Technology and Social Change in Rural America* (Baltimore: Johns Hopkins University Press, 2000), 4–5.

18. Sher, "Will Feller's Boy," 24–30; *Dallas County News*, Feb. 17, 1915; Jan. 23, 1918; Jan. 20, 1943; Sneeden and Sneeden, *Iowa: Dallas County Records*, 2:139; Leah D. Rogers and Clare L. Kernek, "Survey of Buildings, Sites, Structures, Objects, and Districts Related to the Development of Team Sports in Iowa, 1859–1960," July 2003, 64–80, SHSI-DM; Stockton, "Bob Feller—Storybook Ball Player," 12; "Feller Coached by Dad"; Eric McKinley Eriksson, "Baseball Beginnings," *Palimpsest* 8 (Oct. 1927): 329–338; Writers Program of the Iowa WPA, "Baseball! The Story of Iowa's Early Innings," *Annals of Iowa* 22 (Apr. 1941): 625–654; Raymond A. Smith Jr., "Sports and

Games in Western Iowa in the Early 1880s," *Palimpsest* 65 (Jan.–Feb. 1984): 9–16, 25 (1st quote 15); John Liepa, "Baseball Mania Strikes Iowa," *Iowa Heritage Illustrated* 87 (Spring 2006): 3–6; Gene Schoor, *Bob Feller: Hall of Fame Strikeout Star* (Garden City, NY: Doubleday, 1962), 8 (2nd quote); Feller and Gilbert, *Now Pitching*, 33–34; Feller and Rocks, *Bob Feller's Little Black Book*, 4–8; Bob Feller, *Bob Feller's Strikeout Story* (New York: A. S. Barnes, 1947), 1–8; Sickels, *Bob Feller*, 6.

19. *William Feller v. The Consolidated Independent School District of Van Meter, Iowa* (1922), Dallas Co., District Court Case Files, no. 8979, Dallas Co. Archives; H. E. Stone, *Consolidated Schools in Iowa* (Des Moines, IA: Department of Public Instruction, 1926); Viggo Justesen, "Is the District School Doomed?" *Wallaces' Farmer*, Feb. 8, 1930, 1, 18; *Van Meter Centennial History*, 63–70; Harvey Frommer and Frederic J. Frommer, eds., *Growing Up Baseball: An Oral History* (Dallas, TX: Taylor Trade Publishing, 2001), 87; Danbom, *Born in the Country*, 164, 169–172; Barron, *Mixed Harvest*, 43–77.

20. James H. Shideler, *Farm Crisis: 1919–1923* (Berkeley: University of California Press, 1957), 46–75; Fite, *American Farmers*, 34–35; Danbom, *Born in the Country*, 176–197.

21. Shideler, *Farm Crisis*, 46; Morain, *Prairie Grass Roots*, 220–232; Schwieder, *Iowa*, 148–150. Ross, *Iowa Agriculture*, 136–162; *Dallas Morning News*, Nov. 6, 1929.

22. Dallas County, Probate Case Files, Elizabeth Feller, no. 5258 (1930), Dallas Co. Archives; *William Feller v. Frederick W. Meyer and Dorothy Meyer*, no. 8979 (1937), Dallas County, Judgment Docket Book A4, 143, Dallas Co Archives; "Plat of Van Meter Township," *Atlas and Plat Book of Dallas County, Iowa, 1929* (Des Moines, IA: Kean Map Co., 1929), SHSI-IC; Iowa State Census, Population Schedules for Van Meter Township, Dallas County, 1925, SHSI-DM; Crichton, "High School Hero," 22 (quote); Bob Feller, foreword to *The Farm Tractor: 100 Years of North American Tractors*, by Ralph W. Sanders (St. Paul, MN: Voyageur Press, 2007), 8–9; *Van Meter Centennial History*, 96; *Dallas County News*, Feb. 1, 1928; June 13, 1928; Aug. 28, 1929; Feller and Gilbert, *Now Pitching*, 21, 33; Donald Honig, *Baseball When the Grass Was Real* (New York: Berkeley, 1975), 245–246; Fay Vincent, *The Only Game in Town: Baseball Stars of the 1930s and 1940s Talk about the Game They Loved* (New York: Simon & Schuster, 2006), 46.

23. *Feller v. The Consolidated Independent School District of Van Meter* (quote); *Van Meter Centennial History*, 63–70; Stone, *Consolidated Schools in Iowa*, 8, 16–17, 38–39; Justesen, "Is the District School Doomed," 1, 18; Danbom, *Born in the Country*, 172, 193; Barron, *Mixed Harvest*, 43–77.

24. *Dallas County News*, June 28, 1916; Aug. 2, 1916; Aug. 16, 1916; Nov. 9, 1927; Jan. 25, 1928; Aug. 13, 1930; Fite, *American Farmers*, 38–40; Grant McConnell, *The Decline of Agrarian Democracy* (Berkeley: University of California Press, 1953), 19–43; John L. Shover, *Cornbelt Rebellion: The Farmers' Holiday Association* (Urbana: University of Illinois Press, 1965); Morain, *Prairie Grass Roots*, 233–235; Wall, "Iowa Farmer Crisis," 116–127.

25. *Dallas County News*, Nov. 23, 1927; Shideler, *Farm Crisis*, 274–279; David Brody, "On the Failure of U.S. Radical Politics: A Farmer-Labor Analysis," *Industrial*

Relations 22 (Spring 1983): 141–163; McConnell, *Decline of Agrarian Democracy*, 55–65; Wall, "Iowa Farmer Crisis," 116–127; Schwieder, *Iowa*, 149–150; Fite, *American Farmers*, 38–57; Ross, *Iowa Agriculture*, 148–162.

26. Brody, "On the Failure of U.S. Radical Politics," 155–156; McConnell, *Decline of Agrarian Democracy*, 66–83; Danbom, *Born in the Country*, 197–202, 208.

27. McConnell, *Decline of Agrarian Democracy*, 66–83; Brody, "On the Failure of U.S. Radical Politics," 155–156; Danbom, *Born in the Country*, 208–211; Wall, "Iowa Farmer Crisis," 126–127; Fite, *American Farmers*, 54–57; Ross, *Iowa Agriculture*, 163–177.

28. *Dallas County News*, Jan. 11, 1933; Aug. 16, 1933; Donald E. Fish, "Donald and Marian," unpublished manuscript, 1994, 207–208, SHSI-IC; Don Fish, "Warming up Feller," *Iowa Heritage Illustrated* 87 (Spring 2006): 19; Danbom, *Born in the Country*, 173; David Vaught, *Cultivating California: Growers, Specialty Crops, and Labor, 1875–1920* (Baltimore: Johns Hopkins University Press, 1999), 148–149 (quote).

29. *Dallas County News*, July 16, 1930; Aug. 13, 1930; July 15, 1931; U.S. Bureau of the Census, *Census of Agriculture, Vol. 2: Reports by States with Statistics for Counties, Part 1: The Northern States*, 1930 (Washington, DC: Government Printing Office, 1932), 920; Feller, foreword, 8–9; "History of the Feller Farmstead," Bob Feller Museum; Terry Pluto, "One Last Trip Home to Iowa, with Bob Feller," *Cleveland Plain Dealer*, Dec. 17, 2010 (quote); *Des Moines Tribune*, Apr. 5, 1937; Stockton, "Bob Feller—Storybook Ball Player," 12; Feller and Rocks, *Bob Feller's Little Black Book*, 20; Mary Ann Lickteig, "Caterpillar Tractors Keep Feller down on the Farm," *Des Moines Register*, May 21, 1992, Feller HOF file; Hurt, *American Agriculture*, 251–252.

30. *Dallas County News*, Jan. 11, 1933; July 12, 1933; July 19, 1933; July 26, 1933; Aug. 2, 1933; Aug. 9, 1933; Aug. 16, 1933; Sept. 16, 1933; Sept. 13, 1933; Sept. 20, 1933; Sept. 27, 1933; Dec. 6, 1933; Mar. 14, 1934; Oct. 10, 1934; May 8, 1935; Nov. 13, 1935; Apr. 29, 1936; Jan. 20, 1943; Fish, "Donald and Marian," 207–208; Wall, "Iowa Farmer Crisis," 126–127.

31. Fite, *American Farmers*, 1–19.

32. *Dallas County News*, May 23, 1934; Feller and Rocks, *Bob Feller's Little Black Book*, 10–12, 20 (quote 11); Feller, *Bob Feller's Strikeout Story*, 6; Honig, *Baseball When the Grass Was Real*, 245; Frommer and Frommer, *Growing Up Baseball*, 87; Feller and Gilbert, *Now Pitching*, 33–34; Sickels, *Bob Feller*, 7; Schoor, *Bob Feller*, 16–17; Fite, *American Farmers*, 66–69; Joseph M. Flora, "Baseball as Passionate Preference in *No Fun on Sunday*," in *The Lizard Speaks: Essays on the Writings of Frederick Manfred*, ed. Nancy Owen Nelson (Sioux Falls, SD: Center for Western Studies, 1998), 180–195; Pamela Riney-Kehrberg, *Childhood on the Farm: Work, Play, and Coming of Age in the Midwest* (Lawrence: University Press of Kansas, 2005), 126–157.

33. *Dallas County News*, May 14, 1932; June 1, 1932; June 8, 1932; June 15, 1932; June 22, 1932; Aug. 17, 1932; Sept. 28, 1932; May 24, 1933; June 21, 1933; July 18, 1934; Aug. 15, 1934; May 8, 1935; June 12, 1935; July 17, 1935; *Des Moines Tribune*, July 5, 1935; July 26, 1935; July 30, 1935; Aug. 24, 1935; June 26, 1957; Bob Feller as told to Hal Lebovitz, "What Baseball Has Done for Me," *Sporting News*, Dec. 8 and 15, 1954, Feller HOF file; "Feller Coached by Dad"; Bob Feller as told to Hal Lebovitz, "Feller Flashback:

'Legion Ball Launched My Career in Game,'" *Sporting News*, July 20, 1963, Feller HOF file; Bob Feller, "Bob Feller and American Legion Baseball: How a Shy Youngster Started on the Road to Major League Greatness," www.legion.org/baseball/753/bob-feller-and-american-legion-baseball (accessed Mar. 15, 2011); Feller and Rocks, *Bob Feller's Little Black Book*, 4–8; Frommer and Frommer, *Growing Up Baseball*, 86–88; Feller and Gilbert, *Now Pitching*, 34–37; Feller, *Bob Feller's Strikeout Story*, 6–11.

34. *Dallas County News*, Sept. 25, 1929; Mar. 12, 1930 (2nd quote); Feller and Gilbert, *Now Pitching*, 21, 34 (1st quote); Feller and Rocks, *Bob Feller's Little Black Book*, 14, 20.

35. *Dallas County News*, Sept. 7, 1932; Sept. 21, 1932; Oct. 5, 1932; Sept. 19, 1934; May 15, 1935; June 19, 1935; June 26, 1935; *Des Moines Tribune*, Aug. 24, 1935 (quote); Red Smith, "Catfish Hunter of His Day," *New York Times*, May 11, 1975, Feller HOF file; Ed Fitzgerald, "Bob Feller—Incorporated," *Sport* 2 (June 1947): 60–67, Feller HOF file; Feller and Gilbert, *Now Pitching*, 36, 140; Feller and Rocks, *Bob Feller's Little Black Book*, 16; Vincent, *Only Game in Town*, 46; Paul Fisher, "The Splitter," in *The Fireside Book of Baseball*, ed. Charles Einstein (New York: Simon & Schuster, 1956); 124–132; Roland A. White, *Milo Reno, Farmers Union Pioneer: The Story of a Man and a Movement* (1941; reprint, New York: Arno, 1975), 118; Timothy M. Gay, *Satch, Dizzy, and Rapid Robert: The Wild Saga of Interracial Baseball before Jackie Robinson* (New York: Simon & Schuster, 2010), 156.

36. *Des Moines Tribune*, Aug. 24, 1936; Aug. 25, 1936 (quote); *Dallas Morning News*, Aug. 26, 1936.

37. Franklin Lewis, "Feller Leaps from Farm Field to Major Stardom," *Cleveland Press*, Aug. 26, 1936, Feller HOF file; "Feller Coached by Dad"; Ed McAuley, "Young Feller, Who Assaults Old Records, Called Fastest Pitcher since Walter Johnson," *Sporting News*, Sept. 24, 1936; Honig, *Baseball When the Grass Was Real*, 248 (1st quote); *Dallas County News*, Sept. 16, 1936; Jan. 20, 1937 (2nd quote).

38. Sher, "Will Feller's Boy," 24–30; "Bill's Faith Spurred Bob," *Des Moines Register*, Jan. 11, 1943; "Pitchers and Geography," *Sporting News*, Dec. 4, 1924 (quote); Waite Hoyt, "Farm Boys in Baseball," *Farm Quarterly*, 13 (Spring 1958), 72–75, 144–148; Richard C. Crepeau, "Urban and Rural Images in Baseball," *Journal of Popular Culture* 9 (Fall 1975); 315–324; Barron, *Mixed Harvest*, 226. The numerous articles Will may have read over the years include J. Howard Berry, "Play Ball," *Country Gentleman*, May 2, 1925, 11, 34; Cullen Cain, "Dazzy Vance: From Farm to Diamond," *Country Gentleman*, Feb. 21, 1925, 5–6, 24; "Country Boys in the Big Leagues," *Literary Digest*, Apr. 18, 1925, 60–62; "'Hick' Baseball as the Basis of the Game," *Literary Digest*, May 19, 1923, 64–68; Robert H. Reed, "Where Do Big League Ball Players Come From?" *Country Gentleman*, Mar. 14, 1925, 9, 26; and Robert H. Reed, "A Big-League Farm Team," *Country Gentleman*, Apr. 4, 1925, 9, 52. Historian Steven A. Riess is the principal debunker of the farm-boy-dominated-big-leagues myth; see especially his *Touching Base: Professional Baseball and American Culture in the Progressive Era* (1980; rev. ed., Urbana: University of Illinois Press, 1999), 175–184, and "Professional Baseball and Social Mobility," in *Baseball History from Outside the Lines: A Reader*, ed. John E. Dreifort (Lincoln: University of Nebraska Press, 2001), 34–46.

39. *Des Moines Tribune*, Apr. 5–20, 1937 (quotes Apr. 5); H. G. Salsinger, "The Umpire," *Cleveland Plain Dealer*, Feb. 21, 1937, Feller HOF file; Sickels, *Bob Feller*, 30, 39. Many of the photographs published in the series can be viewed at www.desmoinesregister.com/section/bobfeller (accessed Mar. 18, 2011).

40. *Des Moines Tribune*, Oct. 25, 1928; Oct. 30, 1928; Apr. 5–20, 1937; *Dallas County News*, June 22, 1932; Aug. 17, 1932; Rocks, *Bob Feller's Little Black Book*, 14–16; Colonel Red Reeder, *Three Great Pitchers on the Mound* (Champaign, IL: Garrard, 1966), 13–21; Bogue, *From Prairie to Corn Belt*, 133; Ross, *Iowa Agriculture*, 178–186.

41. *Des Moines Tribune*, Apr. 5–20, 1937; Feller, *Bob Feller's Strikeout Story*, 11 (quote). *Strikeout Story* and "My Own Story" follow very similar story lines; in effect, the former is an enlarged version of the latter. See also Hal Lebovitz, "Iowa Farm Boy—to Hall of Fame," *Sporting News*, Feb. 7, 1962, Feller HOF file; Smith, "Catfish Hunter of His Day"; Honig, *Baseball When the Grass was Real*, 246; Vincent, *Only Game in Town*, 39; Feller and Gilbert, *Now Pitching*, 37–38. Slapnicka's signing of Feller soon became controversial. Major league rules discouraged teams from signing players directly from the sandlots, but Feller, as it turned out, never played for a minor league team. The flap ultimately had to be resolved by Commissioner Kenesaw Mountain Landis, who ordered the Indians to pay a Des Moines farm team $7,500 in damages. For a full account, see Sickels, *Bob Feller*, chap. 4.

42. *Des Moines Tribune*, Apr. 6, 1937; Feller, *Bob Feller's Strikeout Story*, 2, 6; Feller and Rocks, *Bob Feller's Little Black Book*, 9–10; Feller and Gilbert, *Now Pitching*, 33; "Feller Surveys Ornament"; Sec Taylor, "Death of Bill Feller, 56, Ends Baseball's Famous Father-Son Partnership," *Des Moines Register*, Jan. 11, 1943; Leighton Housh, "Bob Back on Sandlots for 'Feller Day' in Hometown Van Meter, Iowa," *Sporting News*, Oct. 27, 1947, Feller HOF file; Bob Feller as told to Ken W. Purdy, "I'll Never Quit Baseball," *Look*, Mar. 20, 1956, 53–60, Feller HOF file.

43. *Des Moines Tribune*, Apr. 8 (1st quote), 9, and 10, 1937; *Dallas County News*, May 6, 1931; Feller and Gilbert, *Now Pitching*, 4–8, 35 (2nd quote); George O. Carney, "Cow Pasture Ball: Images of a Folk Sport Place," in *Baseball, Barns, and Bluegrass: A Geography of American Folklife*, ed. George O. Carney (New York: Rowman & Littlefield, 1998), 181–191; Richard Critchfield, *Those Days: An American Album* (Garden City, NJ: Anchor/Doubleday, 1986), 150; Harold Seymour, *Baseball: The People's Game* (New York: Oxford University Press, 1990), 189.

44. The *Chicago Herald-Examiner*, *Cleveland Press*, *Toledo News-Bee*, *St. Louis Star-Times*, *New York American*, among many other papers, ran the series in the second half of Apr. 1937.

45. Gordon Cobbledick, "From the Cornfields to Cooperstown (Bob Feller)," *Cleveland Plain Dealer*, July 22, 1962, Feller HOF file; Lebovitz, "Iowa Farm Boy"; Deford, "Rapid Robert Can Still Bring It," 60–69 (quote 66); Pluto, "One Last Trip Home."

46. Morris Eckhouse, *Bob Feller* (New York: Chelsea House, 1990); Schoor, *Bob Feller*; Sickels, *Bob Feller* (the latter being by far the best biography). For a sampling of the many magazine and newspaper articles, see Bob Broeg, "No Fireball Any

Swifter Than Feller's," *Sporting News*, July 3, 1971, and "Fastballers: Feller Emerged 50 Years Ago Today," *St. Louis Post-Dispatch*, July 6, 1986, both Feller HOF file; "Feller Will Get Record $30,000," *New York Daily News*, Jan. 24, 1941, Feller HOF file; "Feller Means Business," *Newsweek*, June 2, 1947, Feller HOF file; Fitzgerald, "Bob Feller—Incorporated," 60–67; Burton Hawkins, "Bob Feller's $150,000 Pitch," *Saturday Evening Post*, Apr. 19, 1947, 25, 148, 170, Feller HOF file; Hal Lebovitz, "Rapid Robert Relives Top Feats," *Sporting News*, Feb. 14, 1962, Feller HOF file; Grantland Rice, "Reg'lar Fellers: The Story of Bob and His Dad—and How a Dream Came True," *Sport*, Sept. 1946, Feller HOF file; Sher, "Will Feller's Boy," 24–30; Smith, "Catfish Hunter of His Day"; Red Smith, "Feller on Threshold of Hall of Fame," *Arizona Republic*, Jan. 13, 1962, Feller HOF file.

47. "Feller Will Get Record $30,000"; "Feller Means Business"; Fitzgerald, "Bob Feller—Incorporated," 60–67; Hawkins, "Bob Feller's $150,000 Pitch," 25, 148, 170; Virginia Feller as told to Hal Lebovitz, "He's My Feller," *Baseball Digest*, May 1952, 91–106; Vincent, *Only Game in Town*, 49 (quote); Sickels, *Bob Feller*, 136; Gay, *Satch, Dizzy, and Rapid Robert*, 151–260.

48. Feller, *Bob Feller's Strikeout Story*; Feller and Gilbert, *Now Pitching*; Feller and Rocks, *Bob Feller's Little Black Book*; Feller, "Feller Flashback," "What Baseball Has Done for Me," and "Bob Feller and American Legion Baseball"; Bob Feller as told to Ken W. Purdy, "I'll Never Quit Baseball," *Look*, Mar. 20, 1956, 53–60, Feller HOF file; Frommer and Frommer, *Growing Up Baseball*, 86–91; Honig, *Baseball When the Grass Was Real*, 241–263; Vincent, *Only Game in Town*, 34–56.

49. Feller and Gilbert, *Now Pitching*, 20, 33 (1st and 2nd quotes); Hawkins, "Bob Feller's $150,000 Pitch," 25 (3rd and 4th quotes).

50. Feller, "What Baseball Has Done for Me" (1st quote); Pluto, "One Last Trip Home" (2nd quote); Virginia Feller, "He's My Feller," 101–102 (3rd quote 102); "Feller Success Buys Home for His Parents," unidentified clipping dated Aug. 22, 1940, Feller HOF file (4th quote); "History of the Feller Farmstead"; Anthony Castrovince, "Feller Takes Stroll Down Memory Lane: Indians Hall of Fame Pitcher Returns Home to Iowa," *Indians News*, July 20, 2007, http://cleveland.indians.mlb.com/news/article.jsp?ymd=20070720&content_id=2098350 (accessed Mar. 30, 2011); Sickels, *Bob Feller*, 90; Morris Engelberg and Mary Schneider, *DiMaggio: Setting the Record Straight* (Minneapolis: Motorbooks International, 2003), 162.

51. Feller, foreword, 8–9 (1st quote 8); Lickteig, "Caterpillar Tractors"; "History of the Feller Farmstead"; Pluto, "One Last Trip Home"; Castrovince, "Feller Takes Stroll Down Memory Lane," (2nd quote).

CHAPTER 5: THE MILROY YANKEES AND THE DECLINE OF SOUTHWEST MINNESOTA

1. *Redwood Gazette*, Sept. 11, 1947 (quotes); Sept. 16, 1947; *Marshall Messenger*, Sept. 16, 1947; Sept. 18, 1947; Richard Kramer, interview by author, Apr. 12, 2007, Lucan, MN, transcript in author's possession; Mark "Spike" Dolan, interview by author, Apr. 12, 2007, Milroy, MN, transcript in author's possession; Armand Peterson

and Tom Tomashek, *Town Ball: The Glory Days of Minnesota Amateur Baseball* (Minneapolis: University of Minnesota Press, 2006), 354.

2. Zane Grey, "Inside Baseball," *Baseball Magazine* 3 (Aug. 1909): 11–18 (1st and 3rd quotes); Hugo Münsterberg, *The Americans* (Garden City, NY: Doubleday, Page, 1914), 543 (2nd quote); Harold Seymour, *Baseball: The People's Game* (Oxford: Oxford University Press, 1990), chap. 13; Thomas Harvey, "Small-Town Minnesota," in *Minnesota in a Century of Change: The State and Its People Since 1900*, ed. Clifford E. Clark (St. Paul: Minnesota Historical Society Press, 1989), 109–113; Richard O. Davies, Joseph A. Amato, and David R. Pichaske, eds., *A Place Called Home: Writings on the Midwestern Small Town* (St. Paul: Minnesota Historical Society Press, 2003), 16; Joseph Amato, "It's Root, Root, Root for the Home Team," in *Southwest Minnesota: A Place of Many Places*, ed. Joseph Amato and David Pichaske (Marshall, MN: Crossings Press, 2007), 77–81.

3. David B. Danbom, *Born in the Country: A History of Rural America* (Baltimore: Johns Hopkins University Press, 1995), chap. 11; Joseph Amato and John W. Meyer, *The Decline of Rural Minnesota* (Marshall, MN: Crossings Press, 1993).

4. Hamlin Garland, *Main-Travelled Roads* (New York: Harper & Brothers, 1891); Sinclair Lewis, *Main Street* (New York: Harcourt, Brace, 1920); Jane Smiley, *A Thousand Acres* (New York: Alfred A. Knopf, 1991); Laura Ingalls Wilder, *Little House on the Prairie* (New York: Harper & Brothers, 1935); Garrison Keillor, *Lake Wobegon Days* (New York: Viking, 1985); Harvey, "Small-Town Minnesota," 100–104.

5. Richard Hofstadter, *The Age of Reform: From Bryan to FDR* (New York: Vintage Books, 1955); Wendell Berry, *The Unsettling of America: Culture and Agriculture* (San Francisco: Sierra Club Books, 1977).

6. David R. Pichaske and Joseph Amato, eds., *Southwest Minnesota: The Land and the People* (Marshall, MN: Crossings Press, 2000), viii (2nd quote), x (1st quote). Many of the region's talented writers, poets, and photographers contributed to this insightful anthology. See also Joseph A. Amato, *Rethinking Home: A Case for Writing Local History* (Berkeley: University of California Press, 2002); Anthony J. Amato, Janet Timmerman, and Joseph A. Amato, *Draining the Great Oasis: An Environmental History of Murray County, Minnesota* (Marshall, MN: Crossings Press, 2001); Joseph Amato, *Countryside, Mirror of Ourselves: Essays about Calling Farmers Names, Peasants Living in the City, and other Rural Gleanings* (Marshall, MN: Amati Venti, 1981); Leo Dangel, *Home from the Field: Collected Poems* (Granite Falls, MN: Spoon River Poetry Press, 1997); Amato and Pichaske, *Southwest Minnesota: A Place of Many Places*; and Davies, Amato, and Pichaske, *Place Called Home*, 153.

7. John Dolan, interview, in Joe Paddock and Nancy Paddock, "Milroy Memories," typescript, 1977, 3–5, Minnesota Historical Society Library, St. Paul (MHS); Carl Rowland, interview, in Paddock and Paddock, "Milroy Memories," 6–8 (quote 6); Martha Van Dorsten, interview in Paddock and Paddock, "Milroy Memories," 11–12; Robert Zwach, interview in Paddock and Paddock, "Milroy Memories," 23–24; Amato and Meyer, *Decline of Rural Minnesota*, 22; David L. Nass, "The Rural Experience," in *Minnesota in a Century of Change*, 129; Wayne E. Webb, *Redwood: The Story of a County* (St. Paul: North Central Publishing, 1964), 149.

8. *Wabasso Standard*, Mar. 28, 1902; Apr. 13, 1902; Dennis A. Gimmestad and James K. Nestingen, "Five Redwood County Towns: An Architectural Survey of Lucan, Milroy, Sanborn, Wabasso, and Walnut Grove," 1977, typescript, 11, 76, MHS; Edith Ousky et al., *100 Years of Milroy Memories and 75 Years of Baseball* (Milroy: Milroy Centennial History Book Committee, 2002), 3–9 (2nd quote 5), Southwest Minnesota Baseball Collection, Southwest Minnesota Regional Research Center, Southwest Minnesota State University, Marshall (SMBC); Webb, *Redwood*, 174–175, 182–184, 395 (1st quote 184); Amato and Meyer, *Decline of Rural Minnesota*, 22; Davies, Amato, and Pichaske, *Place Called Home*, 8; John C. Hudson, *Plains Country Towns* (Minneapolis: University of Minnesota Press, 1985), chap. 3–5.

9. Webb, *Redwood*, 174–175, 182–184, 331; Amato and Meyer, *Decline of Rural Minnesota*, 19–24, 33, 53; Ousky, *100 Years of Milroy Memories*, 3–5; Davies, Amato, and Pichaske, *Place Called Home*, 8.

10. Torgny Anderson, "When Baseball Was King in the Prairie Country," 1990, typescript, SMBC; Torgny Anderson, "Cottonwood Baseball through the Years," n.d., typescript, SMBC; John Franklin Smart, "Daggett Brook Sketches," n.d., typescript, chap. 6, MHS; John Dolan, interview in Paddock and Paddock, "Milroy Memories," 3–5; Louie Dolan, interview by Joseph M. Kemp, Jan. 15, 1996, cassette tape, box 1, SMBC; Mark "Spike" Dolan, interview by Joseph M. Kemp, Jan. 8, 1996, cassette tape, box 1, SMBC; Joseph M. Kemp, "Baseball and Milroy: A Fifty Year Love Affair," undergraduate paper for History 487, Southwest State University, Feb. 26, 1996, 13–14, SMBC; Cecil O. Monroe, "The Rise of Baseball in Minnesota," *Minnesota History* 19 (June 1938): 162–181; George S. Hage, "Games People Played: Sports in Minnesota Daily Newspapers, 1860–1890," *Minnesota History* 47 (Winter 1981): 321–328.

11. Ousky, *100 Years of Milroy Memories*, 109–115; Sheridan "Shorty" Young, interview by Joseph M. Kemp, Jan. 28, 1996, cassette tape, box 1, SMBC; Kramer, interview by author (3rd quote); Lewis E. Atherton, *Main Street on the Middle Border* (Bloomington: Indiana University Press, 1954), 101; Eugene McCarthy, "Confessions of a Fair Country Ballplayer," *Look*, Oct. 8, 1968, 67–74 (1st and 2nd quotes 72); Richard Critchfield, *Those Days: An American Album* (Garden City, NY: Anchor/Doubleday, 1986), 148–151; Richard Lingeman, *Small Town America: A Narrative History, 1620–The Present* (New York: G. P. Putnam's Sons, 1980), 303; Bruce Catton, "The Great American Game," *American Heritage* 10 (Apr. 1959): 16–25, 86; David L. Cohn, *The Good Old Days: A History of American Morals and Manners as Seen through the Sears Roebuck Catalogs, 1905 to the Present* (New York: Simon & Schuster, 1940), 453–454.

12. Richard O. Davies, *Main Street Blues: The Decline of Small-Town America* (Columbus: Ohio State University Press, 1998), 146–148; Peterson and Tomashek, *Town Ball*, 3–11; Ousky, *100 Years of Milroy Memories*, 110; Kemp, "Baseball and Milroy," 5–6; Zwach, interview in Paddock and Paddock, "Milroy Memories," 23–24 (quote); Bob Zwach, interview by Joseph M. Kemp, Jan. 8, 1996, cassette tape, box 1, SMBC. Basketball also became popular in postwar rural Minnesota, especially at the high school level; see Steven R. Hoffbeck, "Hayloft Hoopster: Legendary Lynd and the State High School Basketball Tournament," *Minnesota History* 55 (Winter 1997–1998): 334–349.

13. Zwach, interview by Kemp; Ousky, *100 Years of Milroy Memories*, 110; Peterson and Tomashek, *Town Ball*, 41, 302–303; Spike Dolan, interview by Kemp; Kemp, "Baseball and Milroy," 6.

14. Peterson and Tomashek, *Town Ball*, x, 356–362; Reed Lovsness, interview by author, Apr. 12, 2007, Marshall, MN, transcript in author's possession (quote); *Redwood Gazette*, Sept. 9, 1954.

15. Louie Dolan, interview by Kemp; Ousky, *100 Years of Milroy Memories*, 39–46; Spike Dolan, interview by author; U.S. Census, Population Schedules for Milroy Village and Westline Township, Redwood County, Minnesota, 1930, Ancestry Library, http://ancestrylibrary.com (accessed Apr. 20, 2011); Kramer, interview by author (quote); Amato, "It's Root, Root, Root for the Home Team," 78; Webb, *Redwood*, 408–410.

16. Joseph A. Amato and John W. Meyer, "If the Home Team Doesn't Win," in Davies, Amato, and Pichaske, *Place Called Home*, 340–341; Amato and Meyer, *Decline of Rural Minnesota*, 22, 51–62.

17. Zwach, interview by Kemp; Kemp, "Baseball and Milroy," 5–6; Webb, *Redwood*, 492; *Redwood Gazette*, July 27, 1948; July 29, 1948; Aug. 5, 1948; Aug. 17, 1948; Aug. 24, 1948; *Marshall Messenger*, Aug. 19, 1948; Doris Zwach, interview by Joseph M. Kemp, Jan. 25, 1996; cassette tape, box 1, SMBC.

18. "76th Annual Tournament, Minnesota Amateur Baseball Association, Aug. 19–22, Aug. 26–29, Sept. 3–6, 1999, Granite Falls, Minnesota," 129–133, folder 2, Minnesota Amateur Baseball Association Records, MHS (for Marshall baseball history); Peterson and Tomashek, *Town Ball*, x, 43–44 (1st set of quotes 44), 159–160; John Radzilowski, *Prairie Town: A History of Marshall, Minnesota, 1872–1997* (Marshall, MN: Lyon County Historical Society, 1997), 33, 302; Zwach, interview in Paddock and Paddock, "Milroy Memories," 24 (2nd set of quotes); Reed Lovsness, interview by Joseph M. Kemp, Jan. 8, 1996, cassette tape, box 1, SMBC (last quote); Louie Dolan, interview by Kemp; Kramer, interview by author; Lovsness, interview by author.

19. Zwach, interview in Paddock and Paddock, "Milroy Memories," 24 (1st quote); Amato, "It's Root, Root, Root for the Home Team," 78; Kramer, interview by author; Spike Dolan, interview by author; Lovsness, interview by author (2nd quote); Zwach, interview by Kemp; *Redwood Gazette*, July 29, 1948; Sept. 28, 1954; *Marshall Messenger*, July 27, 1948; Sept. 28, 1954; Aug. 17, 1955; Sept. 1, 1955; Sept. 9, 1955; Ousky, *100 Years of Milroy Memories*, 111–112.

20. Zwach, interview by Kemp (quotes); Lovsness, interview by author; Lovsness, interview by Kemp; Amato, "It's Root, Root, Root for the Home Team," 80; Peterson and Tomashek, *Town Ball*, 88–89.

21. *Redwood Gazette*, Aug. 10, 1954; Aug. 26, 1954 (1st quote); Aug. 31, 1954; Sept. 7, 1954 (2nd quote); Sept. 9, 1954 (3rd, 4th, and 5th quotes); *Marshall Messenger*, July 22, 1954; Aug. 26, 1954; Aug. 31, 1954; Sept. 2, 1954; Sept. 7, 1954; Sept. 9, 1954; Kramer, interview by author; Lovsness, interview by Kemp; Zwach, interview by Kemp; Lovsness, interview by author; Peterson and Tomashek, *Town Ball*, 90.

22. *Redwood Gazette*, Sept. 16, 1954; Sept. 21, 1954 (2nd quote); Sept. 23, 1954 (1st quote); *St. Paul Pioneer Press*, Sept. 22, 1954; *Marshall Messenger*, Sept. 16, 1954; Sept.

21, 1954; Sept. 23, 1954; *Vesta (MN) Vision*, Sept. 23, 1954; Lovsness, interview by author (3rd quote); Ousky, *100 Years of Milroy Memories*, 111–112.

23. *Redwood Gazette*, Sept. 28, 1954; *St. Paul Pioneer Press*, Sept. 22, 1954; Sept. 23, 1954; Sept. 27, 1954; *Marshall Messenger*, Sept. 28, 1954; "31st Annual Tournament, Minnesota Amateur Baseball Association, Sept. 10–19, 1954, St. Cloud, Minnesota," folder 1, Minnesota Amateur Baseball Association Records, MHS; Zwach, interview by Kemp; Spike Dolan, interview by Kemp; Peterson and Tomashek, *Town Ball*, 11, 176–178, 373–375; Kemp, "Baseball and Milroy," 9.

24. *Marshall Messenger*, Sept. 30, 1954; Oct. 14, 1954; *Vesta Vision*, Oct. 14, 1954 (1st four quotes); Lovsness, interview by author; Zwach, interview by Kemp (5th quote); Ousky, *100 Years of Milroy Memories*, 39.

25. Village of Milroy, "Clerk's Register of Receipts and Disbursements," folder 1, Milroy, MN, Records, 1895–1979, MHS; Zwach, interview by Kemp (quotes); Lovsness, interview by author; Ousky, *100 Years of Milroy Memories*, 110; Kemp, "Baseball and Milroy," 7.

26. John Kagel, interview by Joseph M. Kemp, Jan. 31, 1996, cassette tape, box 1, SMBC (quote); Zwach, interview by Kemp; Louis Dolan, interview by Kemp; Gimmestad and Nestingen, "Five Redwood County Towns," 77; Ousky *100 Years of Milroy Memories*, 112; Kemp, "Baseball and Milroy," 9–11.

27. *Marshall Messenger*, Aug. 1, 1955; Aug. 5, 1955; Aug. 25, 1955; Ousky, *100 Years of Milroy Memories*, 112; Amato, "It's Root, Root, Root for the Home Team," 80–81; Peterson and Tomashek, *Town Ball*, 89–90, 107.

28. *Marshall Messenger*, Aug. 5, 1955; Aug. 8, 1955; Aug. 10, 1955; Aug. 12, 1955; Aug. 15, 1955; Aug. 16, 1955; Aug. 17, 1955 (1st quote); Aug. 18, 1955; Aug. 19, 1955; Aug. 25, 1955; Aug. 25, 1955; Aug. 26, 1955; Aug. 29, 1955 (2nd quote); Lovsness, interview by Kemp; Zwach, interview by Kemp; Ousky, *100 Years of Milroy Memories*, 112.

29. *Marshall Messenger*, Sept. 1, 1955; Sept. 2, 1955; Sept. 6, 1955.

30. *Marshall Messenger*, Sept. 9, 1955; Sept. 12, 1955; Sept. 14, 1955; "32nd Annual Tournament, Minnesota Amateur Baseball Association, Sept. 8–18, 1955, Chaska, Minnesota," folder 1, Minnesota Amateur Baseball Association Records, MHS; Lovsness, interview by author; Lovsness, interview by Kemp; Ousky, *100 Years of Milroy Memories*, 112 (quote); *Milroy Minnesota Diamond Jubilee, 1902–1977: An Historical Anthology: July 9 & 10, 1977* (Cottonwood, MN: Cottonwood Current, 1977), 67, MHS; Amato, "It's Root, Root, Root for the Home Team," 80–81; Peterson and Tomashek, *Town Ball*, vii, 96–97.

31. On the decline of southwest Minnesota from the 1920s to the 1960s, see the series of articles in the *Worthington Daily Globe*, Oct. 18, 19, 20, 21 (quote), 22, 23, and 24, 1971; and Gerald Heil, "Southwest Minnesota Population Study," typescript, Southwest Planning of the Office of Economic Opportunity, Southwest State College, Marshall, MN, Aug. 1971. See also, Amato and Meyer, *Decline of Rural Minnesota*; Davies, *Main Street Blues*, 137–144; Davies, Amato, and Pichaske, *Place Called Home*, 213–216, 260; Peterson and Tomashek, *Town Ball*, 129; John T. Schneider, *Redwood: The Story of a County, 1963–1987* (Redwood Falls, MN: Redwood

County Board of Commissioners, 1988), chap. 1; and Danbom, *Born in the Country*, chap. 11.

32. *Worthington Daily Globe*, Oct. 18, 19, 20, 21, 22, 23, and 24, 1971; Heil, "Southwest Minnesota Population Study"; Kemp, "Baseball and Milroy," 5; Ousky, *100 Years of Milroy Memories*, 13–15; Schneider, *Redwood*, 65–73.

33. Armand Peterson, interview by author, Apr. 13, 2007, Marshall, MN, transcript in author's possession; Ousky, *100 Years of Milroy Memories*, 112–120; Davies, *Main Street Blues*, 137–162; Davies, Amato, and Pichaske, *Place Called Home*, 213–216, 260, 340–341; Peterson and Tomashek, *Town Ball*, 127–132; Amato, "It's Root, Root, Root for the Home Team," 81.

34. Ousky, *100 Years of Milroy Memories*, 112–113; *Milroy Minnesota Diamond Jubilee*, 67–68; Amato and Meyer, *Decline of Rural Minnesota*, 56–62; Pat Dolan, interview by Joseph M. Kemp, Jan. 31, 1996, cassette tape, box 1, SMBC.

35. See *Marshall Independent*, May 26, 1984 (quotes) and other unidentified clippings on the Wheaties contest in box 1, SMBC.

36. Pat Dolan, interview by Kemp; Spike Dolan, interview by author; Kramer, interview by author; Lovsness, interview by author; *Marshall Independent*, Apr. 13, 2007.

CHAPTER 6: GAYLORD PERRY, THE SPITTER, AND FARM LIFE IN EASTERN NORTH CAROLINA

1. Gaylord Perry with Bob Sudyk, *Me and the Spitter: An Autobiographical Confession* (New York: Saturday Review Press, 1974), 11–22 (1st quote 14; 2nd quote 16); Bob Sudyk, "Spitting Images: A Little Dab Took Gaylord Perry to the Hall of Fame," *Hartford (CT) Courant*, July 21, 1991; Tyler, "Spitting Image: Gaylord Perry, a Man, and His Myth," *North Carolina's Down East Magazine*, 3 (Summer 2006): 30–32.

2. Sudyk, "Spitting Images," 12; Ira Berkow, "Perry, at Age 43, Must Prove Himself Again," *Raleigh News and Observer*, Mar. 7, 1982 (quote), North Carolina Collection Clipping File, Wilson Library, University of North Carolina at Chapel Hill (NCCCF-UNC). A lifelong friend of Perry's emphasized his "survival skills"; Jim Ward, interview by author, May 23, 2008, Williamston, NC, transcript in author's possession. Perry has not been the subject of a full-length biography; for a thorough treatment of his baseball career, see Mark Armour, "Gaylord Perry," Baseball Biography Project, Society for American Baseball Research, http://sabr.org/bioproj/person/f7cbod3e (accessed Sept. 25, 2007).

3. In contrast to baseball, links between rural southern culture and other major elements of American popular culture, such as radio, stock-car racing, rock 'n' roll, and jazz, have received considerable attention from historians; see, for example, Randal L. Hall, *Lum & Abner: Rural America and the Golden Age of Radio* (Lexington: University of Kentucky Press, 2007); Pete Daniel, *Lost Revolutions: The South in the 1950s* (Chapel Hill: University of North Carolina Press, 2000); and Court Carney, *Cuttin' Up: How Early Jazz Got America's Ear* (Lawrence: University Press of Kansas, 2009).

4. W. H. Scarborough, "Williamston: Future Is Anything but Rosy," *Chapel Hill Weekly*, Aug. 30, 1964; "Griffins Was Smallest of Nine Townships in County in 1880," *Williamston Enterprise*, Tobacco Edition, Aug. 1964; U.S. Bureau of the Census, *A Report of the Seventeenth Decennial Census of the United States, Census of Population: 1950*, Vol. 2: *Characteristics of the Population . . . Part 33: North Carolina* (Washington, DC: Government Printing Office, 1952), 15–16; Francis M. Manning and W. H. Booker, *Religion and Education in Martin County, 1774–1974* (Williamston, NC: Enterprise Publishing, 1974), 46–56, 224–226; J. A. Dickey and E. C. Branson, *How Farm Tenants Live: A Social-Economic Survey in Chatham, County, N.C.* (Chapel Hill: University of North Carolina Press, 1922), 7–8; Melton A. McLaurin, *Separate Pasts: Growing Up White in the Segregated South* (Athens: University of Georgia Press, 1987), 3. Farm Life and Griffins Township are one and the same; locals have called the township "Farm Life" since the 1920s, when the local public school bearing that name was established; Linda M. Taylor, comp., "The Making of a Community: The Story of Farm Life," typescript, 1974, 3, Francis Manning Room, Martin Community College Library, Williamston, NC.

5. Gaylord Perry, telephone interview by author, May 28, 2008, transcript in author's possession; "Griffins Was Smallest"; Taylor, "Making of a Community," 22–67; Shelby Jean Nelson Hughes, ed., *Martin County Heritage* (Williamston, NC: Martin County Historical Society, 1980), 105–107, 211–240, 384–403, 463–473, 500–528; Thomas R. Butchko, ed., *Martin Architectural Heritage: The Historic Structures of a Rural North Carolina County* (Williamston, NC: Martin County Historical Society, 1998), 188–213; "Martin County Has Contributed Many Important Events in History and Has Many Honors," *Robersonville Weekly Herald*, Dec. 1, 1916, NCCCF-UNC; Perry, *Me and the Spitter*, 52.

6. U.S. Bureau of the Census, *United States Census of Agriculture: 1950*, Vol. 1: *Counties and State Economic Areas, Part 16: North Carolina and South Carolina* (Washington, DC: Government Printing Office, 1952), xviii–xix (quote xviii); "Farm Tenancy in North Carolina," *University of North Carolina News Letter*, May 7, 1947, copy in NCCCF-UNC; Dickey and Branson, *How Farm Tenants Live*, 12–14; Perry, *Me and the Spitter*, 58.

7. "Tobacco Counties Lead in Tenancy," *Raleigh News and Observer*, May 29, 1961, in North Carolina Collection Clipping File, Joyner Library, East Carolina University, Greenville (NCCCF-ECU); Susan Gibbs and Becky Harrison, "The Old vs. the New in the Culture of Tobacco," in *Smoke to Gold: The Story of Tobacco in Martin County*, ed. Stephen Klinedinst et al. (Greenville, NC: Era Press, 1998), 21–24 (1st quote 24); Bill Humphries, "Time Meant Little on N.C. Farms in Depression Days," *Fayetteville Observer-Times*, Jan. 13, 1985, NCCCF-UNC; Roy Blount Jr., "Return of the Natives," *Sports Illustrated*, Mar. 29, 1971, 58–64; Perry, *Me and the Spitter*, 49 (2nd quote), 52, 58; U.S. Bureau of the Census, *The Eighteenth Decennial Census of the United States, Census of the Population: 1960*, Vol. 1: *Characteristics of the Population . . . Part 35: North Carolina* (Washington, DC: Government Printing Office, 1961), 191, 281; Scarborough, "Williamston"; Pete Daniel, *Breaking the Land: The Transforma-*

tion of Cotton, Tobacco, and Rice Cultures since 1880 (Urbana: University of Illinois Press, 1986), 184–202.

8. Dan Collins, "Gaylord Perry: Tarheel Sketch," *Winston-Salem Journal*, July 16, 1989, NCCCF-UNC; "Will Expand Power Potential in Section," *Williamston Enterprise*, May 10, 1951; Perry, interview by author; Perry, *Me and the Spitter*, 55–58 (quote 58); Sudyk, "Spitting Images," 12; Pat Jordan, "Forkballer of the Year," *Sports Illustrated*, June 17, 1974, 38; Ron Fimrite, "Bound for Glory," *Sports Illustrated*, Aug. 24, 1981, 105–106; Linda Flowers, *Throwed Away: Failures of Progress in Eastern North Carolina* (Knoxville: University of Tennessee Press, 1990), 192–194.

9. Ward, interview by author; Perry, interview by author; Lawrence Wright, "The Old Man and the Spitter," *Atlanta Journal Constitution*, Apr. 12, 1981, clipping in Gaylord Jackson Perry player file, A Bartlett Giamatti Research Center, National Baseball Hall of Fame and Museum, Cooperstown, NY (Perry HOF file); Dave Distel, "A Country Pitcher," *Los Angeles Times*, Jan. 10, 1979, Perry HOF file (1st quote); Larry Keech, "Roots of a Pitcher: Perry Thrives on Work Ethic," *Greensboro News and Record*, July 19, 1981, NCCCF-UNC (2nd quote); Perry, *Me and the Spitter*, 51 (3rd quote), 53.

10. David Ward, "Take Me out to the Ballgame," *Huskanaw* 1 (June 1984): 17–20, copy in Francis Manning Room; "Jimmy Brown Went to Big Time but Returns to a Small Town," in "A Tribute to Jimmy Brown," Jamesville School, Dec. 3, 1977, James Roberson Brown Papers, Special Collections Research Center, North Carolina State University, Raleigh; Tommy Misselle, "Jimmy Brown Went to Big Time but Returns to a Small Town," *Williamston Enterprise*, Oct. 27, 1977 (2nd quote); Perry, *Me and the Spitter*, 47–60 (1st quote 47; 3rd quote 50; 4th quote 51; 6th quote 52); Archie, "Spitting Image," 31 (5th quote); Blount, "Return of the Natives," 59–64.

11. "Farm Life Wins First Two Tilts," *Williamston Enterprise*, June 12, 1952; Archie, "Spitting Image," 31; Blount "Return of the Natives," 60 (1st and 2nd quotes); Perry, *Me and the Spitter*, 50–51.

12. Perry, *Me and the Spitter*, 53 (1st quote); Perry, interview by author; Blount, "Return of the Natives," 64 (2nd quote); Manning and Booker, *Religion and Education in Martin County*, 54–56; "J. David Coltrain Died at Home in Griffins Tuesday," *Williamston Enterprise*, Jan. 26, 1950; "Robert Coltrain Died Near Here Sunday Morning," *Williamston Enterprise*, Aug. 22, 1950; "Church Is Now among Largest in Rural Sections of County," *Williamston Enterprise*, Tobacco Edition, Aug. 1957; Pete Daniel, *Standing at the Crossroads: Southern Life in the Twentieth Century* (Baltimore: Johns Hopkins University Press, 1986), 8 (3rd quote); Daniel, *Breaking the Land*, 191; Lu Ann Jones, *Mama Learned Us to Work: Farm Women in the New South* (Chapel Hill: University of North Carolina Press, 2002).

13. On Gaylord's high school basketball career, see the bundle of clippings marked "Gaylord Perry and Basketball," Perry HOF file; see also Perry, *Me and the Spitter*, parts of chap. 5 and 6.

14. "Green Wave Gets Opening Victory in Regional Tilts," *Williamston Enterprise*, May 24, 1955; "Green Wave Defeats Coopers in Regionals," *Williamston Enterprise*, May 31, 1955; "Williamston Defeats Morehead City Twice to Enter State Fi-

nals," *Williamston Enterprise*, June 7, 1955; "Williamston High Green Wave Captures State Championship," *Williamston Enterprise*, June 14, 1955; "Gaylord Perry Is Anxious to Join Club at Phoenix," *Williamston Enterprise*, June 5, 1958 (2nd quote); Wright, "Old Man and the Spitter" (1st quote); Blount, "Return of the Natives," 64–65; Perry, *Me and the Spitter*, 84–87.

15. "Perry Throttles Rock Ridge with Fifth No-Hitter," *Williamston Enterprise*, May 23, 1957; "Gaylord Perry Nears Decision," *Williamston Enterprise*, May 27, 1958 (1st quote); "G. Perry Talking with the Scouts," *Williamston Enterprise*, June 3, 1958; "Gaylord Perry Is Anxious to Join Club"; "Gaylord Perry Signs with Giants, Given Estimated $75,000," *Raleigh News and Observer*, June 4, 1958; Dick Herbert, "The Sports Observer," *Raleigh News and Observer*, June 4, 1958 (2nd quote); Bob Stevens (title missing from clipping), *San Francisco Chronicle*, July 23, 1966, Perry HOF file; Bob Fowler, "20 Is the Name of Perry's Game," *Sporting News*, Oct. 3, 1970, Perry HOF file; Collins, "Gaylord Perry: Tarheel Sketch"; Phil Pepe, "How Gaylord Learned to Pitch," *Sport* 42 (Nov. 1966): 63–65; Armour, "Gaylord Perry"; Perry, *Me and the Spitter*, 91–99.

16. "Gaylord Perry Is Anxious to Join Club" (1st quote); "Funeral Today at the Home for Mrs. A. J. Manning, Sr.," *Williamston Enterprise*, Jan. 21, 1954; "Williamston Splits with Jamesville in Two Games Here," *Williamston Enterprise*, Jan. 7, 1954; "Williamston Boys Edge Bear Grass; Girls Lose by 62–17," *Williamston Enterprise*, Jan. 12, 1954; "Mrs. Gaylord Jackson Perry Is Former Miss Blanche Hodges Manning," *Williamston Enterprise*, Dec. 29, 1959; "Griffins Was Smallest"; Hughes, *Martin County Heritage*, 384–403; Butchko, *Martin Architectural Heritage*, 201–204, 213; Perry, interview, by author; Lucia Peel, "Baseball Annies? Blanche Perry Trusts the Star in the Family, Gaylord," *People Magazine*, July 23, 1979, 44; Fimrite, "Bound for Glory," 106 (fourth quote); Perry, *Me and the Spitter*, 78–81, 103 (2nd quote 80; 3rd quote 79; 5th quote 81).

17. Perry, *Me and the Spitter*, 119 (1st quote); Martin Co., Deeds F-7:701, Martin Co. Register of Deeds, Williamston, NC (MCRD); Roy Hardee, "Gaylord Perry: Pitcher for Giants," *Raleigh News and Observer*, Apr. 2, 1967, NCCCF-ECU (2nd quote); "Back at Home Base," *Raleigh News and Observer*, Feb. 16, 1975, NCCCF-UNC.

18. Berkow, "Perry, at Age 43, Must Prove Himself Again"; Sudyk, "Spitting Images," 15; Ward, interview by author; Fimrite, "Bound for Glory," 106 (1st quote); Collins, "Gaylord Perry: Tarheel Sketch"; Armour, "Gaylord Perry"; Keech, "Roots of a Pitcher"; "Gaylord Perry Minor League Statistics and History," Baseball-Reference.com, www.baseball-reference.com/minors/player.cgi?id=perry-001gay.

19. Richard Bilotti, "A Successful Bum," *Durham Morning Herald*, July 14, 1974, NCCCF-UNC; Charles Maher, "Many Use Spitter but Only a Few Throw It Well," *Baseball Digest* 25 (Dec. 1966): 40–42; Ron Rapoport, "Should They Legalize the Spitball?" *Baseball Digest* 31 (Dec. 1972): 39–44; Herman Weiskopf, "The Infamous Spitter," *Sports Illustrated*, July 31, 1967, 13–17; Perry, *Me and the Spitter*, 35 (quote); Sudyk, "Spitting Images," 12.

20. Weiskopf, "Infamous Spitter," 15 (1st quote), 17; Rapoport, "Should They Legalize the Spitball?" 42; Ron Fimrite, "Every Little Movement," *Sports Illustrated*,

July 16, 1973, 24, 27; Armour, "Gaylord Perry"; Sudyk, "Spitting Images," 16 (2nd quote); Peter Morris, *A Game of Inches: The Stories behind the Innovations That Shaped Baseball: The Game on the Field* (Chicago: Ivan R. Dee, 2006), 140–153.

21. Fimrite, "Every Little Movement," 24, 27; Sudyk, "Spitting Images," 10, 13 (1st quote); Barry Bloom, "All Hail Gaylord: The King of Grease," *Sport* 73 (Aug. 1982): 58 (2nd quote); Frederick C. Klein, "New Tricks from an Old Spin Doctor," *Wall Street Journal*, Jan. 20, 1995 (3rd quote); Perry, *Me and the Spitter*, 148–149, 161.

22. Collins, "Gaylord Perry: Tarheel Sketch" (quote); Keech, "Roots of a Pitcher"; Ira Berkow, "297, 298, 299: The Wait Is Almost over for Gaylord Perry," *Fort Myers News-Press*, Mar. 9, 1982, Perry HOF file; Jordan, "Forkballer of the Year," 38–39; Klein, "New Tricks from an Old Spin Doctor"; Fimrite, "Every Little Movement," 23–27; Sudyk, "Spitting Images," 13–14; Armour, "Gaylord Perry."

23. Sudyk, "Spitting Images," 13; Armour, "Gaylord Perry"; Perry, *Me and the Spitter*, 12 (1st and 2nd quotes).

24. Perry, *Me and the Spitter*, 28–29 (Aaron/Baptist wedding quotes), 191 (Allison quote); Sudyk, "Spitting Images," 14 (mosquito quote); Tracy Ringolsby, "Gaylord Slips into the 300 Club," *Sporting News*, May 17, 1982, 22 (300 wins quote); Bilotti, "Successful Bum" (savvy quote); Dick Schapp, "Sport Talk: Streaker in Cleveland," *Sport* 58 (Sept. 1974): 8; Jordan, "Forkballer of the Year," 38; Fimrite, "Bound for Glory," 95.

25. Armour, "Gaylord Perry"; Fimrite, "Every Little Movement," 23–27; Sudyk, "Spitting Images," 12 (2nd quote), 16 (1st quote).

26. Ward, interview by author; Perry, interview by author; Perry, *Me and the Spitter*, 199–200; Martin Co., Deeds L-9:421, MCRD; Distel, "Country Pitcher"; "Back at Home Base," *Raleigh News and Observer*, Feb. 16, 1975, NCCCF-UNC; Fimrite, "Bound for Glory," 95–96, 103 (1st quote); Keech, "Roots of a Pitcher" (2nd quote).

27. Perry, interview by author (1st, 7th, and 8th quotes); Ward, interview by author; "'Perry Brothers' Day' to Draw Capacity Crowd," *Williamston Enterprise*, Nov. 5, 1970 (2nd quote); "Williamston and Martin County People Extend Cordial 'Welcome Home' to Jim and Gaylord Perry," *Williamston Enterprise*, Nov. 10, 1970; "'Perry Brothers' Day' Here Huge Success Tuesday, *Williamston Enterprise*, Nov. 12, 1970; Blount, "Return of the Natives," 59; Distel, "Country Pitcher"; Fimrite, "Bound for Glory," 92, 96 (3rd quote); "After Last Out, Perry Comes Home," *Raleigh News and Observer*, Nov. 26, 1978, NCCCF-UNC; Perry, *Me and the Spitter*, 49 (4th quote), 62 (5th quote), 178; Peel, "Baseball Annies," 44 (6th quote).

28. U.S. Bureau of the Census, *Census of the Population: 1960*, vol. 1, part 35, 79; Ward, interview by author; Manning and Booker, *Religion and Education in Martin County*, 46–56, 224–226; Hughes, *Martin County Heritage*, 384–385, 394; Martin County Genealogical Society, *Our Heroes, 1861–1865: Sketches of Civil War Soldiers with Connections to North Carolina* (Williamston, NC: Martin County Genealogical Society, 1994); James H. McCallum, *Martin County during the Civil War* (Williamston, NC: Enterprise Publishing, 1971); "Jamesville Riot in the Seventies," *Williamston Enterprise*, Tobacco Edition, Aug. 1954 (for example); Daniel, *Standing at*

the Crossroads, 160; Jack Temple Kirby, *Rural Worlds Lost: The American South, 1920–1960* (Baton Rouge: Louisiana State University Press, 1987), 235–248; McLaurin, *Separate Pasts*, 12–14, 34–41.

29. W. H. Scarborough, "'Segregated-est Town in the U.S.,'" *Chapel Hill Weekly*, July 26, 1964; W. H. Scarborough, "Golden Frinks: 'The Sparkplug,'" *Chapel Hill Weekly*, Aug. 2, 1964; W. H. Scarborough, "The Charges of Brutality," *Chapel Hill Weekly*, Aug. 9, 1964 (1st quote); David C. Carter, "The Williamston Freedom Movement: Civil Rights at the Grass Roots in Eastern North Carolina, 1957–1964," *North Carolina Historical Review* 76 (Jan. 1999): 1–42 (2nd quote 7).

30. W. H. Scarborough, "The Strange Case of Joe Cross," *Chapel Hill Weekly*, Aug. 19, 1964; Carter, "Williamston Freedom Movement," 1–5. For descriptions of race relations as "cordial," see *Williamston Enterprise*, Nov. 14 and Dec. 3, 1963, as quoted in Carter, "Williamston Freedom Movement," 5.

31. Scarborough, "'Segregated-est Town in the U.S.,'" (1st and 2nd quotes); W. H. Scarborough, "The Klan Rises Again," *Chapel Hill Weekly*, July 29, 1964; Scarborough, "Charges of Brutality" and "Williamston"; "Rebirth of Klan Counters Moderate Action in State," *Raleigh News and Observer*, Aug. 23, 1964, NCCCF-UNC; Reese Hart, "Williamston Mayor Says His People Are Not Yet 'Ready,'" *Greenville Daily Reflector*, Apr. 8, 1964, NCCCF-ECU; Carter, "Williamston Freedom Movement," 1–42; Amanda Hilliard Smith, "The Broken Promise of Brown: A Look at Williamston, NC" (BA honors thesis, Meredith College, 2005), copy in Francis Manning Room.

32. Perry, *Me and the Spitter*, 66 (1st quote); "Farm Life Club Holds Meeting," *Williamston Enterprise*, Jan. 24, 1950; "Ruritans Meet in Farm Life School," *Williamston Enterprise*, Jan. 28, 1950; "Humber Talks to Farm Life Ruritan Club on Tuesday," *Williamston Enterprise*, Sept. 21, 1950; "Ruritans of Farm Life in Meeting," *Williamston Enterprise*, Mar. 20, 1952 (2nd quote); "Minstrel Parade by Farm Life Club," *Williamston Enterprise*, Apr. 20, 1954 (3rd quote); John Strausbaugh, *Black Like You: Blackface, Whiteface, Insult, and Imitation in American Popular Culture* (New York: Tarcher/Penguin, 2006).

33. "Segregation Held Unconstitutional," *Williamston Enterprise*, May 18, 1954; "Not Settled," *Williamston Enterprise*, June 1, 1954 (quote); "Prejudices Are Seen in All Races," *Williamston Enterprise*, June 3, 1954; McLaurin, *Separate Pasts*, 4–5.

34. Perry, *Me and the Spitter*, 67–68 (1st and 2nd quotes); Daniel, *Standing at the Crossroads*, 160; Timothy B. Tyson, *Blood Done Sign My Name* (New York: Three Rivers Press, 2004), 31–32.

35. Charles Einstein, *Willie's Time: A Memoir of Another America* (New York: J. P. Lippincott, 1979), 60, 191 (3rd quote), 225–226; Perry, interview by author; Fimrite, "Bound for Glory," 98; Perry, *Me and the Spitter*, 66–67 (2nd quote); Gaylord Jackson Perry, induction speech, National Baseball Hall of Fame and Museum, Cooperstown, NY, July 21, 1991, http://baseballhall.org/node/11248 (accessed Mar. 26, 2008); Chris Haft, "Gaylord Perry Recalls a Different Era in Baseball," *San Jose Mercury News*, July 23, 2005, Perry HOF file.

36. Jack Patterson, "Gaylord Boils, Hints at Trade," *Akron Beacon Journal*, Sept. 27, 1974, Perry HOF file; Russell J. Schneider, *Frank Robinson: The Making of a*

Manager (New York: Coward, McCann & Geoghegan, 1976), 34–60, 145–156 (1st quote 38; 2nd quote 41); Fimrite, "Bound for Glory," 96–97 (3rd quote 97); Frank Robinson and Roy Blount Jr., "I'll Always Be Outspoken," *Sports Illustrated*, Oct. 21, 1974, 31–38; Frank Robinson with Dave Anderson, "How a Pair of Perrys and One Blue Moon Left Cleveland," *Sport* 62 (May 1976): 56–66; Pete Axthelm, "The Conquering Con Man," *Newsweek*, May 17, 1982, 89; "Frank Robinson's Cleveland Indians," *Black Sports* 4 (May 1975): 26–28; Frank Robinson with Dave Anderson, *Frank: The First Year* (New York: Holt, Rinehart, and Winston, 1976); Armour, "Gaylord Perry"; McLaurin, *Separate Pasts*, 50, 114–116, 133–134.

37. Manning and Booker, *Religion and Education in Martin County*, 296–297 (1st quote 296); Smith, "Broken Promise of Brown," 24–28; Carter, "Williamston Freedom Movement," 40–42; Tyson, *Blood Done Sign My Name*, 41–42 (2nd quote 42); "After Last Out, Perry Comes Home"; Flowers, *Throwed Away*, 154–180 (3rd quote 174).

38. "After Last Out, Perry Comes Home"; Collins, "Gaylord Perry: Tarheel Sketch"; David Boul, "Gaylord Perry's Farm Bankrupt," *Greensboro News and Record*, Aug. 13, 1986; "Ex-Pitcher May Take Aim at Congress," *Raleigh News and Observer*, Aug. 15, 1985, NCCCF-UNC; "Perry Won't Make Congressional Bid," *Raleigh News and Observer*, Oct. 10, 1985, NCCCF-UNC; William Link, *Righteous Warrior: Jesse Helms and the Rise of Modern Conservatism* (New York: St. Martin's Press, 2008), 1, 19, 75, 98, 99 (1st quote), 125; Jack McCallum, "The Prime of the Ancient Mariner," *Sports Illustrated*, May 17, 1982, 29; Fimrite, "Bound for Glory," 96–97 (2nd quote 97).

39. Fimrite, "Bound for Glory," 92–106 (1st quote 97; 2nd quote 106; 3rd quote from the title of the article). See Timothy M. Gay, *Tris Speaker: The Rough-and-Tumble Life of a Baseball Legend* (Lincoln: University of Nebraska Press, 2005), for a major exception to the tendency among historians and journalists to avoid the issue of race in their accounts of white southern ballplayers. For a similar dynamic in a variety of other cultural contexts, see Benjamin Filene, *Romancing the Folk: Public Memory and American Roots Music* (Chapel Hill: University of North Carolina Press, 2000), and Jack Temple Kirby, *Media-Made Dixie: The South in the American Imagination* (Baton Rouge: Louisiana State University Press, 1978).

40. Bilotti, "Successful Bum"; S. H. Hobbes Jr., "Tar Heel Farming: A Time of Sweeping Change," *Greensboro Daily News*, July 2, 1961, NCCCF-UNC; Jimmy Tart, "Jobs in West Pull Population off Eastern N.C. Farms," *Raleigh News and Observer*, Dec. 12, 1966, NCCCF-ECU; Dick Brown, "Mule and Plow Ghosts of Past," *Fayetteville Times*, Apr. 11, 1976, NCCCF-UNC; Keech, "Roots of a Pitcher"; Distel, "Country Pitcher"; Daniel, *Breaking the Land*, 264–265; McLaurin, *Separate Pasts*, 156–160; Flowers, *Throwed Away*, 50–64.

41. Hobbes, "Tar Heel Farming" (1st quote); "Back at Home Base," *Raleigh News and Observer*, Feb. 16, 1975, NCCCF-UNC; Distel, "Country Pitcher"; Ward, interview by author; E. L. Evans, "Troubles on the Farm Spread to North Carolina," *Fayetteville Observer-Times*, Mar. 3, 1985, NCCCF-UNC; Martin Co., Deeds P-9:295, S-9:29, T-9:518, V-9:221, B-10:814, B-10:817, B-10:822, C-10:469, D-10:768, E-10:452,

L-10:456, D-11:528, MCRD; *In the Matter of Gaylord J. Perry and Blanche M. Perry* (1986), U.S. Bankruptcy Court, Eastern District of North Carolina, Case 86-01723-MA4, Schedule A, National Archives and Record Administration, Southeast Region, Ellenwood, GA (Perry bankruptcy case); Fimrite, "Bound for Glory," 95–99 (2nd quote 99); David B. Danbom, *Born in the Country: A History of Rural America* (Baltimore: Johns Hopkins University Press, 1995), 254–262.

42. David Zucchino, "Price Outlook Worries Farmers," *Raleigh News and Observer*, Apr. 2, 1978, NCCCF-UNC; Bruce Siceloff, "Farmers Caught in Squeeze," *Raleigh News and Observer*, Oct. 10, 1982, NCCCF-UNC; Lee Freeland Hancock, "N.C. Farmers in Debt-Driven Spiral," *Raleigh News and Observer*, Oct. 26, 1986, NCCCF-UNC; Evans, "Troubles on the Farm Spread to North Carolina"; Elizabeth Leland, "A Southern Rural Depression: Farm, Factory Failures Leave Many in Region 'Without Nothing but Their Dignity,'" *Charlotte Observer*, May 16, 1986 (quote); Ward, interview by author; Danbom, *Born in the Country*, 262–266; Neil E. Harl, *The Farm Debt Crisis of the 1980s* (Ames: Iowa State University Press, 1990).

43. Perry bankruptcy case, Schedule A, Schedule B; Evans, "Troubles on the Farm Spread to North Carolina"; Peter Richmond, "Bankruptcy Closes Perry's Farming Career," *Miami Herald*, Oct. 4, 1986, Perry HOF file; Jerry Allegood, "Gaylord Perry, Wife File for Bankruptcy," *Raleigh News and Observer*, Aug. 13, 1986, NCCCF-UNC; "Perry Gets Farmed Out," *Boston Globe*, Aug. 15, 1986, Perry HOF file (1st, 2nd, and 4th quotes); "Sports People: Perry's Farm Fails," *New York Times*, Aug. 14, 1986 (3rd quote); David Boul, "Gaylord Perry's Farm Bankrupt," *Greensboro News and Record*, Aug. 13, 1986; Ginger Bishop, "Gaylord Perry Files for Chapter 7 Bankruptcy," *Williamston Enterprise*, Aug. 12, 1986; "N.C. Loses Over 13,000 Farms in 5 Years, Census Reports," *Fayetteville Observer-Times*, Apr. 15, 1989; Bruce Martin, "Farm a Failure, but Gaylord Keeps Pitchin'," *Sporting News*, Jan. 19, 1987, Perry HOF file.

44. The literature on the 1980s farm crisis is extensive, but for an especially poignant analysis of how farmers talked about their losses, see Melissa Walker, *Southern Farmers and their Stories* (Lexington: University of Kentucky Press, 2006), 164–176 (quote 170).

45. "Wife of Perry Dies in Accident," *New York Times*; Sept. 12, 1987; "Mrs. Perry is Killed in Florida Accident," *Williamston Enterprise*, Sept. 15, 1987; "Evan Perry Drowns in Accident," *Williamston Enterprise*, Nov. 10, 1988; "Gaylord Jackson Perry, Jr. (Jack)," *Williamston Enterprise*, Jan. 21, 2005; Ward, interview by author; Sudyk, "Spitting Images," 15 (1st quote); Archie, "Spitting Image," 32 (2nd and 3rd quotes).

46. Fimrite, "Bound for Glory," 95, 104; Sudyk, "Spitting Images," 15; Perry, interview by author.

47. Martin, "Farm a Failure"; Gary Caruso, "Schooldays Agree with 'Coach Perry,'" *National Sports Daily*, Feb. 11, 1991, 23; Jim Green, "Gaylord Perry to Be Inducted Sunday," *Williamston Enterprise*, July 18, 1991; Klein, "New Tricks from an Old Spin Doctor"; Armour, "Gaylord Perry."

EPILOGUE: VINTAGE BALL

1. Author's observations, Fourth Annual Veterans Cup, Boerne City Lake Park, Boerne, TX, Nov. 6, 2010, notes in author's possession; "Vintage Base Ball Games to Be Held Saturday at Boerne City Lake Park," *Boerne Star*, Nov. 5, 2010; Kristy "Horseshoe" Watson, report on the Presidents Cup, Richmond Texas, Sept. 1, 2007, Boerne Vintage Baseball, www.vintagebaseball.org/richmond07.html (accessed May 16, 2011); "What in the World is Vintage Baseball?" Texas Vintage Baseball League, www.vbbtexas.org/whatisvbb.html (accessed May 14, 2011).

2. Jeff Siegel, "The Old Ball Game: The Texas Vintage Base Ball League Captures the Small-Town Spirit of America's Pastime," *Texas Journey* (Mar.–Apr. 2009): 22–24; Randy Mallory, "Show Some Ginger! Huzzah for Vintage Base Ball in Texas," *Texas Highways* (Apr. 2008): 48–53; Doug Stewart, "It's Two, Three, Four Strikes You're Out at the Old Ball Game," *Smithsonian* 29 (Oct. 1998): 98–106; Diane Jennings, "Going Back, Back, Back: Texans Step into 1800s in the Name of Vintage Base Ball—Yep, 2 Words," *Dallas Morning News*, Mar. 25, 2007; Erika Janik, "The Old Ball Game," *My Midwest*, Mar.–Apr. 2009, http://mymidwestmagazine.com/2009/03/01/the-old-ball-game (accessed Mar. 22, 2009); James R. Tootle, *Vintage Base Ball: Recapturing the National Pastime* (Jefferson, NC: McFarland, 2011).

3. Siegel, "Old Ball Game," 23; Jennings, "Going Back, Back, Back" (1st Wettemann quote); Mallory, "Show Some Ginger," 48–53 (2nd Wettemann quote 53).

4. Author's observations, Fourth Annual Veterans Cup; Siegel, "Old Ball Game," 22–24; Stewart, "It's Two, Three, Four Strikes You're Out," 101.

5. Author's observations, Fourth Annual Veterans Cup (all quotes); Kim Richardson, "Old School: Base Ball Takes a Look Back," *Houston Villager*, Sept. 27, 2006, www.vbbtexas.org/TheVillager.html (accessed May 14, 2011); Janik, "Old Ball Game"; Siegel, "Old Ball Game," 24; Mallory, "Show Some Ginger," 48–53.

6. Jennings, "Going Back, Back, Back"; Siegel, "Old Ball Game," 22–24; Janik, "Old Ball Game."

7. Author's observations, Fourth Annual Veterans Cup; Siegel, "Old Ball Game," 23–24 (quote).

8. Marc Bloch, *The Historian's Craft* (New York: Alfred A. Knopf, 1953), 29–35 (quotes, 32, 35); Jules Tygiel, *Extra Bases: Reflections on Jackie Robinson, Race, and Baseball History* (Lincoln: University of Nebraska Press, 2002), x–xi. Bloch's "idol of origins" has much in common with Erik Erikson's "originology." Erikson criticized psychoanalysis for fixating on the pathological origins of behavior, which he believed reduced every human situation to an analogy of an earlier one; see Hetty Zock, A *Psychology of Every Concern: Erik A. Erickson's Contribution to the Psychology of Religion* (Atlanta, GA: Rodopi, 1990): 56.

ESSAY ON SOURCES

The Farmers' Game is grounded in a wide range of primary sources and a rich body of secondary literature. This short essay highlights the evidence and interpretations most crucial to the making of the book. For additional bibliographical information and complete citations, readers should consult the chapter notes.

I began my research by reading through several large, general collections of archival materials, not yet knowing the specific subject matter of my case studies or, for that matter, that the book would be conceived in that manner. My first stop was the A. Bartlett Giamatti Research Center, National Baseball Hall of Fame and Museum, Cooperstown, New York. Like many before me, I found myself mesmerized by the correspondence, newspaper clippings, and magazine articles on the Mills commission in the John T. Doyle Collection, Albert Spalding Scrapbooks, A. G. Mills Papers, Origins of Baseball File, and Henry Chadwick File. The Giamatti Center keeps extensive clippings files on every major league player, two of which—Bob Feller and Gaylord Perry—proved especially valuable. One hundred miles to the west, in Ithaca, in the Harold and Dorothy Seymour Papers, Division of Rare Manuscript Collections, Carl A. Kroch Library, Cornell University, researchers will find ninety-one boxes packed full with the Seymours' research notes for all their books—a veritable gold mine of source materials (though largely unexploited). Boxes 46 through 50, covering *Baseball: The People's Game* (Oxford: Oxford University Press, 1990), made the drive from Cooperstown well worth it for me. More accessible are the wealth of resources available on the Society of American Baseball Research Web site. The Baseball Index, a searchable bibliography of books, articles, and other documents, and the Baseball Biography Project are worth the price of membership by themselves.

In terms of secondary sources on the general history of the game, in addition to the well-known books by the Seymours, David Q. Voigt, Benjamin G. Radar, and Steven A. Riess, I found John R. Betts, "Organized Sport in Industrial America" (PhD diss., Columbia University, 1952); Gunther Barth, *City People: The Rise of Modern City Culture in Nineteenth-Century America* (Oxford: Oxford University Press, 1980); and Jules Tygiel, *Past Time: Baseball as History* (Oxford: Oxford University Press, 2000), particularly useful, even with their urban, professional biases. On the origins of the game, see especially David Block, *Baseball before We Knew It: A Search for the Roots of the Game* (Lincoln: University of Nebraska Press, 2005), and John Thorn, *Baseball in the Garden of Eden: The Secret History of the Early Game* (New York: Simon & Schuster, 2011).

Most of my research on Cooperstown in the early nineteenth century took place a couple of miles from the Hall of Fame at the New York State Historical Association Research Library on the west shore of Lake Otsego, not far from where the Doubleday family played ball on Uncle Seth's farm. An entire wing of the reading room contains genealogical materials on local families, including the previously uncited (to my knowledge) Margaret B. Curfman and Stephen W. D. Rockstroh, *Doubleday Families of America* (Port Charlotte, FL: Stephen W. D. Rockstroh, 1993), which allowed me to trace the comings and goings of several generations of Doubledays. While newspaper research has gone out of vogue lately, especially papers not available on the Internet, my efforts to read through the files of the *Freedman's Journal*, *Otsego Herald*, *Otsego Republican*, and *Cooperstown Watch-Tower* were richly rewarded. Several local, county, and regional histories offer useful biographical, geographical, and community information; see especially Duane Hamilton Hurd, *History of Otsego County, New York* (Philadelphia: Everts & Fariss, 1878), and its comprehensive unpublished index on site in the reading room. Many village, township, county, and state census materials can be found there as well, but researchers should also familiarize themselves with the wonders of Ancestry.com, if they have not already done so. My work in the population census schedules for Otsego County, which would have taken me several days (and many headaches) the old way of scrolling through rolls of microfilm, took me just a few hours on Ancestry.

Anyone familiar with the secondary literature of the region will recognize my debt to Alan Taylor, *William Cooper's Town: Power and Persuasion on the Frontier of the Early American Republic* (New York: Vintage, 1995); Marvin Meyers, *The Jacksonian Persuasion: Politics and Belief* (Stanford, CA: Stanford University Press, 1957); and James Arthur Frost, *Life on the Upper Susquehanna, 1783–1860* (New York: King's Crown, 1951). I also benefited considerably from Tom Heitz, "In Our Past," a multipart local history with an emphasis on baseball, published in the *Cooperstown Crier* in the fall of 1999; the many works of village historian Hugh Cooke MacDougall, especially *Cooper's Otsego County: A Bicentennial Guide to Sites in Otsego County Associated with the Life and Fiction of James Fenimore Cooper, 1789–1851* (Cooperstown: New York State Historical Association, 1989); and Jared Van Wagenen Jr.'s *The Golden Age of Homespun* (Ithaca, NY: Cornell University Press, 1953). Also on the library's shelves are several dozen master's theses, mostly on local topics, from the State University of New York College at Oneonta, Cooperstown Graduate Program, many of which offer valuable substantive and bibliographical insights.

My analysis of the spirited rivalry between the Davisville Oletas and Dixon Etnas stems from my previous work on rural life in the Sacramento Valley. In addition to the primary sources cited in the notes, researchers should consult the essay on sources in my book *After the Gold Rush: Tarnished Dreams in the Sacramento Valley* (Baltimore: Johns Hopkins University Press, 2007), 295–300. My most valuable source for this chapter, Elijah Brown's weekly "Davisville Doings" column in the *Dixon Tribune*, gives readers a front row seat to the "epidemic of baseball" in these two towns during the 1880s. I also mined the *Weekly Solano Press, Yolo Weekly Mail, Knights Landing News*, and *Sacramento Daily Union* for information on community life and the region's other favorite pastime, horse racing. Several published works document the early history of baseball in California—again, however, from a largely urban perspective; see especially Kevin Nelson, *The Golden Game: The Story of California Baseball* (San Francisco: California Historical Society Press, 2004); John E. Spalding, *Always on Sunday: The California Baseball League, 1886–1915* (Manhattan, KS: Ag Press, 1992); and the articles by Joel Franks cited in the notes. On gambling, two essential sources are Jackson Lears, *Something for Nothing: Luck in America* (New York: Viking, 2003), and T. H. Breen, "Horses and Gentlemen: The Cultural Significance of Gambling among the Gentry of Virginia," *William and Mary Quarterly* 34 (Apr. 1977): 239–257.

My inspiration to explore multicultural ball in south-central Texas came from Thad Sitton and Dan K. Utley, *From Can See to Can't: Texas Cotton Farmers on the Southern Prairies* (Austin: University of Texas Press, 1997), and a collection of early-twentieth-century baseball-related photographs at the Fayette Heritage Museum and Archives, La Grange, Texas (two of which are reprinted in this book). With regard to newspapers, the *La Grange Journal* proved especially valuable because it regularly published articles and box scores of community teams from throughout Fayette County, as did the *Brenham Daily Banner-Press* for Washington County. Many of the other newspaper and magazine articles cited in the notes come from the extensive vertical files and scrapbooks of clippings housed at the Briscoe Center for American History, University of Texas at Austin, and the Institute of Texan Cultures, University of Texas at San Antonio. Several oral histories and memoirs contributed to my understanding of the cultural significance of baseball in the region, most notably Kermit W. Fox, *A Son of La Bahia Remembers* (Austin, TX: Aus-Tex Print & Mailing, 1991); W. F. "Boy" Hasskarl Jr., *Remembering Brenham: A Collection of Stories as Told by Dr. "Boy" Hasskarl* (Brenham, TX: Webb Printing, 2005); Robert L. Skrabanek, *We're Czechs* (College Station: Texas A&M University Press, 1998); and the detailed, insightful interviews with Grover Williams, Thomas Oliver Whitener, Robert Lee Dement, and several other Burton (and vicinity) residents cited in the notes from the Baylor University Institute for Oral History, Waco.

Historians of the state and region will already be familiar with the *Handbook of Texas Online*, but others would do well to acquaint themselves with this invaluable resource. On Texas Germans, the standard remains Terry G. Jordan, *German Seed in Texas Soil: Immigrant Farmers in Nineteenth-Century Texas* (Austin: University of Texas Press, 1966), but see also the books and articles cited in the notes by Walter D. Kamphoefner and Wilfred O. Dietrich. The literature on Texas Czechs is extensive as well, but particularly useful are Clinton Machann and James W. Mendl, *Krásná Amerika: A Study of the Texas Czechs, 1851–1939* (Austin, TX: Eakin Press, 1983); Sean N. Gallup, *Journeys into Czech-Moravian Texas* (College Station: Texas A&M University Press, 1998); and Robert L. Skrabanek's scholarly articles cited in the notes. On African Americans, the essential study is Thad Sitton and James H. Conrad, *Freedom Colonies: Independent Black Texans in the Time of Jim Crow* (Austin: University of

Texas Press, 2005); see also Mance Lipscomb and Glen Alyn, *I Say Me for a Parable: The Oral Autobiography of Mance Lipscomb, Texas Bluesman* (New York: W. W. Norton, 1993), and Thad Sitton's entry, "Freedmen's Settlements," in the *Handbook of Texas Online*.

Bob Feller's player file at the Hall of Fame proved indispensable to my research. It contains several thick folders of clippings from New York, Cleveland, Chicago, and Iowa newspapers, as well as articles from the *Saturday Evening Post*, *Collier's*, *Sporting News*, *Sports Illustrated*, and a host of other popular magazines. Locally, the *Dallas County News* provides extensive coverage of agricultural and community developments in the 1920s and 1930s and of Bob's spectacular career before and after he broke into the major leagues. The two contemporary Des Moines papers, the *Tribune* and the *Register*, covered the story closely as well. My analysis of four generations of Feller farmers in Iowa since the 1850s stems primarily from research in land records, obituaries, maps, probate files, census materials, court cases, and other local records scattered across four archives in the state: the Roy R. Estle Memorial Library, Dallas Center; the State Historical Society of Iowa Library and Archives, both the Des Moines and Iowa City branches; and the Dallas County Archives, Adel. The many county and local histories cited in the notes—most notably *Van Meter Centennial History, 1868–1970* (Van Meter, IA: Van Meter Centennial Committee, 1970)—are conveniently housed in the Van Meter Public Library.

Feller himself published three full-length autobiographies and numerous "in-his-own-words" articles in newspapers, magazines, and book chapters; the most revealing accounts may be found in Bob Feller with Burton Rocks, *Bob Feller's Little Black Book of Baseball Wisdom* (Chicago: Contemporary Books, 2001); Donald Honig, *Baseball When the Grass Was Real* (New York: Berkeley, 1975), 241–264; Fay Vincent, *The Only Game in Town: Baseball Stars of the 1930s and 1940s Talk about the Game They Loved* (New York: Simon & Schuster, 2006), 34–56; and Harvey Frommer and Frederic J. Frommer, eds., *Growing Up Baseball: An Oral History* (Dallas, TX: Taylor Trade, 2001), 86–91. Of several biographies, the best by far remains John Sickels, *Bob Feller: Ace of the Greatest Generation* (Dulles, VA: Potomac Books, 2004). See also Don Fish, "Warming up Feller," *Iowa Heritage Illustrated* 87 (Spring 2006): 19, and the many other fine articles in this special edition devoted to Iowa baseball history.

Several secondary sources on the changing economics and ideology of agriculture in the last half of the nineteenth and first half of the twentieth centuries helped shape my analysis, most notably Dorothy Schwieder, *Iowa: The Middle Land* (Ames: Iowa State University Press, 1996); Thomas J. Morain, *Prairie Grass Roots: An Iowa Small Town in the Early Twentieth Century* (Ames: Iowa State University Press, 1988); Earle D. Ross, *Iowa Agriculture: An Historical Survey* (Iowa City: State Historical Society of Iowa, 1951); Gilbert C. Fite, *American Farmers: The New Minority* (Bloomington: Indiana University Press, 1981); and Hal S. Barron, *Mixed Harvest: The Second Great Transformation in the Rural North, 1870–1930* (Chapel Hill: University of North Carolina Press, 1997). See also Barron's article, "Rural America on the Silent Screen," *Agricultural History* 80 (Fall 2006): 383–410, for an illuminating cultural analysis of rural life in this period of transition.

An abundance of materials documents the Milroy Yankees' storied past in the midst of a prolonged period of decline in southwest Minnesota. Interviews with Bob Zwach, Reed Lovsness, Spike Dolan, Rich Kramer, and other former players—some published, some archival, some my own—provide special insights into the team itself, game details, individual personalities, and family histories; see Joe Paddock and Nancy Paddock, "Milroy Memories," typescript, 1977, Minnesota Historical Society Library, St. Paul; Joseph M. Kemp interviews, January 1996, box 1, Southwest Minnesota Baseball Collection, Southwest Minnesota Regional Research Center, Southwest Minnesota State University, Marshall (along with numerous newspaper clippings in that same collection); Edith Ousky et al., *100 Years of Milroy Memories and 75 Years of Baseball* (Milroy, MN: Milroy Centennial History Book Committee, 2002); and *Milroy Minnesota Diamond Jubilee, 1902–1977: An Historical Anthology: July 9 & 10, 1977* (Cottonwood, MN: Cottonwood Current, 1977). While Milroy had no newspaper of its own, the *Redwood Gazette* (Redwood Falls) and *Marshall Messenger* provide detailed game stories and box scores of most Yankee games in the late 1940s and early 1950s. For more information on the annual tournament, see the Minnesota Amateur Baseball Association Records, Minnesota Historical Society Library.

No one understands southwest Minnesota's highly complex economy, culture, and environment better than Joseph Amato. Of his many works (authored and coauthored) cited in the notes, see especially *The Decline of Rural Minnesota* (Marshall, MN: Crossings Press, 1993); *Rethinking Home: A Case for Writing Local History* (Berkeley: University of California Press, 2002); and "It's Root, Root, Root for the Home Team," in *Southwest Minnesota: A Place of Many Places*, ed. Joseph Amato and David Pichaske (Marshall, MN: Crossings Press, 2007), 77–81. For additional perspective, see Clifford E. Clark, ed., *Minnesota in a Century of Change: The State and Its People since 1900* (St. Paul: Minnesota Historical Society Press, 1989); Richard O. Davies, Joseph A. Amato, and David R. Pichaske eds., *A Place Called Home: Writings on the Midwestern Small Town* (St. Paul: Minnesota Historical Society Press, 2003); and Richard O. Davies, *Main Street Blues: The Decline of Small-Town America* (Columbus: Ohio State University Press, 1998). Armand Peterson and Tom Tomashek, *Town Ball: The Glory Days of Minnesota Amateur Baseball* (Minneapolis: University of Minnesota Press, 2006) enhanced my understanding of the game's popularity and cultural significance in the North Star State in the postwar era.

Its frivolous title notwithstanding, Gaylord Perry with Bob Sudyk, *Me and the Spitter: An Autobiographical Confession* (New York: Saturday Review Press, 1974), offers much insight into the last generation of sharecroppers in the American South. Three huge clipping files provide an abundance of information—not only Perry's player file at the Hall of Fame, but also the North Carolina Collection Clipping File, Wilson Library, University of North Carolina at Chapel Hill; and North Carolina Collection Clipping File, Joyner Library, East Carolina University, Greenville. The *Williamston Enterprise* proved invaluable as well, along with two other local sources, Linda M. Taylor, "The Making of a Community: The Story of Farm Life," typescript, 1974, and Stephen Klinedinst et al., *Smoke to Gold: The Story of Tobacco in Martin County*

(Greenville, NC: Era Press, 1998)—all available in the Francis Manning Room, Martin Community College Library, Williamston. Over the course of his baseball career, *Sports Illustrated* featured Perry in several articles, the most revealing being Roy Blount Jr., "Return of the Natives," March 29, 1971, 58–64, and Ron Fimrite, "Bound for Glory," Aug. 24, 1981, 92–106. The *Chapel Hill Weekly* provides extensive coverage on race relations in Martin County in the 1960s, and Perry's bankruptcy file documents his farm's failure in the agricultural crisis of the 1980s.

Perry has not been the subject of a full-length biography, but much can be learned from Mark Armour's entry in the Baseball Biography Project, Society of American Baseball Research; Bob Sudyk, "Spitting Images: A Little Dab Took Gaylord Perry to the Hall of Fame," *Hartford (CT) Courant*, July 21, 1991; and Tyler Archie, "Spitting Image: Gaylord Perry, a Man and His Myth," *North Carolina's Down East Magazine*, 3 (Summer 2006): 30–32. In my efforts to understand Perry's life in historical context, I benefited immensely from Melton A. McLaurin, *Separate Pasts: Growing Up White in the Segregated South* (Athens: University of Georgia Press, 1987); Linda Flowers, *Throwed Away: Failures of Progress in Eastern North Carolina* (Knoxville: University of Tennessee Press, 1990); Timothy B. Tyson, *Blood Done Sign My Name* (New York: Three Rivers, 2004); Pete Daniel, *Standing at the Crossroads: Southern Life in the Twentieth Century* (Baltimore: Johns Hopkins University Press, 1986); David C. Carter, "The Williamston Freedom Movement: Civil Rights at the Grass Roots in Eastern North Carolina, 1957–1964," *North Carolina Historical Review* 76 (January 1999): 1–42; and Melissa Walker, *Southern Farmers and Their Stories* (Lexington: University of Kentucky Press, 2006). For a concise analysis of the 1980s farm crisis, see David B. Danbom, *Born in the Country: A History of Rural America* (Baltimore: Johns Hopkins University Press, 1995), 254–266.

On vintage ball, James R. Toole, *Vintage Base Ball: Recapturing the National Pastime* (Jefferson, NC: McFarland, 2011), offers the most comprehensive treatment. One cannot fully appreciate this rather striking phenomenon, however, by reading about it. Go to a game! Huzzah!

INDEX